The Ultimate Guide to Cheerleading

For Cheerleaders and Coaches

Leslie Wilson

THREE RIVERS PRESS

NEW YORK

Published by Three Rivers Press, New York, New York.
Member of the Crown Publishing Group, a division of Random House, Inc.
www.randomhouse.com

THREE RIVERS PRESS and the Tugboat design are registered trademarks of Random House, Inc.

Printed in the United States of America

Design by Melanie Haage

LIBRARY OF CONGRESS CATALOGING-IN-PUBLICATION DATA
Wilson, Leslie (Leslie M.)
    The ultimate guide to cheerleading : for cheerleaders and coaches / Leslie Wilson.
        p.   cm.
    Includes index.
    1. Cheerleading. I. Title.
LB3635 .W55   2003
791.6'4—dc21   2003001166
ISBN 0-7615-1632-8

10 9 8 7 6 5 4 3 2 1

First Edition

611   1898

All Glory to God

Contents

Foreword

When I see the word *ultimate* used to describe something, my knee-jerk response is "yeah, right." To use the word *ultimate* to describe anything in an industry that reports staggering growth and almost-daily changes would be like using *ultimate* to describe a computer—knowing it will not be "ultimate" tomorrow and it could be "obsolete" next week.

However, there is no better word to describe the book you are about to read. *The Ultimate Guide to Cheerleading* is, quite simply, the *ultimate* printed information source for today's cheerleading coach and/or today's cheerleader. Nothing I have written or read about the sport of cheerleading comes close to being as comprehensive as this book. In the four-part, sixteen-chapter format of *The Ultimate Guide to Cheerleading*, the reader will find a plethora of information covering everything from a brief history of cheerleading and the first "Sis Boom Bah" to the proper execution of a Rewind + Cupie + TickTock + Cradle + Regrab + Liberty stunt combination!

Along with this wealth of information, Leslie Wilson provides logical progressions and timelines for starting a team, making a team, preparing for a competition, and creating a budget. The variety of sample forms and schedules she includes are impressive, and coaches in particular can adapt any of them to suit their own unique situations.

I am frankly amazed at the seamless way Wilson writes for both audiences at the same time. Each of the four sections of the book carries a title for both coach and cheerleader. The "Coaches' Corner" sections bring into focus creative yet practical ideas for team management, while the "Tip" sidebars punctuate various chapters throughout the book with little gems designed to make both coaches' and cheerleaders' jobs easier.

From quizzes to determine whether you are best suited for a school team, an all-star team, or a community team to a glossary of cheerleading terminology, Wilson has not missed a thing. Cheerleaders and coaches will even find a how-to section of well-illustrated cheers, chants, and jumps that are extremely easy to follow.

Who should read this book? The young pre-teen who wants to learn how to cheer, as well as the college coach who wants to determine the correct progression of elite partner stunts; the aspiring entrepreneur who wants to start an all-star cheerleading gym, as well as the 20-year veteran coach who wants to update her knowledge. It's all here within the 288 pages of this remarkable book.

The cheerleading industry has waited a long time for a book like this. This book is so good I wish I had written it! Wilson's research is flawless, her grasp of our multi-dimensional sport is strong, and her clarity about the athletic nature of cheerleading is cutting edge.

At Cheer Ltd. Competitions and Camps, we are constantly receiving requests for a magical book that will "tell me how to cheer" or that will "tell me how to coach this team." For the first time ever, I can say with honesty, "I've got *just* the book for you—*The Ultimate Guide to Cheerleading!*"

—**Gwen Holtsclaw,** president and CEO of Cheer Ltd. Inc., founder of the National Cheerleading Coaches Conference, author of *101 Exciting New Tips to Energize Your Cheerleaders,* and coauthor of *Cheerleader's Little Instruction Book.*

Acknowledgments

So many have been instrumental in bringing this project to fruition that I hardly know where to start thanking you all! I want everyone who provided encouragement and guidance throughout this exciting adventure to know how appreciative I am.

I'm grateful to my agent, Nancy Love, who took me under her wing, gave me this opportunity, and believed in me every step of the way. You're wonderful!

To the staff at Prima Publishing, thank you for the countless hours you've spent transforming this project into an amazing book. I'm fortunate to have worked with a wonderful team of professionals, especially my acquisitions editor, Denise Sternad, and my project editor, Michelle McCormack. Your invaluable guidance and constant flow of innovative ideas brought immeasurable value to this book of ours for coaches and cheerleaders everywhere.

I'm grateful to my photographer Julia Sumner from Photo Images by Julia for taking such wonderful pictures for the book. Your endless patience and utter commitment to this project has never gone unnoticed. I had such fun working with you!

Thanks to Elizabeth Vasas who edited my work before I dared send it out. I'm appreciative of your many ideas and suggestions. Kim Bosch, thank you for your 24-hour edit marathon and impromptu game photography. Thanks also to Alexis Williams for assisting with the fitness content. I bet you all know much more than you thought there was to know about cheerleading.

I especially want to thank my friend Jim Wegener and his staff (Kesha Harris, Katie Hoefer, Andrew Fitzpatrick, and Philip Pierce) from the Cheerleading Stunt Academy. Jim, I've been blessed with your friendship and will be forever

thankful for your dedication to ensuring that we got great pictures for this book. Thank you also to the incredibly talented Dundee-Crown High School cheerleading team from Carpentersville, Illinois, especially Lindsay Revera, Michelle Beck, Nicole Alexander, Hollie Benedik, Alina Petre, Nikki Knight, Erica Bernard, and Eiffel Santos. I can't tell you how much I appreciate your grueling weekend of stunting. We ended up with great shots, didn't we?

Thank you to the Oakville Trafalgar High School cheerleaders and their coach Nicole McKenzie, and also to Steph Russell, Susan McSporran, and Mailie Harris for being great "stunt models" for hours under the hot sun. To all of you: Your friendship means so much to me.

My thanks and appreciation goes out to the United Spirit Association (USA), the United Performing Association (UPA), the USA Spirit Team, Kilgore College, and to the Cedar Falls High School cheerleading team for providing photos for the book.

I'm also grateful to the University of Guelph Athletics and Athletic Director Richard Freeman for granting permission to photograph games and athletic events. Thank you also to the talented athletes and coaches from the cheerleading teams of both University of Guelph and Wilfred Laurier University. I learned much from all of you!

I never would have experienced starting and participating on a varsity cheerleading program had the staff and teachers at Notre Dame High School in Burlington, Ontario, not supported the idea from the beginning. Thank you especially to Peter Visser, Mike Harris, and Anna Antolovich, among numerous others who liberally gave time and energy to the cheerleading team over the years. Without your efforts in organizing the program, providing instructors, supervising practices, and cheering us on at competitions, this book may never have materialized.

My enthusiasm for cheerleading was cultivated by one of my first coaches, Sarah Johnston, who generously shared her knowledge, enthusiasm, and friendship, all the while being one of my most looked-up-to role models. Thank you for taking me on as your "unofficial sister." I wish you happiness and success wherever you may be. To my other first coach, Mandy Cheetham, thank you for taking me along on your cheerleading adventures! I will always be grateful for the many opportunities you provided to share my knowledge of cheerleading with others. (He is faithful indeed, isn't He?) Thanks also to Sharon Hollingsworth, who was so kind to me—the kid at summer cheerleading camp who came all by herself.

Suzy, I don't have the words to thank you for the life lessons, friendship, and love. Who would I have based with without you? And Joshua, you've been there every step of the way, from the rejected query letters to the actual publication of my biggest accomplishment. For your encouragement, love, and everything else with which you've blessed my life, I love you.

To my dear family: Dad Glenn, Mom Elaine, and Brother Tyler—your constant encouragement, patience, and love have helped immeasurably with not only this project and my business, but with everything I do. Thanks for taking me to and from practice, hosting end-of-the-year parties, and putting up with my cheerleading-crazed moments. I love you all so very much. Dad, you'll be happy to know that I'm still "keeping my eye on the carrot."

Thank you to all my coaches, teammates, instructors, and campers who positively shaped my cheerleading experience, and to the hundreds of thousands of coaches and cheerleaders around the world who, despite many challenges, work hard to cultivate this sport we've all come to love. Stick together, and enjoy every second with one another as you practice, compete, perform, and *lead*.

And last, but actually first, thank you to the One who blessed me in so many ways, including the ability to share my cheerleading knowledge and talent with others around the world.

Rah! Rah! Sis Boom Bah!? Not anymore—that's yesterday's cheer. Modern day cheerleading is a sport of dedication, strength, and talent in which over 4.3 million young men and women participate. Once predominant only in North America, cheerleading is now exploding across the globe, increasing in both popularity and competitiveness. Coaches and cheerleaders are constantly searching for new ideas and resources that will help propel them to the top of the cheerleading ranks. They know that only those with excellent ability and knowledge of the sport will succeed. And that is why I've written this book: to give you the skills you need to take your team to the next level of cheerleading—to the level of a sport.

I once made a $100 bet with a guy who argued that cheerleading *wasn't* a sport. He reasoned that just about anyone could be a cheerleader because it "didn't require any skill." So, I did what any cheerleader would have done: I challenged him. Mr. Basketball was soon $100 poorer when he learned that stunting wasn't as easy as he had once thought. (Actually, he *should* have been $100 poorer, but I forgave him because he put such a commendable effort into learning a Walk Hands.) I didn't earn any money for the month I spent coaching him, but I did earn respect for cheerleading as well as a life-long friend.

Like my friend before our bet, many people are uneducated about cheerleading. A lot of this ignorance has to do with the fact that cheerleading, while growing rapidly, still receives relatively low exposure compared to other sports. With limited or no first-hand experience, people rely on secondary information, such as commonly held stereotypes and suggestions from the media to form opinions. As a result, inaccurate perceptions have emerged, labeling cheerleaders as "bimbos" and "sideline eye candy" who lack real athletic talent. Those of us involved in cheerleading know that nothing could be further from the truth. Today's cheerleaders are talented athletes, leaders, and role models—and are *very* far from the "cheerleader" stereotype. Indisputably, athletic ability, skill, and technique form the foundation upon which modern-day cheerleading is built.

Whether you're an experienced cheerleader or a novice, a veteran coach or brand-new one, you can find a wealth of information in *The Ultimate Guide to Cheerleading*. Within these pages you'll discover valuable step-by-step photos, creative ideas, helpful advice on techniques, and useful coaching guidelines. Given the resources found in this book, you'll have everything you need to participate in, or coach, a successful cheerleading program.

The book is divided into four main parts. In Part One: "Coaches: How to Create the Team; Cheerleaders: How to Make the Team," coaches and cheerleaders will learn how to start a cheerleading program from scratch, hold tryouts, and run an effective cheerleading program. Cheerleaders will learn how to prepare for tryouts and how to improve skills and strength during the season. Part Two: "Motions, Cheers, Chants, and Jumps: Everything For Cheerleaders to Learn and Coaches to Know" contains resources that teach the actual cheerleading techniques and jump skills. Part Three: "Moving Beyond the Basics: Important Stunt Information for Cheerleaders and Coaches" covers all the stunting information you need to safely stunt, form pyramids, perform tosses, and more. Finally, Part Four: "Getting It Together for Competition: Choreographers' Organization and Cheerleaders' Preparation" covers all the information you need for routine choreography and competitions.

Whether you're a novice or a veteran, I have three important pieces of advice for you to consider before putting into practice the cheerleading skills and ideas found in this book:

1. ***Stay Safe.*** I know you're excited about the section on stunting (it's my favorite part, too!), but you must read the guidelines on safety *first.* Learn proper spotting techniques and always take the proper precautions before putting a flyer in the air. Staying safe also means taking care of your body. Keeping healthy through proper exercise and nutrition is essential for stunting with one another. You can't safely catch or be caught by another if you don't have a strong, well-fed body.

2. ***Build up*** one another, *not just pyramids.* There's one thing that is unique to cheerleading: Cheerleaders cheer for one another, regardless of what team they're on. If a team builds an awesome pyramid, cheerleaders will encourage the other team by cheering for them. You'd be hard-pressed to see this among the players in football, basketball, or other competing teams. Supporting one another is vital to both increasing public awareness and increasing the skill level of cheerleading in general. This unique sportsmanlike characteristic is responsible for the fact that cheerleading continues to grow at such a rapid pace. Building up your own teammates is also important. Encouragement is one of the most important gifts you can give to one another.

3. ***Keep it fun.*** Don't get so caught up in competitiveness that you forget why you like to cheerlead in the first place. Train seriously and be a dedicated member of the team, but don't let competitiveness with your own teammates or other teams take over. Participating in cheerleading will build your confidence, introduce you to lifelong friends, and take you on an awesome adventure.

You, the readers, are the reason I wrote this book. So many people have generously coached and guided me along my cheerleading journey that I want to give back to the cheerleading community. I'm thankful for the opportunity to share my knowledge of cheerleading with you in the hope that you will gain a renewed sense of enthusiasm for cheerleading. I know I have while doing the research and writing! And I trust that, in turn, you will share your knowledge with others so that one day the public will recognize and appreciate cheerleading as a sport.

With the help of this book, your dreams of being involved in cheerleading may soon become reality. Whether you want to cheer or coach, this book will open doors to opportunities you never knew existed. Cheering for games, performing at community events, or going across the continent to participate in the competitions you've always watched on TV—there's a whole new world out there waiting for you! Who knows? Maybe you'll become a member of an All-Star team. Or you may be the one coaching that team. You might even use your cheerleading experience to create your own business or become a professional cheerleader or even a fitness competitor. With cheerleading, your opportunities are endless.

Now that you've decided that you want to become involved in cheerleading, get ready for your life to change! Are you ready to become part of the fastest-growing and what those involved consider the most exciting sport in the world? You are going to meet amazing people, see incredible talent, and enrich the lives of the young men and women with whom you will be working. Cheerleading is undeniably different from any other sport. The uniqueness of cheerleading, whether you are coaching or cheerleading, is that *all* participants support one another. This camaraderie sets cheerleading apart from other sports. At what other competition do you see *all* competitors cheering excitedly for one another?

Are you ready to take on this challenge? It's time to start making your dreams a reality. . . .

PART ONE

Coaches:
How to Create the Team

Cheerleaders:
How to Make the Team

Chapter One

Where Do I Begin?

For Cheerleaders and Coaches Starting a Team

So you love watching cheerleaders defy gravity with their spectacular stunts and tumbling skills, do you? And you feel a rush of excitement when you see dynamic routines with perfectly synchronized dancing and jumps? Can't help but cheer along? You're definitely a cheerleader at heart!

Whether you want to create a team, or become an athlete on a cheerleading team, before you bring out the pom-poms, you have a few big decisions to make. Let's start with the easy questions:

1. Are you going to create/participate in a high school, college/university, all-star, open, or a city or club team?
2. Will it be a co-ed or all-girl team?

— Deciding on a Team Type —

Take into consideration the following when selecting the type of team you are going to create/participate in.

High School/Varsity

Comprised of athletes from grades 9 to 12, this type of team represents its school and participates in activities such as competitions, game cheering, and pep rallies, as well as school or community events.

College/University

Athletes on a university team are most likely experienced cheerleaders. More often than not, your team will consist of both males and females, although all-girl university teams are popular as well.

All-Star

Composed of the most elite cheerleaders in your region, this team will likely participate in competitions above all else. All-star teams have no affiliation with particular schools and thus allow cheerleading athletes from any school to participate. Athletes generally pay to be on this type of team, and are from already-established cheerleading programs. If your area has no current cheerleading programs, you might consider creating an all-star team. Although divisions vary among organizations, the most common ones for all-star teams are:

Open: any number of males and females, any age

Large Co-Ed: four or more males plus females, generally a maximum of 20 athletes on the floor, from grades 9 to 12

Small Co-Ed: three or fewer males plus females, generally a maximum of 20 athletes on the floor, from grades 9 to 12

Super Varsity: all female, 21 to 30 athletes, from grades 9 to 12

Large Varsity: all female, 16 to 20 athletes, grades 9 to 12

Medium Varsity: all female, 13 to 15 athletes, grades 9 to 12

Small Varsity: all female, 12 or fewer athletes, grades 9 to 12

Junior: male and female (both all-girl and co-ed divisions), grades 9 and under

Open

Open teams can consist of both males and females who are either still enrolled in school or have graduated. This type of team provides an opportunity for "older" cheerleaders to continue competing and participating in cheerleading.

City/Club Teams

Similar to all-star teams, club teams are usually made up of athletes who pay to be on the team and come from a number of different schools. Unlike all-star teams, club teams may consist of individuals with varied previous experience. This is the perfect team type if you cannot find enough interest in one school to form a team, or if you are having difficulties with school administration. Club teams most commonly cheer for city games and events, in addition to entering cheerleading competitions. Once again, whether you field a club team or another type depends largely on the team's focus.

— What Is Your Team's Purpose? —

You will base your team choice on a number of factors so think carefully before you make a decision. Keep in mind the best type of team to fit your situation. How much cheerleading experience do you have? If you're just starting out, you may not want to jump into coaching an all-star team just yet. What age group is expressing the most interest in starting a team? If you are thinking about joining a team, which one caters to your age and experience?

Will you be more community-oriented, participating in events such as parades and cheering for city teams? Will your purpose be to evoke school spirit by performing at school events and pep rallies or cheering for school sports such as wrestling, football, and basketball? Will your main focus be to design and execute winning routines and compete across the country in prestigious competitions such as those seen on TV sports channels? Or will your team be involved in all three types of activities? Once you have decided what your main focus will be, you can start to design your cheerleading program for maximum success and effectiveness. Read on to begin!

— Getting the "Go-Ahead" —

Cheerleading teams are a welcome addition to any school or city. They draw fans to games, excite the crowd during pep rallies or events, and bring attention to the city or school they represent. Your first challenge is to convince the athletic department or city officials of this fact. Will this be an easy feat? Yes—*if* you create a dynamic proposal.

Preparing Your Proposal

Doing proper research and writing a well-composed proposal to support your plan is the best way to get school or city officials to accept your idea. First, establish the type of team it will be and clarify its main objectives. Next, list all the benefits of having a cheerleading team represent your school or city. Your list of benefits may include ideas such as these:

1. *To promote and publicize the school or city.*
If you live in a city with a population of 10,000 or less, chances are slim that the majority of out-of-town people will recognize the name of your school or city when they hear it. Cheerleading teams often increase the public's awareness of a

school or city and in turn may lead to benefits for its residents or students. It's even possible that an appearance at an event could lead to scholarships, grants, or funding from a business or organization.

2. *To evoke pride and spirit.*

Feeling proud of, rather than indifferent toward, your school or community creates an awesome sense of unity. Those who share the feeling that they are part of something bigger than just themselves encourage everyone to work together to achieve common goals. Teams especially thrive on community spirit and will work even harder knowing that as many as twenty other athletes—the cheerleaders—are encouraging school or community pride.

3. *To increase attendance at games.*

Other than a few diehard fans, people generally won't come to games when they're boring. But when games offer additional entertainment (a cheerleading routine) and interactive activities (cheering), they tend to draw a bigger crowd. Increasing the number of fans has many advantages, including higher revenue from ticket sales, food/snack sales, and other fundraising activities. This is financially rewarding for the team and community organizations that use games to raise funds. Additionally, athletes perform better when they're encouraged. What better way is there to encourage a team than filling the stadium with enthusiastic supporters? And when teams perform well, even more people will want to come to the next game.

4. *To add excitement to school pep rallies and events (see chapter 4).*

5. *To encourage sports teams.*

Cheerleaders aren't fickle like the kind of fans who climb on the bandwagon only to disappear at the slightest hint of trouble. Even losing sports teams know that the cheerleading team will still be at the next game or pep rally, providing support and encouragement.

6. *To represent the school or city at competitions and community events.*

7. *To provide young women and men with the opportunity to build self-confidence, stay healthy, and have fun by participating in athletics.*

RECRUITING CHEERLEADERS

Keep in mind that school or city officials want to know that their time and funds will go toward a productive endeavor. Therefore, you'll want to list interested prospective cheerleaders to reinforce the fact that a demand for a cheerleading team clearly exists in your area. You can gather these names through a variety of ways, including advertising at schools and around the city. Some ideas include:

★ Advertising in local or school newspapers

★ Advertising on local radio or TV stations

★ Posting flyers around the community (bus shelters, community boards, grocery stores, schools, etc.)

★ Making an announcement over a school P.A. system

★ Performing demonstrations by an existing cheerleading team at malls, schools, or other public events

After this list, include the name and qualifications of the coach (whom you may want to bring along to the meeting).

The next section should include your proposed practice schedule. Include when the gym or other practice area is available, and how many times per week the team will practice. A typical school team practices two to three times a week for approximately 1½ to 2 hours, and may have additional gymnastics practices as well. City and club teams usually have similar practice schedules. All-Star teams typically practice more often or for longer periods of time than high school and club

ESTABLISHING CREDIBILITY

If *you* are coaching the team, include in your proposal why you feel you are a qualified coach. Think of questions the decision makers might ask, such as: Have you ever taken or taught dance or gymnastics? Do you have experience in coaching a team of young adults? Why are you excited about coaching cheerleading? What can you offer the program? If you don't have any experience directly related to cheerleading, emphasize that you are enthusiastic about beginning this new program.

---

teams. Remember that the amount of practice time also depends on your focus for the team. For example, teams preparing for competition will require more practice time than a team focusing on game cheering only.

As with all sports, funding is a key concern. Bring a list of the projected costs for running the team. Here are some items to consider including on your list:

★ Fees and gas money for coaches (if not volunteer coaching)

★ Uniform costs (bows, shell, skirt, bloomies, and shoes)

★ Travel costs to games, events, and competitions

★ Judging fees for tryouts

★ Facility fees

★ Gymnastics fees

★ Props, such as mats, pom-poms, megaphones, or signs

In addition to listing projected costs, also include fundraising ideas or a list of possible sponsors who might help pay some of the costs, and list what the cheerleaders will pay for individually.

Here's a review of what your proposal package should include:

PROPOSAL PACKAGE CONTENTS

1. Type of team and why it would be a valuable addition to the city or school

2. A list of interested athletes
3. The coach's name and qualifications
4. Proposed practice location and schedule
5. Projected costs

Be sure to include all these written sections in your proposal. This not only demonstrates that you are organized and responsible, but that you are committed to making this team a success. In addition, you are also making important decisions and plans. This will ensure a quick and easy set-up and make filling out the necessary paperwork as painless as possible. We all know we'd much rather be stunting than organizing details at the last minute!

Presenting Your Proposal

In addition to preparing a written proposal, you may be asked to personally present your proposal to the individual, committee, or group that will decide whether to approve and/or support your team. Whether you present your proposal to the school principal, a committee of teachers and administrators, or an entire school board or parent-teacher association, be sure you carefully plan, prepare, and practice your proposal presentation so it's brief and to the point. Your presentation outline will probably look similar to this:

1. Briefly introduce yourself, potential coaches, performers, and any others involved in the presentation.

2. Explain how the school/organization will benefit from a cheerleading team and outline the

events that cheerleaders will participate in (such as competitions, game cheering, or both).

3. Briefly describe the interest that has been shown in starting a team (such as lists of interested athletes, teachers, or sponsors).

4. Introduce the coach and his or her qualifications in more detail. Outline practice details such as when (days per week), where (practice location), and who will be responsible (names of supervisors).

5. Describe financial requirements and break down where funding will come from (such as athlete fees, school contributions, fund-raising).

6. Give a live performance or show a video of cheerleaders performing.

7. Allow for a question and answer period.

8. Thank officials for coming and state that you look forward to their response.

It is a good idea to rehearse beforehand what you will say and how you will answer questions. Be prepared for initial resistance to the proposal; some school officials may be opposed to cheerleading teams, thinking they are inappropriate or outdated.

One way to overcome this resistance and educate those who have misconceptions about the sport is to show a video clip of performances and competitions that illustrates what contemporary cheerleading is really like. This visual tool is great for demonstrating that cheerleading has evolved into a sport. You can *tell* administration what cheerleading teams do, but by far the best way is to *show* them what cheerleading is all about. A video of a cheerleading team performing a routine can help clear up any negative stereotypes.

As long as you prove that you are serious about starting a team, the people considering your proposal will be more motivated to support your request. Don't ever give up on creating a cheerleading team! If school administration is tough to convince, even if the answer is a stern "No," you can take lots of other routes. For example, you might take a group of athletes to summer cheerleading camp (no permission needed from the school). It is likely that when the "campers" come back in the fall, they will be excited about cheering and may put pressure on administrators to agree to sponsor a team. The decision makers will find it harder to say no if you have everything ready to go. If, after your second proposal the answer is still "no," consider creating a club team that allows students from any high school to participate. A club team has no affiliation with schools, and in many cases is easier to run because you are only required to obtain permission from parents, not the school administration.

Or try talking to other local coaches or cheerleaders. They will have good advice about getting the approval you need to start a team and making your team a success. Make friends with these people—you will see them around at numerous events and you can draw on one another's experiences to help *each others'* teams. Keep in mind that cheerleading is not like other sports. We cheer for one another because we love our sport and we know that the only way to advance it and enhance our image is to work together. Now, you may be asking yourself, "So after all this hard work, what do cheerleading teams get out of this game-cheering, team-supporting deal?" Well, you get to:

1. Have Fun!

Cheering games can be a lot of fun! Granted, cheering at a particularly unfriendly away game or supporting the football team during a November snowfall may not exactly be fun, but for the most

---

— TIP —

Invite a cheerleading company or local team to perform a demonstration at the meeting.

part, the high-energy atmosphere makes games enjoyable events in which to participate.

2. Build Confidence.

Cheering in front of a large group of fans helps to build cheerleaders' confidence and eases their anxiety. Even cheering in front of unfriendly crowds has its benefits. While athletes may feel intimidated at first, they eventually gain enough confidence to perform in any situation. Cheerleaders who learn to feel comfortable in front of a crowd typically have fewer competition jitters, which helps the whole team perform better in front of judges.

3. Increase Exposure.

When cheerleaders perform at pep rallies or cheer at games, both the sports team and the cheerleading team benefit from the increased exposure. Cheerleading teams let the public (including potential sponsors) know they exist and show everyone (including prospective cheerleaders) what cheerleading is about.

So, once you've finished the proposal and received the "thumbs up," give yourself a big pat on the back. You're now on the path to an exciting cheerleading career . . . so let the fun begin!

Simple Steps to Starting a Team

*Help for Cheerleaders and Coaches from
Preparation to Tryouts and Beyond*

To start a team requires detailed preparation and organization. While your first instinct might be to hold tryouts right away, there are several prerequisites to ensure successful tryouts. For example, communicating your goals and requirements to parents through a parents meeting is an essential primary step. After this initial meeting, you can then contact judges and recruit athletes. Once you're well prepared and your parents, participants, and judges are ready, you can schedule tryouts and select your team.

So you can be sure your careful organization, hard work, and patience pay off in the form of a solid group of dedicated cheerleading athletes eager to attend your first practice, follow the necessary steps.

— Step 1: Hold a Parents Meeting —

Holding a parents meeting is essential to get your cheerleading team off to a good start. That's because good relationships with your cheerleaders' parents is an important element in creating a successful team. Parents can assist the team in a number of ways, such as volunteering to help with fund-raising, carpooling to community events, and sponsoring your

team, just to name a few. The coach should really be in charge of this meeting, with any other cheerleaders or team advisors there to help.

Sample Tryout Release and Waiver

Releases and waivers are important for protecting the school or organization hosting tryouts, the volunteers and coaches running tryouts, and the participating athletes. Ensure all athletes have releases signed before they are allowed to participate in tryouts. (See sample Tryout Release and Waiver form on page 11.)

— Step 2: Contact Judges and Set Criteria —

The next step after the parents meeting is to contact judges for the tryout. Three to five individuals is considered an appropriate number of judges. Judges should be mature, responsible individuals with prior knowledge of cheerleading. They may be, for example:

★ Instructors from cheerleading companies and organizations

★ A coach whose team is not in your division

(continues on page 12)

THE PARENTS MEETING

Dealing with parents effectively and professionally is an invaluable skill for all coaches, regardless of experience. Before tryouts, hold an open meeting for any interested cheerleaders and their parents. Make sure you hold the meeting at a convenient time, such as in the evening, when working parents can attend.

The parents meeting should be the first of many contacts the team has with parents throughout the year. Stay in contact with parents throughout the season via newsletters, calendars, and meetings. Communication with parents is important; they will appreciate your including their input, and in turn you will benefit from their support.

On the Parents Meeting Agenda

As athletes and parents come in, have them fill out a tryout form with the athlete's basic information (name and address; previous dance, gymnastics, and cheerleading experience) as well as a medical form and waiver (see Athletic Tryout Release and Waiver Form sample on page 11). Introduce yourself and any other coaches or advisors or cheerleaders and summarize your qualifications. State your goals for the team and what you hope to accomplish. Also cover these important points:

★ Practice schedule and team commitments for the year

★ Projected costs (uniforms, travel, and other expenses)

★ Team Constitution, which should include this information:

1. Team purpose
2. Team structure (co-ed and competitive, for example)
3. Team rules and regulations (tryouts, practices, games, attendance, travel)
4. Consequences (penalties for absences, late arrivals, other)
5. Physical qualifications for participants (skills, attitude, other)
6. Team captain(s) (selection process, responsibilities)
7. Safety/Accident/Illness/Insurance

At the end of the meeting, ask for input and questions from parents and cheerleaders, mention tryout dates, and thank them for coming.

Parent Problems

There are hundreds of thousands of awesome cheerleader-parents out there—the ones who book gym time for you or hand-make thirty beautiful bows. Unfortunately, there are also difficult ones, including some parents who force cheerleading on their children. They'll saunter into practice unannounced, insist on making suggestions to the coaches ("Well, when *I* was a cheerleader, we always used to . . .") and may drive you crazy with their obsessive cheerleader-parent behavior ("Why isn't *my* daughter/son in the front?!").

As a coach, the best thing you can do is understand that these parents just want the best for their children. Listen to what their underlying message is, rather than their actual words. Remember that, as a qualified coach, you don't have to explain yourself, but do give those who ask fair questions the courtesy of answers. Firmly but congenially (remember, you want parents on your side!) reiterate that you are qualified and have been designated to make decisions for the team. Stand your ground and don't let difficult parents intimidate you. They will respect you for your confidence and dedication to the program.

— Sample Tryout Release and Waiver —

Athletic Tryout Release and Waiver Form

I, _____, understand that cheerleading
  (athlete's name)

has an inherent danger in participation, and that in spite of all precautions and accident preventatives, injuries do occur. I intend to be legally bound and do, hereby, for myself, my heirs, executors, and administrators, waive, release and forever discharge all claims which may arise now or in the future which I may accrue against _____,
                                          (school or organization)

and any of its employees for any and all injuries suffered by me while attending and participating in cheerleading tryouts and activities.

In order that I receive the necessary medical treatment in the event of an injury or illness, I hereby authorize _____ to
                       (school/organization name)

obtain medical treatment for myself for such injury or illness during any event, and I hold _____ harmless in their exercise of the authority.
  (school/organization name)

To the best of knowledge, I do not have any diseases or injuries that would medically prohibit my participation in practices while trying out for and participating in cheerleading activities at

_____.
        (school/organization name)

I further certify that I have read and understood the above statements and that the information provided is truthful to the best of my knowledge.

_____   _____
  (athlete's signature)   (date)

_____
  (athlete's printed name)

Parent/Guardian Acknowledgment Statement (*required* if athlete is under age 18)*

I/We have read the above statement and agree to the conditions of this tryout release and waiver as outlined above. I/We consent to allow our son/daughter to tryout for the cheerleading team at

_____
        (school/organization name)

_____   _____
  (parent/guardian signature)   (date)

_____
        (school/organization name)

If you are under the age of 18 years old, you must have this signed by a parent or legal guardian. No one can be admitted to cheerleading activities held by _____ unless this form has been properly filled out and signed by a parent or legal guardian.
        (school/organization name)

(continued from page 9)

★ Collegiate cheerleaders

★ Teachers with cheerleading experience (if it's a school tryout)

★ Other adults with cheerleading experience who have no affiliation with any of the athletes trying out

Do *not* ask cheerleaders from the team (or anyone else who might be biased toward individual athletes who are trying out) to judge tryouts for you.

Judging Criteria

Judges should take the following points into consideration when judging athletes at tryouts.

SAMPLE JUDGING CRITERIA

✓ *Stunting:* coordination, ease, poise, technique, level of difficulty, safety

✓ *Cheer:* execution, motions, voice, face, projection, confidence, enthusiasm, eye contact

✓ *Tumbling:* coordination, technique, ability, willingness to learn

✓ *Fight Song/Dance:* expressions, interaction with the crowd, rhythm, technique, ability to learn quickly, sharp execution, timing

✓ *Jumps:* technique, timing, skill, sharpness

✓ *Personal Interview:* confidence, poise, communication, attitude, personality

The judging sheet (see Sample Tryout Judge Sheet on page 13) and score breakdown should reflect the requirements of the cheerleading team. For example, stunting skills may be worth more points than cheer if the athlete is trying out for a competition team, whereas performance on the cheer component may be more important to a game-cheering team. Having a panel of judges rather than just one can be beneficial to gaining an accurate perception of an athlete's suitability for the team.

Be sure to contact your judges early and give them a score sheet ahead of time so that they know exactly what kind of athletes you're hoping to recruit for the team. You may also want to hand out score sheets at the parents meeting so that athletes can prepare for the tryout.

— Step 3: Bring the Talent to the Tryout —

Advertising is crucial for a good turnout at tryouts. Generally, the larger the number of athletes from which the judges can choose, the higher the skill level the resulting team will have.

You can advertise in a number of effective ways. For example:

★ Perform during assemblies or do demonstrations in gym classes at feeder schools for students coming to your school in the following year, hand out tryout sheets, and send posters to homeroom teachers.

★ Print tryout posters and tape them up around your campus or residence.

★ Put in a message for the morning announcements at school.

★ Visit homerooms and have cheerleaders hand out flyers.

★ Perform demonstrations at dance studios, gymnastics clubs, and even malls.

★ Put up flyers around the city, at community centers, and other recreational facilities.

★ Advertise in the newspaper.

Advertising is a year-round task. The more publicity your team gets, the more talented people will want to try out for your team the next year. Performances, appearances, parades, halftime shows, advertisement in recreational guides, and community service are some of the many great ways you can both serve the community and increase public awareness of your team and cheerleading.

— Step 4: Get Organized —

Though it's helpful for everyone involved in the team to be organized, it's the coach's responsibility to make sure the team stays that way. But help your

(continues on page 15)

— Sample Tryout Judge Sheet —

Athlete's name and/or tryout number: _____

TECHNICAL SKILLS
Stunting: judging on coordination, ease, technique, "solid" stunts (i.e. no wobbles or falls), athletic ability, level of difficulty of optional skill.

Required skills: Skills chosen by the coach as the minimum skills/skill level required for an athlete to be on the team (worth 10 points):
1.
2.
3.

Optional skill(s): skill(s) chosen by the athlete to demonstrate his or her abilities (worth 10 points):
1.
2.
3.

Total score (out of 20): _____

Tumbling: judging on coordination, rhythm, technique (toes pointed, legs straight, etc.), athletic ability, level of difficulty of optional skill, consistency:

Required skills/tumbling pass (worth 10 points):
1.
2.

Optional skill/tumbling pass (worth 10 points):
1.
2.

Total score (out of 20): _____

Jumps: judging on technique, height, pointed toes, straight legs, timing, and clean landing:

Required skills/combinations (worth 5 points):
1.
2.

(continues)

— Sample Tryout Judge Sheet, continued —

Optional skill/combination (worth 5 points):

1.

2.

Total score (out of 10): _____

PERFORMING SKILLS

Cheer: judging on sharp motions, crowd interaction, eye contact, clear/crisp words, good volume, enthusiasm/spirit, crowd appeal, and confidence (up to 10 points):

Total score (out of 10): _____

Fight Song: judging on enthusiasm, crowd interaction, sharp motions, technique, overall execution, confidence, poise, and crowd appeal (up to 10 points):

Total score (out of 10): _____

Dance: judging on rhythm, technique, crowd interaction, confidence, poise, eye contact, and crowd appeal (up to 10 points):

Total score (out of 10): _____

INTERVIEW

Judging on ability to communicate, positive attitude, and personality (up to 10 points):

Total score (out of 10): _____

OVERALL PRESENTATION

Judging on neatness, poise, confidence, positive self-image, posture, athleticism, and enthusiasm (up to 10 points):

Total score (out of 10): _____

Grand total score (out of 100): _____

NOTES

(continued from page 12)

coach in any way you can (see the Volunteer Task List on page 16 for ideas on how you can help).

Different Tryout Styles

How tryouts are conducted will depend on a number of factors, including your judges' preferences, the general skill level of the athletes trying out, and your time frame. The most common ways to select athletes are through Clinic Tryouts, Gradual Selection Tryouts, and Multiple-Day Tryouts.

CLINIC TRYOUTS

There is only one "judging" day in Clinic Tryouts. Before tryouts, Clinics are held for new cheerleaders to come and learn new skills or for experienced cheerleaders who want to brush up on existing skills. These "practice" tryouts are great for teams in which the majority of those trying out are inexperienced cheerleaders. Clinics, because of their relaxed nature, help to eliminate the participants' anxiety and nervousness.

C O A C H E S '   C O R N E R

ORGANIZED COACHING—KEEPING YOUR SANITY

Every coach, new or experienced, will have to organize team tryouts at one point or another. As veteran coaches can testify, running tryouts can be either a major headache or a minor event, depending on how efficiently they are organized.

For every coach who has dreaded tryouts because of the time they can take and the stress they can bring, this step is the answer to saving time and eliminating unnecessary aggravation. Read on for practical ideas and checklists for running hassle-free tryouts.

SMART TRYOUTS

What distinguishes a hassle-free tryout from a stressful one?

1. *Preparation*
2. *Task Delegation*

These two simple factors can determine whether your tryouts are successful or disastrous. Doing anything without planning ahead is like driving into the jungle without a map. Soon you'll find yourself stressed—stuck in the middle of chaos and evading angry parents and participants. Not a pleasant situation.

Additionally, although we may think we can do everything ourselves, that's impossible in reality. Just as you can't be the cook, waiter, and busperson for a large group, neither can you simultaneously organize, instruct, and judge tryouts. This is where task delegation comes in. Don't mistake task delegation with loading your responsibilities onto others (which is classified more appropriately as taking advantage of others!). Task delegation entails enlisting others to help, especially with the more mundane tasks, so that you can concentrate on being the best possible coach for your cheerleaders.

As you read through the next few sections, keep these two important concepts in mind. If you want to run manageable tryouts, preparation and delegation are the secrets to your success.

The Value of Volunteers

Volunteers are crucial to the success of a cheerleading program. They are the people willing to take on extraneous tasks and thus enable you to focus on coaching; typically, they love every minute of it.

(continues)

ORGANIZED COACHING—KEEPING YOUR SANITY, continued

VOLUNTEER TASK LIST

You'll need volunteers for tasks such as these:

★ Pre-tryout advertising (creating and handing out or posting flyers, posting signup lists)

★ Registering athletes (collecting forms and fees, answering questions about the cheerleading program)

★ Floating (assisting other volunteers, organizing groups, doing errands for the judges)

★ Organizing athletes into tryout groups

★ Teaching tryout material

★ Spotting tumbling skills (using qualified spotters only)

★ Tabulating scores

★ Videotaping the tryouts/clinics

FINDING VOLUNTEERS

Suitable tryout volunteers are easy to find. Here are some sources:

★ Senior or alumni cheerleaders

★ Parents of senior or alumni cheerleaders

★ Faculty

★ An unbiased coach from a different school or organization (A coach familiar with your type of team who coaches a different type is best. For example, a college or university coach would be a suitable volunteer to help with all-star team tryouts.)

AVOIDING VOLUNTEERS

Avoid using the following individuals as volunteers:

★ The parent, sister, brother, or other relative of an athlete trying out

★ Biased faculty members and judges

★ Your arch rival team's coach

★ Any unreliable individual

GRADUAL SELECTION TRYOUTS

Gradual Selection Tryouts ("weeding outs") are held a few days in a row, and only athletes still "in the running" are asked to return the next day. This type of tryout is suitable for teams with a large number of athletes trying out and teams for which competition is tough.

MULTIPLE-DAY TRYOUTS

The Multiple-Day Tryout is a combination of the Clinic and the Gradual Selection Tryouts. Each day is classified as a "tryout," but no cuts are made until the end of the last day. Many coaches use this tryout method because it gives the judges a few (usually three) separate days to see each athlete in action.

Scheduling Reminders

Preparing to hold tryouts involves so many tasks that it's easy to forget important details. Use the following reminders to stay organized and ensure that tryouts run as smoothly as possible.

ONE MONTH BEFORE

✓ Book the tryout facility. (As it gets closer to the tryout dates, confirm the dates and times so you're not stuck without a gym.)

✓ Begin advertising.

✓ Select a supervisor for tryouts.

✓ Find a team manager.

✓ Recruit judges and other volunteers.

✓ Determine what style of tryouts will be held.

✓ Set a preliminary date for the parents meeting. Draft the handouts and begin preparing your presentation.

✓ Sign up a supervisor for the upcoming season. This adult (over age 18) can be a parent, teacher, or coach who has been approved by the school as a qualified supervisor (where applicable) so that the cheerleaders will be covered by school insurance policies when they participate in athletic events.

✓ Determine judging criteria.

✓ Prepare judging sheets.

✓ Organize and print out tryout schedule.

✓ Design participant tryout form.

✓ Print out tryout forms, copy releases/parental consent forms, and judging sheets.

ONE WEEK BEFORE

✓ Increase advertising efforts (announcements, posters, other).

✓ Hold the parents meeting.

✓ Make the judges' packets.

✓ Determine tryout material. That is, select the cheers, chants, dances, and stunts that participants will be taught and/or judged on.

✓ Arrange to have a videographer (amateur is fine) with fresh tapes at tryouts.

✓ Organize tryout supplies: boom box, music for warm-up and dance segments, labels, pens, markers, and a first-aid box.

Holding tryouts can be a lot of fun, provided you plan them out well ahead of time and stay as

★ ★ ★ ★ ★ ★ ★ ★ ★ ★ ★ ★ ★ ★ ★ ★ ★

Judges' Packets

Whether you have judges from an outside source or you judge tryouts yourself, a pre-made package makes judging efficient and easy. On a clipboard or in a clipboard folder, put together the judging sheets, tryout schedule, and blank sheets. Along with the clipboards, include pens, pencils, and calculators.

★ ★ ★ ★ ★ ★ ★ ★ ★ ★ ★ ★ ★ ★ ★ ★ ★

organized as possible. Stick to your schedule and rely on volunteers to do a lot of the groundwork for you. For example, volunteers can do the photocopying, put up posters, be responsible for advertising tryouts, and even videotape tryout material. And finally, take a deep breath . . . just follow the pointers in this chapter, and tryouts will be only a minor event in your cheerleading season.

— Step 5: Hold Tryouts —

The big day has arrived! In this section you'll find a sample three-day tryout clinic for coaches and some last-minute reminders for all team members to help get your tryouts off to a great start.

JUST BEFORE TRYOUTS BEGIN

Ensure Safety

✓ Pull up all basketball nets.

✓ Sweep the floors.

✓ Put out mats.

✓ Make sure that all props you will be using (such as bleachers for stunting drills) are sturdy.

Set Up

✓ Set up the judges' table, complete with judges' packets and bottles of water. (*Note:* On the

Start the Music!

While cheerleaders are registering and getting ready for tryouts, playing music is an effective way to reduce stress and nervousness and keep the atmosphere fun and upbeat.

final day of tryouts, set up the judges' table in a separate room from the practice area.)

✓ Set up the registration table (extra forms, labels, markers, pencils, and a cash box if there is a tryout fee).

✓ Make sure the volunteers are clear on their responsibilities.

✓ Check to be sure the boom box works and the right music is nearby.

— Sample Three-Day Tryout Schedule —

This sample schedule is for coaches to follow, but it's a great way for cheerleaders and other team members to know what to expect. Coaches can add to and rearrange the following schedule to suit their own tryouts based on the needs of the team. For example, you can devote more time to tumbling and less time to stunts if tumbling is an important element for the team. Notice that the sample schedule ends at 6:00 P.M., and the times are back-to-back. The schedule may run over because you should allow a few minutes in between each time slot.

DAY 1 (CLINIC)

4:00 P.M. to 4:10: Welcome

Before tryouts begin, welcome all applicants and introduce yourself. Make sure everyone has signed a tryout form and a release form. Outline the aims and objectives of the program, as well as the expectations of cheerleaders. You may also want to list the judging criteria and tryout agenda. Review rules (such as no jewelry) and mention that only those who come to *all* tryouts will be considered for positions. *Here's a good rule of thumb:* If participants can't come to all the tryouts, they won't come to all the practices.

4:10 to 4:25: Warm Up

Lead 10 minutes of cardio (such as running or aerobic exercise) to warm muscles and 5 minutes of stretching. (See chapter 3 for more specifics on cardio and stretching.)

4:25 to 4:40: Cheer Skills

Teach motions and a simple sideline.

4:40 to 4:55: Jump Skills

Teach the basic elements of jumping. Go through simple drills (timing, straight jumps, "frog jumps") before teaching Toe Touches.

4:55 to 5:00: Break

5:00 to 5:30: Stunting Skills

Even if the majority of those trying out are experienced cheerleaders, it is important that you review safety and spotting before you have participants do any stunting. Depending on the overall level of the group, you may need to begin with a few drills before going onto the basic stunts such as the Thigh Stand, Elevator (all-girl/Quad Base), and Toss Chair (co-ed/Single Base). For a complete list of drills and stunts, refer to chapters 7 through 12.

5:30 to 5:45: Gymnastics Skills

Provide qualified spotters to spot athletes if needed. Look for technique (tight bodies, solid landings, consistency) as well as for potential. If any athletes show good basic technique but have not yet perfected their skills, you might still want to consider them for the team if they show a willingness to improve.

5:45 to 5:55: Dancing

Teach a simple dance (four eight counts is a good length) to assess overall dancing ability and style. Remember to use windowed lines and switch lines often so that everyone has a chance to be in the front row. Keep the teaching pace congruent with the skill of the group. If most of those trying out are having trouble, slow down the teaching speed to match the group's average ability—but don't wait for those who are lagging behind.

5:55 to 6:00 P.M.: Goodbye

Thank everyone for coming. Give the next tryout date and remind athletes to practice at home.

DAY 2 (CLINIC)

4:00 P.M. to 4:05: Welcome

Welcome everyone back and briefly review the tryout schedule for that day. Mention important details such as whether or not cuts will be made that day. Remind participants to take off all jewelry and to stunt safely.

4:05 to 4:20: Warm Up

Warm up with 10 minutes of cardio and 5 minutes of stretching.

4:20 to 4:35: Cheer Skills

Review the motions and the sideline taught the day before. Teach a more difficult chant or sideline.

4:35 to 5:05: Stunting Skills

Teach more difficult stunts, relying on the skill level from the previous day to guide the teaching pace. Break everyone up into groups and allow them to practice while you watch, looking for good partner combinations. Change groups around often, challenging participants to stunt with different people.

5:05 to 5:10: Break

5:10 to 5:25: Jump Skills

Review the Toe Touch and teach a new jump, such as the Front Hurdler. Remember to change the lines so that everyone can be seen.

5:25 to 5:40: Gymnastic Skills

As during the previous practice, ensure that qualified spotters are on hand to spot athletes.

5:40 to 5:55: Dancing

Review the four counts of eight from the day before and add on a few more counts of eight. Run the dance full out with music.

5:55 to 6:00 P.M.: Goodbye

Review the dates and agenda for the next tryout session. Mention that the next tryout will require groups to come up with their own routines incorporating skills taught from previous clinics. Have the sign-up sheet ready so you don't waste time during the final tryout day waiting for them to get organized. Participants should be in groups consisting of one flyer, two bases, and a third. A qualified spotter should be provided. Athletes can either put themselves into groups or you may group them where appropriate (a particularly good idea if you want to see how they work with others). Once the sheet is filled out with participant names, copy it for all judges and volunteers.

DAY 3 (ACTUAL TRYOUT)

4:00 P.M. to 4:05: Welcome

Outline the agenda and details for the last day of tryouts.

4:05 to 4:20: Warm Up

Warm up as on the previous days.

4:20 to 5:55: Judging

With the judges in a separate room, call in each group one by one, according to the scheduled sign-up sheet. Designate a volunteer as the "runner," responsible for organizing the groups to be brought in one after another so that time isn't wasted waiting for people.

5:55 to 6:00 P.M.: Goodbye

Let the athletes know when and where the final list will be posted. Mention other available opportunities for those who don't make the team this year (such as a junior varsity team, recreational team, or management positions). Thank everyone for coming and tell everyone when the first scheduled practice will be.

— So . . . Now What? —

Tryouts leave coaches with two gifts: the exciting potential of building a successful team, and athletes eager to practice. These advantages can diminish, however, when coaches fail to create a plan to guide their program. Coaches should address important issues at the beginning of the season to ensure that everyone's hard work in starting up a team will bring success. To help this happen, a Team Goal-Setting Worksheet is provided on page 21 for coaches to follow. An Individual Goal-Setting Worksheet that athletes should fill out with their coaches is also provided on page 22. Cheerleaders should review both of these forms to know what is expected of the coach and the team. If the whole team works together on the worksheets, the team is bound to be a success.

When you take a moment to specify your goals, it becomes easy to create a plan to accomplish them. For every goal, both long term and short term, list the ways you plan to work toward achieving them. For example, if a long-term team goal is to have full-team back handsprings, you'll want to schedule a team practice at a gymnastics club with tumbling coaches to help you reach that goal. If a short-term individual goal is to perfect your Toe Touch, consider taking 15 minutes a day to work on jump drills, followed by doing ten Toe Touches in a row. You can use the Plan of Action Worksheet on page 23 to help create your own plan.

If you're fairly new to the cheerleading scene, a little bit of extra assistance can go a long way in helping you reach your objectives. In addition to the information found in this book, you should consider a number of other sources, such as these:

★ Coaches from other teams

★ Veteran cheerleaders or cheerleaders from another team (for example, university cheerleaders)

(continues on page 24)

C O A C H E S '   C O R N E R

GOAL SETTING

While the general purpose of the team has already been established in the proposal, it's essential that specific long-term and short-term goals be set. To determine your long-term goals as a coach, ask yourself these questions: What are your aspirations for your team this year? If you plan on competing, to what competitions do you want to go? If game cheering is your priority, to what teams are you going to commit and in how many events can you participate?

Once you have answered these general questions, move on to a detailed set of short-term goals. For example, ask for details such as these: What stunts do you want perfected by competition date? By the end of the month? Use the Team Goal-Setting Worksheet on page 21 as an aid in developing your team's general and specific goals for the upcoming year.

It's also a good idea to sit down with athletes and have them fill in their own personal goal sheet. This helps to keep them focused on what they want to accomplish as a member of the team. You can use the Individual Goal-Setting Worksheet on page 22 as an example.

— Team Goal-Setting Worksheet —

Our team strengths are:

Our team weaknesses are:

LONG-TERM GOALS

The purpose of our team is:

We plan on participating in the following events this year:

Our long-term goal for team stunting is:

Our long-term goal for team tumbling is:

Our long-term goal for team jumps is:

Our long-term goal for team dancing is:

Other goal(s):

By the end of the year, we want to be able to:

We can commit to practicing _____ practices per week in order to be adequately prepared for these events and technical goals.

SHORT-TERM GOALS

Our first event will be _____ on _____.
　　　　　　　　　　　　　　　(event)　　　　　　　　　(date)

Our short-term goal for team stunting is:

Our short-term goal for team tumbling is:

Our short-term goal for team jumps is:

Our short-term goal for team dancing is:

Other goal(s):

We plan on participating in the following events this month:

By the end of the month we want to be able to (Example: hit our Heel Stretch pyramid perfectly):

By the end of the week we want to be able to:

By the end of this practice we want to be able to:

— Individual Goal-Setting Worksheet —

My strengths as a cheerleader are:

My weaknesses as a cheerleader are:

LONG-TERM GOALS

My ultimate goal for being a cheerleader is:

My long-term goal for stunting is:

My long-term goal for tumbling is:

My long-term goal for jumps is:

My long-term goal for dancing is:

Other goal(s):

SHORT-TERM GOALS

Our first event will be _____ on _____. By then I want to be able to:
                              (event)   (date)

My short-term goal for stunting is:

My short-term goal for tumbling is:

My short-term goal for jumps is:

My short-term goal for dancing is:

Other:

By the end of the month I want to be able to:

By the end of the week I want to be able to:

By the end of this practice I want to be able to:

— Plan of Action Worksheet —

We plan on accomplishing our long-term team goals by:

1.

2.

3.

4.

5.

We plan on accomplishing our short-term team goals by:

1.

2.

3.

4.

5.

I plan on accomplishing my long-term individual goals by:

1.

2.

3.

4.

5.

I plan on accomplishing my short-term individual goals by:

1.

2.

3.

4.

5.

(continued from page 20)

★ Instructional cheerleading companies

★ Cheerleading videos

Don't be afraid to approach an experienced cheerleader or coach for help, as intimidating as they might seem to be. The prospects are pretty good that these people will be enthusiastic about sharing their love of the sport with others. Remember that even the greatest cheerleaders once started out knowing nothing about cheerleading.

— Team Cohesion —

Team bonding is vital in cheerleading—especially since the dynamics of the sport require that all members work closely with one another. Every athlete has an important role (for example, if just one person is missing, an entire pyramid may be impossible to form). It's also natural that cheerleaders who are friends will ultimately perform better. And because a large part of cheerleading is having fun, athletes with friends on the team are likely to enjoy their sport even more. It's important that the coach is aware of these important factors, as well as the other team members.

— Attitude Reflects Leadership —

Positive attitude is essential for any successful team. The coach's responsibility extends far

(continues on page 26)

COACHES' CORNER

KEEPING YOUR TEAM TOGETHER

At the beginning of the season, encouraging friendships and team cohesion is key—especially when veteran cheerleaders are mixed together with new athletes. You can accomplish this through activities such as these:

★ Play "get-to-know-you" games (for example: "twenty questions" and "name games")

★ Form groups to work together on a fundraising project or game/pep rally committee

★ Mix up base groups

★ Run team conditioning drills with partners (for example, piggy-back runs)

★ Have after-practice parties

★ Organize team activities (for example: bowling or mini-putting)

By the end of the first few weeks, teammates should know one another's names and have spent at least some time with each person on the team. Continue to encourage team bonding throughout the year. Your team will soon discover that the best part of cheerleading isn't hitting your pyramid perfectly after all; it's creating friendships that can last a lifetime.

Discipline

A section on coaching isn't complete without mentioning team discipline. Too little discipline leads to an unproductive, disordered team that lacks respect for the coach(es). On the other hand, too much discipline tears down self-esteem, hampers creativity, and fosters discouragement. Finding and maintaining the right balance between these two extremes is a very important aspect of coaching.

Discipline is closely tied to the coach's expectations of the team. Your athletes will strive to meet what you expect of them. If you set expectations too low, you're preventing them

C O A C H E S ' C O R N E R

from realizing their full potential. But if expectations are too high, you're setting your athletes up for failure. Again, finding the right balance is imperative to your becoming a good coach.

Before the season begins, establish what your expectations are and review them once the program has commenced. Use these points (along with your goals) to form the basis of the Team Constitution. Once the season begins, it's also a good idea to discuss with the team their expectations of one another, as well as of you, the coach. Here are a few ideas to get you started:

AS A COACH, I EXPECT

★ Athletes will arrive at practice on time and ready to begin

★ Athletes will show respect to their coach, administrators, and one another

★ Athletes will give 110 percent effort at every practice, event, game, and competition

★ Athletes will represent the cheerleading team in a positive manner at all times, during and outside of practice

Expectations don't have to be solely behavior oriented. They can include physical demands, such as these:

AS A COACH, I EXPECT

★ Athletes will use good technique and teamwork to achieve solid stunts

★ Athletes will take care of one another with good spotting when stunting; there will be *no* falls

★ Athletes will train outside of scheduled practices (weights and cardio) to maintain a healthy body

For every expectation, institute a consequence to discipline an athlete who doesn't meet the requirements for conduct. It's vital that you include the team when determining consequences. Consequences can range from doing pushups for incorrect techniques to removal from the team.

Use discipline responsibly. When implementing consequences, be respectful of your athletes. Openly criticizing or putting down an individual (especially in front of other members of the team) is not only harmful to that athlete's sense of self-worth, but is unacceptable behavior from a coach. Be conscious of the fact that some athletes may be more sensitive than others and act accordingly. Remember, too, that a repetitive discipline problem at practice often reflects a more serious underlying issue.

If you suspect there may be a serious underlying issue behind an athlete who continually requires discipline, consider scheduling a personal meeting with the athlete and ask her to explain her behavior. Provide her with an opportunity to discuss difficulties she may be having. Be careful not to intrude or press the issue if the athlete prefers not to confide in you. If you suspect a serious problem such as abuse, contact an authority immediately.

Discipline must be instituted at the beginning of a program and remain consistent throughout the year. If the coach begins to slack on the disciplining, the actions of athletes will reflect this. Remember to review your expectations and consequences periodically and assess their effectiveness with the team. Make changes to your Team Constitution, if necessary.

Be firm in your discipline, but never be unfair. Verbal abuse and excessive discipline are never appropriate.

— TIP —

It's dangerous to set body weight expectations for athletes. *Never* institute weigh-ins or "maximum weight limits." Make it clear that negative comments regarding body shape or size (about one another or oneself) will not be tolerated.

(continued from page 22)

beyond just teaching technical skills; a coach provides athletes with a positive role model. Because athletes often think highly of their coaches, it's essential that coaches remain role models worthy of such respect. Regardless of whether a coach is sick, tired, or just plain cranky, he or she still owes the team good leadership.

— Not *More* Practices, But More *Efficient* Practices —

Just as you can't go into a game without a game strategy, neither can you go into a cheerleading practice without a plan. A two-hour practice goes by quickly; it's easy to waste time with mundane tasks that can be organized ahead of time. Planned practices are essential to make efficient use of the time the team has together.

It's a good idea for everyone to review the following list under the Team Managers section on this page so you'll know what to expect at the competition practice. This way, if any athletes have suggestions or concerns with the list, they can discuss them with the coach ahead of time.

Of course, every team's practice schedule will be different, depending on the team's objectives, skill level, strengths, and weaknesses. Coaches should allow the flexibility to modify the schedule as the practice goes on. If the team is really close to hitting a pyramid and eager to continue trying, the coach may go ahead and cut the next scheduled time block a little short.

— Team Managers —

In addition to carefully planning your practices, another way to make efficient use of time is delegating tasks to a team manager. The manager serves as the coach's right-hand (wo)man and is responsible for organizing details such as these:

★ Booking gym space and gym time

★ Locating and securing a supervisor (if needed)

★ Organizing buses for competitions and away games

C O A C H E S ' C O R N E R

KEEP THINGS IN CHECK

Your team is a direct reflection of your emotions and attitude. If you're observing problems among team members, first take a look at *your own attitude* and how you're handling the situation. If you notice that your athletes seem worn out, is it *your* enthusiasm that's wavering? If your athletes are acting irritable, is it *your* patience that's running thin? Often all it takes is a five-minute break and a conscious effort on your behalf to remedy the problem.

Make a genuine attempt to keep a positive and encouraging attitude at every practice with your team. Your team's attitude *will* reflect your leadership.

C O A C H E S '   C O R N E R

IS YOUR TEAM PRACTICING TOO MUCH?

Many coaches make the mistake of adding more practices per week in an attempt to increase the team's skill level and ability. The number of appropriate practices in a week depends on many factors (age, skill, goals, and more), but also be aware that too many hours of training can actually lower the overall level of the team. Watch out for these common signs of practice burnout:

★ frequent injuries

★ easily frustrated athletes

★ decreased levels of effort

★ pessimistic attitudes (especially from usually upbeat individuals)

★ lack of interest in practicing

★ repeatedly missed practices without reasonable excuses

★ "sick" athletes who were well until practice time

If you notice any of the above, it's time to rethink the length and number of practices. Never sacrifice your team's health and safety by pushing your athletes beyond a fair and reasonable level of training.

★ Booking the team for charity events, community performances, and fundraising activities

★ Handing out uniforms

★ Ordering warm-ups, practice wear, and uniforms

★ Ordering megaphones, poms (pom-poms), or other props

★ Collecting all monies for athletic fees, apparel, and competitions

★ Organizing paperwork (such as ensuring that all permission/health forms have been filled out)

★ Compiling information letters about upcoming scheduled events, games, and competitions

★ Organizing camps and clinics

★ Serving on the Game/Pep Rally Committee

If your team doesn't already have a team manager, try to find one. A manager is the answer to saving time and running a more efficient cheerleading program. A bonus to having a good manager is that you can live a cheerleading coach's dream: focusing all your energy on coaching.

Making the most of practices is important in any sport. A detailed plan encourages efficient use of time and is invaluable in helping teams reach their goals. Don't have *more* practices; plan more *efficient* ones.

— Uniforms —

Since uniforms can be expensive, you may want to consider buying team shorts and T-shirts to wear until your team can afford uniforms. You can use these sets later for game cheering, pep rallies, and practices—especially if you want to save your uniforms for competing.

When you decide to buy uniforms, consider two alternatives to pay for them:

1. Raise the funds as a team and buy a team set.
2. Have each team member buy his or her own uniform.

— Sample Two-Hour Practice for Competition —

4:00 P.M. to 4:15: Warm up and stretch. Discuss specific goals for the practice.

4:15 to 4:25: Practice cheer and jump skills.

4:25 to 4:40: Warm up tumbling and practice gymnastics skills.

4:40 to 5:00: Practice stunts.

5:00 to 5:05: Break.

5:05 to 5:20: Practice pyramids.

5:20 to 5:35: Practice dance (leave as before).

5:35 to 5:55: Run routine, putting all elements together.

5:55 to 6:00 P.M.: Stretch. Give coach's talk and review goals.

There are pros and cons to each option so make sure you decide carefully. For example, if athletes purchase their own uniforms, when cheerleaders leave the team, their replacements will have to buy new uniforms. If the specific style is no longer available, all athletes will need to buy a new style the following year. On the other hand, uniforms often receive better care when they are individually owned. You may want to have a short meeting with cheerleaders and their parents to discuss the best choice for your team's situation before making the final decision.

— Sponsorship —

Funding for a cheerleading program has to come from somewhere. If the cheerleaders are on a school team, the athletic department is usually

(continues on page 30)

C O A C H E S '   C O R N E R

PLANNING YOUR PRACTICES

Before sitting down to plan out a year's worth of practices, review your team goals. Keep in mind both your long-term and short-term objectives. Using these goals as guidelines, take a calendar and roughly sketch in a timeline for reaching them. This is your framework for building your practice schedule.

Working backward from each main goal, start outlining your plan. For example, if your goal is to compete in six weeks, your general schedule might look something like this:

Week 1: Write the routine and teach main routine elements.

Week 2: Practice technical skills.

Week 3: Put together the routine; make changes to choreography as needed.

Week 4: Add music and run the routine.

Week 5: Clean up the routine.

Week 6: Compete.

For many teams, this short schedule might be cutting it a bit close to competition time. For others, however, six weeks might allow the perfect amount of preparation time. Keep in mind your team's skill level as well as your experience as a coach as you outline your general plan.

Next, specify the basic idea for each practice. Keeping with the previous example, your schedule might look like this:

Sample Practice Schedule

WEEK 1

★ *Practice 1:* Organize team into stunt groups. Teach main routine elements.

★ *Practice 2:* Stunt groups work on partner stunts.

★ *Practice 3:* Stunt groups continue working on stunts. Teach dance. Perform dance with music.

WEEK 2

★ *Practice 1:* Stunt groups work on stunts. Review dance. Teach cheer.

★ *Practice 2:* Stunt groups continue working on stunts. Review dance and cheer. Teach pyramid(s).

★ *Practice 3:* Review dance, cheer, pyramid, and stunts.

WEEK 3

★ *Practice 1:* Review, practice, and put together routine elements.

★ *Practice 2:* Clean up elements. Make changes if necessary.

★ *Practice 3:* Put together the routine. Run the routine to continuous counts.

WEEK 4

★ *Practice 1:* Run the routine with counts. Clean up elements.

★ *Practice 2:* Add music to routine. Begin breaking routine down and clean up elements section by section.

★ *Practice 3:* Continue running routine to music. Remove stunts that aren't working and make any other necessary changes.

WEEK 5

★ *Practice 1:* Run the routine full out. Make only minor changes to clean up the routine.

★ *Practice 2:* Practice in full uniform. Invite press, friends, and family. Run routine full out/clean up routine.

★ *Practice 3:* Conduct short practice. Run routine full out/clean up routine.

WEEK 6

★ Compete.

After you have organized the basic idea of every practice, start to plan out an even more detailed schedule for each practice. *Word of warning:* Don't get ahead of yourself! It's best not to plan specifics too far in advance. Planning practices in detail at the beginning of each week is usually sufficient. This way, you can modify practices the following week based on the amount of progress during the previous week.

Before each practice, you'll need to prepare more detailed plans to ensure that you make efficient use of your time and accomplish your goals for the practice. See the Sample Two-Hour Practice for Competition list on page 28 for a general guideline.

(continued from page 28)

— TIP —

A great way to entice companies to sponsor you is to offer to display the sponsor's name on your team warm-up, T-shirt, or bag.

responsible for footing the bill. But if you're involved in a community, club, or all-star team, athletes are generally responsible for their own costs, which can quickly climb to a sizeable amount. In addition to fundraising, sponsorship is one of the best ways to support a cheerleading program. Such assistance can be in a number of forms:

★ Financial support

★ Product support (a bag company may supply team bags, or a restaurant may offer discount coupons to the team)

★ Non-monetary donations (such as raffle or silent auction prizes)

Before approaching a company for sponsorship, you should do the following:

Check with the appropriate authority in charge of your team. Do this before approaching companies for potential sponsorship. This is an especially important step if your cheerleading team is part of a school's athletic department.

Draft a sponsorship letter. Indicate who you are (your team), what you are requesting (money, product support, donation), why you need sponsorship, and what you can do for the company in return.

Ask for the manager or owner when you approach a company for financial support. The part-time sales clerk won't be able to help you in this situation, so make sure you talk to the person who can help. Start with a phone call requesting the name of the person in charge of sponsorship at the company. Then, schedule a time

— TIP —

After you've made the pitch, don't forget to make follow-up telephone calls or in-person visits to potential sponsors. Refresh the potential sponsor's memory of who you represent, that you have requested sponsorship, and that are now touching base to find out their response to your request.

COACHES' CORNER

MAKING IT WORK

After tryouts, you're faced with the task of creating a team from a group of individual athletes. Whether your team is the first or the twentieth group to represent your school or city, you must address numerous elements. You can generally take care of administrative tasks (such as practices, uniforms, and sponsorship) at the beginning of a season. However, team building blocks (such as goal-setting, cohesion, discipline, and leadership) require continuous effort throughout the year. Attending to both types of team needs at the start of the program and staying on top of them can help guarantee a productive and enjoyable year ahead.

to meet with this individual *in person*. Offering to take them for coffee won't hurt either.

Once you've secured a sponsor and received money, products, or donations, it's important to keep the company involved in your program. For example, invite your sponsor to come to your open practices and performances, send photos of your team in action, and forward competition results and copies of news clippings. You might even offer to perform at a sponsor's important event, such as a grand opening or sidewalk sale. Make sure you let them know how much you appreciate their support and their interest in your team.

After setting goals, establishing practice schedules, buying uniforms, and securing sponsorship, the group of athletes that were once only successful tryout candidates have now evolved into a cohesive team. It only gets better from here!

Chapter Three

Are You Ready to Be a Cheerleader?

Cheerleading demands a great deal from athletes: time, energy, and effort—all in considerable amounts. Do *you* have what it takes? The following quizzes will help you determine whether you're ready to make the commitment to cheerleading.

Are You Ready?

Circle T for true statements; F for false statements.

T F 1. I'm outgoing, friendly, and a good sport.

T F 2. I can keep my enthusiasm and energy levels high for 2- to 3-hour-long practices, 4-hour games, and all-day events. I don't mind practicing or participating in events 2 to 7 days a week.

T F 3. I enjoy and work hard at keeping fit.

T F 4. I love being the center of attention.

T F 5. I enjoy cooperating with others to reach a common goal.

T F 6. I can take constructive criticism, and I don't allow negative comments to hurt my feelings or performance.

T F 7. I'm ready to give full respect to my coaches and their decisions.

T F 8. I'm committed to making *all* practices, even if it means giving up something else I'd rather be doing. When I'm injured or sick, I'm willing to just come in and watch (as long as I'm not contagious!).

T F 9. I like to help raise funds.

T F 10. I enjoy volunteer work.

If you answered "False" to more than two of these, you might not be ready for the responsibilities and commitments that come along with being a cheerleader. Read on to learn why each condition is so important.

1. I'm outgoing, friendly, and a good sport.
Cheerleading is unique in the sense that cheerleaders are constantly interacting with the public. Whether it's at a game, community event, or competition, you have to be approachable and friendly. You *want* people to enjoy having you around. Cheerleaders also need to act and speak with a positive attitude, displaying good sportsmanship at all times. It won't always be easy though, especially when your team is down by 30 points, or when your routine's prized pyramid comes down. You have to be ready for such situations and not let them ruin your morale.

2. I can keep my enthusiasm and energy levels high for 2- to 3-hour–long practices, 4-hour games, and all-day events. I don't mind practicing or participating in events 2 to 7 days a week.
Cheerleading runs all year long; there really isn't an "off season" as with other sports. During the year, participants cheer for football, basketball, and other sports, practice for competitions, and participate in community events. In the summer, cheerleaders attend cheerleading camps and practices. Games can be long, especially if you're cheering back-to-back men's and women's games. By the time you're done, more than 5 hours can go by, or as much as a full day if you're traveling. Community events often take up the whole day as well, and you might have to miss classes or other activities to participate with your team. You have to be ready to keep up your energy and enthusiasm all the time, even when you're tired from cheering hours on end.

3. I enjoy and work hard at keeping fit.
Get ready for some muscles! Cheerleading is a fantastic workout, both anaerobically and aerobically. (See the Basic Strength Training Glossary on page 42 for definitions of these terms.) You're building strength when you stunt and improving your cardiovascular system (heart and blood vessels) when you dance and cheer. Additionally, coaches often mandate that athletes train outside of practice at least a few days a week. You have to be ready to hit the gym and the track in order to keep yourself in top shape.

4. I love being the center of attention.
It's pretty tough to do a good job cheerleading if you're petrified of the crowd. Who's going to want to watch someone who doesn't appear confident in his or her abilities? This isn't to say that shy people don't make good cheerleaders. It just means that their shyness usually goes away pretty quickly—in the first tryout if you're going to make the team! If you don't enjoy being in front of people, cheerleading isn't for you. As a cheerleader, you also must be mindful of the fact that a lot of people look up to you. The crowd is always watching how you conduct yourself and how you act with others, on and off the field. Even when you're not in uniform, people are going to recognize you and associate your actions with cheerleading. Cheerleaders are always in the spotlight.

5. I enjoy cooperating with others to reach a common goal.
Cheerleading is a team sport. When even just one person is missing, the team may not be able to perform its pyramid, dance, or cheer segment. Stunting especially suffers when one person is missing or isn't working with the rest of the group. When you stunt, you need to act as "one," even though there may be many of you. Only then will your stunt work. If you're more an individualist who likes to do things his or her own way, you'll find it difficult to progress as a cheerleader.

6. I can take constructive criticism, and I don't allow negative comments to hurt my feelings or performance.
You have to be able to take constructive criticism from your coaches or teammates, just as you would in any sport. It's important that you not take it as a personal attack on your abilities as an athlete. In fact, listening carefully to constructive criticism can be one of the best ways to help your team improve. That's because others can help you fix

technique errors you may not have noticed before. Unfortunately, whether it's a frustrated teammate or a rude fan, people sometimes say things that aren't "constructive." You simply can't let such unproductive comments affect your performance as a cheerleader.

7. I'm ready to give full respect to my coaches and their decisions.

There will be lots of times when you won't agree with your coach. You might think your cheer doesn't suit your team, or you might not agree with having to run laps after dropping stunts. But even though you might not like their decisions, part of being on a team means respecting yourself, your teammates, and especially your coach.

8. I'm committed to making all practices, even if it means giving up something else I'd rather be doing. When I'm injured or sick, I'm willing to just come in and watch (as long as I'm not contagious!).

Every single teammate is an important part of a cheerleading team. Unlike some other sports where missing athletes are easily replaced, you need every single person to perform your partner stunts, pyramid, or dance in cheerleading. If just one person is missing, an entire segment will suffer. It's essential that every single person is present at all practices. Even when you're feeling sick (but don't have something contagious), you are expected to go to practice and watch.

9. I like to help raise funds.

Cheerleading can be expensive. Often your school or club will supply things such as uniforms and megaphones, but you'll need to foot the bill for warm-ups, shoes, and bloomies, or perhaps plane fares to get to competitions. If you're thinking about becoming a cheerleader, you'll have to be ready to work hard at raising money to cover the costs of being on the team.

10. I enjoy volunteer work.

Volunteering at community events is a big part of cheerleading. A lot of your free time will be devoted to the planning and participating in parades, fundraising for special causes, and entertaining at community events. While you can expect that cheerleading will be very time consuming, it will also be very rewarding.

— Do You Have What It Takes? —

So now that you know you're ready to make the commitment to cheerleading, do you have what it takes? Here's another quiz to help you determine what areas to focus on in preparation for tryouts. Circle the answer that comes closest to describing you.

· ·

Do You Have What It Takes?

Circle the letter of the answer that comes closest to describing you.

1. I currently work out:
a. Three to four times a week.
b. One to two times a week.
c. Never.

2. My flexibility is:
a. Awesome: I can wrap myself into a pretzel.
b. Okay: It needs some work, but I still have a decent Heel Stretch (Y scale).
c. Splits? What are splits?

3. *Being in front of a crowd:*
   a. Gives me the biggest rush!
   b. Makes me a little nervous at first, but once I get going, I can't be stopped.
   c. Scares me. I'd rather run around the track a million times with no one watching than stand on the sidelines in front of thousands.

4. **When it comes to dancing:**
   a. I've danced all my life. I love music and love to move to it.
   b. I enjoy dancing. I might not be the best dancer on the face of the earth, but I like the cheerleading "Hip Hop" funk style of dancing.
   c. I swear I was born with two left feet; "5, 6, 7, 8" just doesn't fit into my vocabulary.

5. **My eating habits:**
   a. Are great. I make an effort to eat healthy foods and drink lots of water to fuel my body, but I don't "diet." If I want that chocolate bar, I'm going to eat it!
   b. Are fairly good, but sometimes I forget to eat when I'm on the run or substitute a junky snack for a meal.
   c. Eat?

6. *The thought of balancing on one foot high in the air or holding someone high above my head:*
   a. Sounds like fun. I'm always up for a challenge and am the first one in line to try it.
   b. Makes me a little nervous at first, but once I see it done, I'm willing to try it.
   c. Scares me to death, even more so than being in front of a crowd.

7. **My gymnastics skills:**
   a. Are pretty good. If someone asked me to do a handspring right now, it wouldn't be a problem.
   b. Are a little rough but I'm willing to put in the time and effort to make a handspring happen.

   c. Are nonexistent . . . and they're staying that way.

8. *Watching football, basketball, and other team sports:*
   a. Makes me so excited that if I weren't cheerleading I'd be right in there playing.
   b. Can be a little boring when I don't understand all the rules but fun to watch when I do.
   c. Puts me to sleep.

9. **My daybook:**
   a. Is full, but organized. Although I have a lot to do, I have things planned so I have time for everything.
   b. Is full, but slightly disorganized. I manage to get almost everything done on time, but sometimes I neglect things like school-work because I didn't budget enough time for everything.
   c. Is full, completely disorganized, and unintelligible. I'm constantly running from A to B and never seem to have enough time to do everything. I struggle with planning my time and organizing my schedule.

Rating Your Cheerleading Potential

Give yourself 2 points for each "a" answer, 1 point for each "b" answer, and 0 points for each "c" answer, then add up your total points.

13 to 18 points

You were born to cheer! Your strength, flexibility, coordination, and enthusiasm for trying new things will contribute to your success as a cheerleader. Keep up the great attitude, healthy eating, and taking good care of yourself, and you'll soon be on your way to being a successful cheerleader.

8 to 12 points

Even though you may not be an amazing gymnast or a fantastic dancer, you're willing to put the time and effort into it. This attitude is exactly what you need to be a good cheerleader. Remember to take good care of yourself, though. Get enough sleep, don't skip meals, and organize your schedule so you have time for all of the most important priorities (like school). With your willingness to work hard on the areas you need improvement, you're going to be a great cheerleader.

0 to 7 points

You need to work on a few things before you consider cheerleading. If you're shy, practice becoming more extroverted the next time you're with a group of others. If your dancing skill or flexibility needs a little work, enroll in a dance class or practice your splits every day. It's also important to take good care of your body so that you will be able to perform at your best. You have to learn to organize your schedule so you don't neglect important factors such as eating well and sleeping enough. If you scored *really* low, you need to look at your approach to trying new things and give your attitude a makeover. A positive attitude will get you cheerleading a lot faster than pessimism. If you want something enough, you *can* make it happen. Don't give up your cheerleading dreams just yet; with determination and some hard work, you can still realize your goal of becoming a cheerleader.

— Getting the Inside Scoop —

Before you try out for a cheerleading team, you need to do some homework. This step can be just as important as your actual tryout. That's because, for example, you don't want to get to the tryout only to find out that a Standing Back Tuck and a Toss Liberty are the minimum skill requirements when you've never tried them before.

Pre-Tryout Homework

Learn as much as you can about the team by getting answers to the following questions from the sources suggested here:

WHAT ARE THE TEAM'S CHARACTERISTICS?

The answers to this question will give you a good idea about the general qualities of the team. For example, is it a stunting or non-stunting team? Is the team all-girl or co-ed? Does the team cheer games or is it competition-only? Finding out these and other characteristics of the team will help you decide if you would enjoy being a member. You can find out more about a team in a number of ways:

★ Look at the team Web pages

★ Ask friends/teammates who know athletes on the team

★ Talk to or e-mail the coach or a current member of the team

★ Watch the team perform at a game or competition

★ Sit in on a practice

When you talk to current members of the team, here are some good questions to ask them:

★ What is it like being on the team? (Their answer to this simple question will often give you a good idea what the team is like.)

★ Who are the coaches? What are they like?

★ How do athletes get along with the coach?

★ What are the minimum skill requirements?

★ What games, events, and competitions does the team participate in?

★ What are the additional commitments and responsibilities of being a member of the team?

WHAT IS THE GENERAL SKILL LEVEL OF THE TEAM?

If the team is still working on perfecting extensions, it's understandable that you wouldn't want to waste your time trying out if you can hit a Double Twist Dismount (see page 133) in your sleep. By the same token, if all members of the team can do extensive stunting and a cartwheel is your best tumbling line, you'd better sign up for some gymnastic classes. If you don't know the general skill level of the team, you'll find it impossible to put your best foot forward at tryouts.

WHAT COMMITMENTS ARE INVOLVED IN BEING A MEMBER OF THE TEAM?

If you're thinking about trying out for a team, it's important that you understand the responsibilities that come along with being a member. You need to determine whether you can commit to these responsibilities *before* you try out, rather than have to quit afterward because you can't meet the obligations. Do you know what days and times practices are held? Will the team practices fit into your schedule? Can you make all the events, games, and competitions? What are the financial requirements? Are you willing to put the effort into fundraising if you're unable to come up with the funds on your own? Be sure you understand the implications of being a member of the team, and that you're both ready and willing to accept the requirements should you become a member of the team.

It's crucial that you discover the answers to these questions *before* you head off to tryouts. The more people you can talk to and the more sources you can investigate, the better. Find out everything about the team, from the coach's personality to financial commitments to minimum skill requirements. This way, you'll not only be able to make an *informed* decision about the best cheerleading program for you, but when the time comes, you'll be better prepared for tryouts.

— University/College Tryouts —

If you've been a cheerleader for a good part of your high school career, chances are you'll want to cheer at the college or university level too. And no wonder post-secondary cheering looks so appealing: Who wouldn't love cheering in front of thousands of fans, stunting with other talented cheerleaders, and competing with the best? In addition, many schools offer scholarships for cheerleaders that cover tuition, residence, and expense bills. In fact, a recent issue of the *American Cheerleader Magazine* College Scholarship Guide mentions over 230 scholarships, which include many substantial financial awards at some colleges and universities.

Getting a good scholarship can definitely influence your decision on which school you'll choose to spend four years of your life. It is not wise, however, to choose a school solely on the basis of whether or not they offer cheerleading scholarships or have a cheerleading program. It's more important that the school's academic program meets your educational needs and future plans.

After you find a school that suits your academic needs, *then* you can look at a school's cheerleading program. Once you've done the necessary homework to find out what the program entails, your next step will be to decide whether you're ready to take on cheerleading *in addition* to your responsibilities as a college/university student. Post-secondary school life, besides being a lot of fun, is filled with exams, deadlines, and distractions that leave little time for activities such as cheerleading. Be prepared to cut back in certain areas, as college cheerleading does have disadvantages such as these:

★ *Less free time.* Because many weekends and evenings will be full of cheering for sporting events and practices, you'll have less free time.

★ *Less time for socializing life.* As your friends head out for the evening, you might be catching up on homework or going to bed early so you can make your 7:00 A.M. practice. Your availability and time for socializing will be significantly reduced as games, competitions, and practices replace it.

On the other hand, while you may have to give up some of your free time and a bit of your social life, there are definitely benefits to cheering in college or university:

★ *Forget the "frosh fifteen."* That's the fifteen extra pounds students often gain in their first year away from home. Cheerleading will keep you in amazing shape, and staying healthy will help you become a more productive student.

★ *It's great for the resume!* Being a college/university athlete definitely has its perks, and one is that you can put this leadership experience on your resume. Employers are always impressed with individuals whose track record demonstrates that they have time-management skills, self-discipline, and the ability to cooperate with others.

★ *It's fun.* In addition to being fantastic exercise and a great addition to your resume, cheerleading at the college/university level is fun!

If you think you're ready for all the responsibility that comes with being a varsity athlete, then do your (cheerleading) homework and get yourself to tryouts!

— Fitness Training for Cheerleaders —

By now you should have a good idea of whether you are ready to commit to and would enjoy being a part of cheerleading. When you've chosen a team you're interested in joining, do as much background investigation as possible and use the information you gain to help you prepare for tryouts. Your next step is to get your skills tryout-ready. A fitness plan is essential for every athlete. Whether you're just starting out and need to get into shape for tryouts, or you're already on a team and want to improve your overall physical condition, a cheerleading training program is a must.

Cheerleading requires these four major physical components:

1. cardiovascular endurance
2. strength
3. flexibility
4. skill

By training your body in all four areas, you will be prepared for the demands of being a cheerleader-athlete.

Cardiovascular Endurance

Cardiovascular endurance is important in cheerleading. Games can stretch on, practices can go for hours at a time, and a competition routine that is only a few minutes long can seem to take forever if you don't have a good aerobic system. Therefore, it's essential that you include cardiovascular training in your schedule.

CARDIOVASCULAR TRAINING SCHEDULE

Participating in physical activity at least three, if not four, times a week is essential for maintaining a healthy body. Not only will you feel great, but exercise has been shown to improve overall physical and mental health. As a cheerleader, you must

★ ★ ★ ★ ★ ★ ★ ★ ★ ★ ★ ★ ★ ★ ★ ★ ★

Note on Weight Training

If you're in your early teens or younger, it's a good idea to stay away from strenuous weight training to avoid overstressing and possibly damaging your still-developing body. It's still important, however, to keep your muscles strong so you're in top shape for cheerleading. Good alternatives to weight training include plyometrics (exercises that use your own body weight, such as push-ups) and participating in other sports (such as dancing, basketball, or swimming). It's also important that everyone, regardless of age, consult a medical doctor before beginning any type of training program (aerobic, anaerobic, or other) mentioned in this chapter.

★ ★ ★ ★ ★ ★ ★ ★ ★ ★ ★ ★ ★ ★ ★ ★ ★

maintain a healthy, athletic lifestyle so that you're prepared to handle the demands placed on your body at practice, at games, and at competitions.

Whether you play another sport such as basketball or tennis, go for regular runs, or take an aerobics class, try to get at least twenty minutes of cardiovascular exercise three times a week or more. A *word of warning:* Be careful not to overdo it, as this could *reduce* the effectiveness of your training by leading to over-exhaustion and injury. If you're just starting out, it's wise to limit your cardiovascular training to every other day for a maximum of three days per week. Gradually increase the number of days you train as your cardiovascular system improves. Cap your cardiovascular activity at a maximum of five to six times a week, giving yourself at least one or two days of rest each week.

You'll want to structure your training so that you have a full day of cardiovascular rest every other day or after two days of aerobic activity. This way, your body will have a full chance to repair itself while giving your muscles and joints a break. Remember to drink lots of water before, during, and after your workouts so that you keep your body hydrated. In addition, be sure you eat healthful foods regularly to keep your body adequately fueled.

If you have previous injuries (such as knee or back problems), you'll want to structure your training to compensate for the severity of the problem. For example, if you have injured knees, you'll want to participate in an activity that doesn't overexert or overuse your knees (such as stationary cycling). If your joints are sore or susceptible to injury, stick to low-impact activities such as swimming or low-

impact aerobics. Remember, no matter how badly you want to achieve your cheerleading goals, it's not worth permanently injuring your body.

SAMPLE CARDIOVASCULAR ACTIVITIES

You can challenge your cardiovascular system in a number of ways such as running, doing aerobics, playing other sports, interval training, and even cheerleading itself.

Running

Running is one of the best ways to improve cardiovascular endurance and also provides you with time by yourself to enjoy some peace and quiet. If you're new to running, start out slowly. Run for one minute, walk for one minute. Gradually build up the amount of time running and reduce the amount of walking until you feel you don't need to walk at all.

Aerobics

With so many aerobics classes from which to choose, you'll find this a fantastic way to build up your cardiovascular endurance. Bring a friend and classes can be even more fun. When you take a class for the first time, go easy until you get comfortable with the program. Taking a variety of classes can help avoid overuse of one particular set of muscles and will keep you from getting bored. Popular aerobics classes include these types:

High/Low Impact: In this type of class, you'll use both high-impact and low-impact movements in a choreographed set of thirty-two or sixty-four counts. Because you're able to choose your own intensity options, this class is great for beginners and advanced athletes alike.

Kickboxing: Combining martial arts and aerobics, kickboxing is great for intense workouts and building lower body strength. Kickboxing classes are available in most areas.

Step: Using risers and a flat plastic step, you'll get your workout by stepping up and off of this

---

— TIP —

Remember to consult your doctor before beginning any type of exercise program, especially if you are currently injured or have previous injuries.

box-type apparatus to choreographed moves and sets.

Interval: Because interval aerobics alternates low-impact movements with intense bursts of energy, it is great training for cheerleading routines.

Playing Other Sports
Shooting some hoops or playing a game of tennis is a great way to get your heart rate going. Grab a bunch of your teammates and let the bonding begin!

Interval Training
With interval training, you alternate low to moderate cardiovascular activity with a more intensive exercise or activity. For example, grab a rope and begin skipping at a medium pace for three minutes. For the next minute, skip intensively. Alternate low/medium and high intensities for a challenging workout. Interval training can be done with weights as well. Warm up with a light aerobic activity and then begin your workout sets. After you have done three sets, go back to your aerobic activity and increase the intensity. Alternate your workout sets with cardio intervals. This is a great way to train your body for a competition routine because it simulates anaerobic work (such as stunting or building pyramids) with aerobic work (such as dances and intensive cheers).

Cheerleading
Cheerleading practice counts as cardiovascular exercise, too—particularly when you've been working intensively on dances or cheers for more than twenty minutes. Cheering games can also count as aerobic and anaerobic exercise, depending on how much cheering/dancing/performing you're doing.

— Strength Training for Cheerleaders —
Strength training is an essential part of cheerleading, especially when you're expected to toss around others or be the one tossed around. Without anaer-obic training (muscle training), your body will be unable to meet the physical requirements of stunting and gymnastics.

An ideal time for an anaerobic workout is on your off days from practice and cardiovascular training. Many cheerleading programs actually require athletes to work out an additional two to four times outside of practice.

Sample Workout Splits
Here are several sample workout schedules you might use. It's best, however, to design a workout schedule that meets your specific needs and goals.

TWO-DAY SPLIT
If you work out twice a week, you'll want to work out your lower body on the first day and your upper body on the second workout day. Remember to keep a few days in between workouts to prevent overworking your body.

Sample Two-Day Split
Day 1: quadriceps, gluteus, hamstrings, calves, and lower back

Day 2: deltoids (shoulders), chest, triceps, biceps, and upper back

This is an ideal workout for someone just starting to work out or for an athlete who wants to maintain strength. Because you're working so many muscle groups in one exercise period, you'll want to do only compound exercises (such as squats, push-ups, and chin-ups) or one to two exercises for each muscle group. Compound movements are great for two-day splits because they work a number of muscles all in one exercise. (See the following list for samples of compound exercises.) You do *not* want to do too many exercises for each muscle group for these reasons:

1. Your workouts will be too long
2. You'll get tired and won't be able to keep proper form
3. Your risk of injury will be greater

Basic Strength Training Glossary

Aerobic Training: Aerobic training refers to activities that increase your overall cardiovascular endurance. Examples of aerobic training include running, aerobics classes, swimming, biking, in-line skating, basketball, and tennis.

Anaerobic Training: Anaerobic training refers to increasing your muscle strength and endurance. You're training your anaerobic system when you engage in short bursts of intense activity (either with or without weights) that increase your overall muscle strength.

Proper Form: Proper form refers to using the correct muscles for an exercise. Near the end of a set, people often "cheat" by using stronger muscles or momentum to finish their exercise. Not only can this lead to injury, but it's also counterproductive. It's best to use just the muscles you're focusing on. If you're using stronger and larger muscles, you aren't really accomplishing your training goals.

Rep: Short for "repetition," a rep is one full movement of an exercise. Usually six to fifteen reps are done of one exercise, depending on the trainee's goals. Lower reps with heavier weights build muscle mass (size) while higher reps with lower weights increase muscle endurance and definition. Performing a rep should take you about 4 to 6 seconds.

Set: A set is a group of reps. If you're just starting out, begin with one set of each exercise and gradually work your way up until you are performing two to three sets for each exercise. For example, if you're doing bicep curls with the intention of increasing your muscle size, you might do three sets of eight to ten reps with a rest in between each set.

Split: A split is how you break up working out your body parts during the week. For example, if you're on a three-day split, one day you might do legs; the next day shoulders, chest, and triceps; and on the last day, back and biceps. This schedule prevents you from overworking any one muscle group and, as a result, improves your anaerobic ability more quickly while decreasing the chances of injury. Depending on the intensity of your cardiovascular and practice schedules, you can decide on taking up a two-day, three-day, or four-day split.

Spotter: Just like in stunting, spotters play an important role in weight training. A spotter is someone who either stands in front of or behind you, depending on the type of exercise. If you need a little help at the end of your set, spotters can assist you with the weight or save you from dropping the weights on yourself. Spotters are also great for ensuring that you have the proper form and for handing you your weights at the beginning of a set. It's important when you're doing an exercise for the first time or when you're getting tired near the end of your workout that you have a spotter nearby.

Here are some pointers to help you get the most out of your Two-Day Splits:

★ Two-day splits are great for weeks with lots of practices.

★ Perform only compound movements or one to two exercises per body part to avoid the chance of injury and fatigue.

★ If you're just starting out, give your body a few days rest in between Day 1 and Day 2.

★ Do cardio workouts up to a maximum of five days to avoid burnout. (Remember that doing lots of dancing or intensive cheering at practices or games counts as a cardio workout, too!)

★ Take one day completely off training (cardiovascular and strength training).

THREE-DAY SPLIT

Three-day splits provide more opportunity for a heavier workout. As with the Two-Day Split routine, remember to allow for at least one day of rest between your workouts. Here's a suggested schedule for a Three-Day Split.

Sample Three-Day Split

WORKOUT 1

Day 1: chest, shoulders, and triceps

Day 2: legs (quadriceps, gluteus, hamstrings, calves, and lower back)

Day 3: upper back, biceps

WORKOUT 2

Day 1: chest, upper back, and calves

Day 2: legs (quadriceps, gluteus, hamstrings, and lower back)

Day 3: deltoids (shoulders), biceps, and triceps

WORKOUT 3

First Week

Day 1: Upper body—deltoids (shoulders), chest, triceps, biceps, and upper back

Day 2: Lower body—quadriceps, gluteus, hamstrings, calves, and lower back

Day 3: Upper body—deltoids (shoulders), chest, triceps, biceps, and upper back

Second Week

Day 1: Lower body—quadriceps, gluteus, hamstrings, calves, and lower back

Day 2: Upper body—deltoids (shoulders), chest, triceps, biceps, and upper back

Day 3: Lower body—quadriceps, gluteus, hamstrings, calves, and lower back

Here are some pointers to help you get the most out of your Three-Day Splits:

★ When starting out, allow at least one day of rest between workouts.

★ If you are an intermediate or advanced weight-trainer, rest at least one day after you complete Days 1, 2, and 3 in a consecutive row.

★ Use light, medium, or heavier weights, depending on your workout goals.

★ Choose compound exercises and one to three exercises per body part.

★ If you're doing Workout 3 (alternating upper and lower body), keep the weights light to avoid injury and overuse of muscles.

★ Limit cardiovascular training to three to four times a week maximum to avoid burnout.

★ Take one day per week completely off from training (cardiovascular and strength workouts).

FOUR-DAY SPLIT

You'll probably only want to work out four times a week if:

1. You practice only two to three times a week
2. You want to put on some serious muscle

When working out on a Four-Day Split, you can increase the number of exercises per body part as well as the weight. Because you're doing a smaller number of body parts per workout session, there's less chance of injury with higher weights and exercise sets. Be careful that you don't overdo things in your eagerness to put on muscle. Start out slowly and listen to your body. If you're still a little sore, that means your body hasn't fully repaired itself and needs more rest. Take an extra day off from weight training if necessary.

Sample Four-Day Splits

WORKOUT 1

Day 1: biceps and triceps

Day 2: legs (quadriceps, gluteus, hamstrings, and lower back)

Day 3: chest and deltoids (shoulders)

Day 4: upper back and calves

WORKOUT 2

Day 1: upper back and biceps

Day 2: legs (quadriceps, gluteus, hamstrings, and calves)

Day 3: deltoids (shoulders) and lower back

Day 4: chest and triceps

Note for Workouts 1 and 2: If you want to get all workouts done in one week, only do Day 1 and Day 2 *or* Day 2 and Day 3 back to back without a day of rest in between. Otherwise, leave at least one non-workout day between your workout days.

WORKOUT 3

Day 1: Upper body—deltoids (shoulders), chest, triceps, biceps, and upper back

Day 2: Lower body—quadriceps, gluteus, hamstrings, calves, and lower back

Day 3: Upper body—deltoids (shoulders), chest, triceps, biceps, and upper back

Day 4: Lower body—quadriceps, gluteus, hamstrings, calves, and lower back

Here are some pointers to help you get the most out of your Four-Day Splits:

★ Be careful which days you work out back-to-back.

★ Never work out the same muscles (or complementary muscles like chest and triceps or back and biceps) two consecutive days.

★ Keep extra activities and cardiovascular training to a minimum, especially if you are using heavy weights. That means no more than two or three times a week.

★ Take an additional day of rest if your body tells you it needs one.

Ten Essential Weight Training Tips

Weight training can result in both short-term and long-term injuries if you don't take the necessary precautions before starting a program. If you've never weight-trained before, or if you're just getting back into it after taking time off, start slowly. Here are ten tips to help you get the most out of your weight training:

1. Be safe.

Warm up before a workout and cool down and stretch after completing one. During your actual workout, begin with one or two sets with low repetitions. Once you become comfortable in your program, you can change your routine according to your goals. Always use a trainer when trying out new exercises or if you're getting tired near the end of your set. And last, but not least, never train by yourself; make sure other people are around to help if you get into trouble.

2. Use proper form.

You're wasting your time if you train without proper form. Not only is it dangerous if you don't use the right muscle groups, but you won't reach your goals. Have a trainer watch your form to make sure you're performing the exercise correctly.

3. Listen to your body.

If you don't feel like working out because you're still stiff and sore from the previous workout, don't bother hitting the weights. Your body is telling you it needs some more time to recover. On the other hand, if you're not feeling challenged by the last rep, increase the weight so you're getting the maximum benefit from your workout. By listening to your body, you'll also be able to tell which exercises do the most and which do the least for your strength.

4. Have a plan before you go into the gym.

Just as you wouldn't get out on the competition floor without a choreographed plan, you shouldn't go to the gym without a workout plan. If you wander around from exercise to exercise without a specific goal, you won't accomplish anything. If you're new to the workout scene, have a fitness professional set you up with an exercise program rather than just jumping into the gym and grabbing random weights. If you choose to set up your own program, decide which muscle groups you're going to work on and plan exactly which exercises you're going to do before you get to the gym. You might have to wait your turn for a machine or for a set of dumbbells, but stick to your plan and you'll see results.

5. Establish goals.

Do you want to build muscle size or just improve muscle endurance? Is your chest a little weaker than your back? If you're not sure of the answers to these questions, it's a good idea to sit down with a trained professional to discuss what you want to get out of your workout program. To build muscle mass, you'll want to use heavier weights and lower reps. Alternatively, to increase muscle endurance and definition, you'll want to choose a lighter weight but more reps of each exercise. Both methods will increase your strength.

6. Rest.

It's important to allow for at least 24 hours of rest between workouts of the same or complementary muscles. Complementary muscles are muscles that work together, such as back and biceps, upper back and rear deltoids (back shoulders), and triceps and chest. If there isn't ample time for the muscle to repair itself, you may get injured and won't achieve results. Rest also includes getting enough sleep at night. Your body does the majority of its repairs while you're sleeping; therefore, if you cheat yourself out of sleep, you're also cheating yourself out of muscle development. Even if you're not working the same muscle groups on consecutive workouts, it's still a good idea to allow for a full day of recuperation before beginning another weight-training session.

7. Drink lots of water.

Keep your body hydrated so it can perform at its full potential. This is true with all types of exercise. Without enough water, you run the risk of dehydration, which can lead to serious side effects. Don't wait until you feel thirsty; if you feel like you need some water, you're already dehydrated. Fill up a water bottle and keep it nearby as you practice, participate in cardiovascular training, or do strength-training sets.

8. Don't overdo your workouts.

Choose the type of workout split that best suits your goals as well as complements your practice schedule and aerobic training schedule. If you practice three to five times a week, it's not practical to attempt a heavy four-day weight-training schedule, nor is it wise to run an additional five miles every day. You might be able to keep it up for a while, but soon your body will start to protest in the form of injuries and exhaustion.

Use the following guidelines to give you an idea of a realistic fitness schedule:

ONE TO TWO PRACTICES/EVENTS A WEEK

★ Do aerobic training up to five times a week (remember, cheerleading practice also counts as one session of aerobic training if you're doing more than twenty minutes of dancing and intensive cheering).

★ Do two-, three-, or four-day weight-training splits, depending on your goals and on how many times a week you're doing cardiovascular training. (More aerobic training equals less weight training; more weight training equals less aerobic training.)

★ Allow at least one full day per week off—without any aerobic training, weight training, or practice.

THREE TO FOUR PRACTICES/EVENTS A WEEK

★ Do aerobic training up to a maximum of three times a week.

★ Do a two-day weight-training split (three or four practices) or a three-day weight-training split (three practices). The intensity of your weight-training workouts should even out the intensity of your practices or events. (Intense practices/events equal lighter workouts; light practices/events equal an option to increase the intensity of your workouts.)

★ Allow one full day of rest each week without any weight training, aerobic training, or practice.

FIVE TO SEVEN PRACTICES/EVENTS A WEEK

★ Do a maximum of one or two sessions of aerobic training in addition to practices.

★ Do a two-day weight-training split or a light three-day weight-training split, depending on the intensity and number of practices.

★ Allow a minimum one day off per week without aerobic or strength training.

9. *Properly schedule your anaerobic and aerobic training around practices.*

As stressed before, it's important not to overdo physical exercise. Keep this in mind when you plan out your aerobic activities and weight-training

---

┌─────────────────────────────────────┐

— TIP —

Remember that these are just guidelines. You will have to adjust your fitness schedule according to your individual needs and personal response to training.

└─────────────────────────────────────┘

schedule around your practices. Avoid scheduling a heavy weight-training session right before a practice. Your performance at practice will noticeably suffer, and your stunting partners likely won't appreciate the fact that you can't lift your arms above your head. Additionally, it's unsafe for both you and your teammates.

If you plan to weight train on the same day as practice, either train after practicing or train long enough before practice that the effects of weight training are minimized. Even so, you will likely notice a reduction in your strength at practice.

You'll also find that your aerobic performance will be affected by a heavy workout. When possible, schedule your cardiovascular training on different days than your weight training. If your cardiovascular training day falls on the same day as practice, train after practice so you're able to give 100 percent of your efforts to your team.

10. *Change things up.*

To prevent reaching a plateau in your training (that is, you stop seeing results), change the type of exercises (anaerobic and aerobic) that you do. Once you've been doing a weight-training workout for about 12 weeks, re-evaluate your goals and make new ones. Consequently, redesign your workout program toward meeting your new goals.

— Flexibility —

Flexibility is vital for performing certain techniques in cheerleading, such as Toe Touches, Basket Tosses, Heel Stretches, Scales, Bow and Arrows, and Scorpions. Although flyers are responsible for hitting these stunts, bases also must be flexible enough to hit elements such as Toe Touches and Side Hurdlers. (See chapter 6 for detailed descriptions of these techniques.)

Hamstrings, hip flexors, and the inner thigh aren't the only muscles that give cheerleaders the benefit of increased flexibility. A greater range of motion in the shoulders and back can also improve stunting and gymnastics skills.

Unless you've been stretching since you were young, regaining a flexible range of motion can take some time. However, by working at it every day, someone with minimal flexibility may end up able to do the splits.

Increasing Your Flexibility

You can increase your flexibility by doing daily stretches while warm and relaxed, and by working with a partner. The following five suggestions will help you reach the level of flexibility you'll need for cheerleading.

1. Stretch every day.

Stretching every day (or every other day if you're just starting) is vital for increased flexibility. Hold your stretches for at least 15 seconds and work up to 60 seconds. Stretch each part of your body. Stretching ideas include doing right, left, and middle splits, and back bridges.

2. Stretch while warm.

Stretching cold (that is, without warming up first) can lead to serious injuries such as pulled or ripped muscles (which, by the way, never perform as well as before an injury). Jog a lap or do some stationary, full-body exercise before attempting any stretches.

3. Relax while stretching.

Relaxed muscles are easier to stretch than tense muscles. Take a deep breath in, and as you breathe out, perform your stretch. This is a much safer and more effective way to increase your range of motion than holding your breath and keeping your muscles tight, as many people tend to do.

4. Stretch after working out.

Stretching after a workout not only serves to increase the range of motion of your muscles, but also promotes increased blood flow. Increased blood flow to the muscles will help to decrease lactic acid, which will help to decrease muscle soreness the next day. Additionally, most permanent changes in flexibility will occur after a workout rather than before.

5. Stretch with a partner.

Even flexible people can benefit from the added help that stretching with a partner can provide. Stretching with someone else can help you concentrate more on your breathing and form, as well as help you stretch to a greater degree than you could by yourself. The next section offers instructions for several stretching exercises you can do with a partner.

Partner Stretching Exercises

Here are several stretching exercises you can do with a partner.

REVERSE SPLITS

Lie down on your back and extend one leg into the air. Have your partner place one of his or her legs just above the knee of your other leg to keep it from bending. Hold onto your extended leg (while your partner gently pushes your other leg down), as you take a deep breath and blow out. Take another deep breath, and as you blow out again, your partner pushes farther. For a final stretch, push against your partner's hands, using the muscles in your extended leg. Have your partner gently lower your leg and switch sides.

STRADDLE STRETCH

Sit down in a straddle position, with your partner kneeling behind you. Have your partner place their hands on the small of your back and push forward and down as you reach for the floor. (The trick is to think about touching your stomach to the floor, rather than just your head.) Remember

Figure 3.1 *Straddle stretch.*

Figure 3.2 *Heel stretch.*

to have your partner push down as you relax and breathe out. Take another deep breath; and as you blow out, reach a little farther, keeping your knees to the ceiling. (See figure 3.1.)

HEEL STRETCH

Standing up, have your partner face you just off to one side. Lift your leg and place it on your partner's shoulder, leaning forward for the stretch. You may need to stand against a wall and have your partner support your leg with his or her hands if placing your leg on his or her shoulder doesn't stretch you well enough. For an extra stretch, push down with your leg against your partner's hands or shoulder. Have your partner slowly release your leg and bring it down to the ground, avoiding letting it just fall. (Dropping it quickly can lead to injuries.) (See figure 3.2.)

— Skills —

A great cardiovascular system and big muscles won't secure you a place on the cheerleading team if you haven't practiced the required skills. (If you're not already familiar with cheerleading skills, take a look at the chapters in Part Two for information on how to properly perform these techniques.)

Solid stunting, sharp motions, clean jumps, and coordinated dancing are among the most important skills in cheerleading. In Table 3.1 on page 49 you'll find exercises to improve your cheerleading skills and techniques.

Training for cheerleading requires no less effort than training for any other sport. When designing a fitness program, take into consideration cardiovascular endurance, strength, flexibility, and skill in order to achieve your maximum potential as a cheerleader.

If you ever get discouraged with your workouts, remember that if you want to be treated like an athlete, you have to train like one. Keep in mind that there are people who don't view cheerleading as a sport. Your athletic training will give you the ability to prove them wrong.

Table 3.1. Beneficial Exercises for Cheerleading Skills

	Exercise	Beneficial for
LOWER BODY	jump squats (using your own body weight)	toss stunts (bases simulate tossing and flyers simulate being tossed), tumbling (especially back tucks), and jumps
	straddle leg lifts	jumps (especially Toe Touches)
	leg extensions	stunting, jumping, dancing
	leg curls	tumbling, jumping
	V-ups	jumps (V-ups are great for hip flexors), mid-air tricks, stunting
UPPER BODY	push-ups	stunting (beneficial for both bases and flyers), tumbling, motions
	shoulder press	stunting (essential for basing extended stunts), motions
	handstand push-ups	stunting, tumbling, motions
	upright rows	stunting (simulates toss stunts)
	bent-over rows	stunting, tumbling
	clean-and-jerks	stunting (simulates basing)
	dips	stunting, tumbling, motions
	bicep curls	stunting, motions
	wrist curls	stunting (strong wrists are key for bases and thirds), tumbling
ABDOMINALS	crunches	stunting (strong abdominal muscles equals better stunting technique)
	V-snaps	jumps, mid-air tricks (helps flyers to snap faster), stunting
	straddle snaps	Toe Touches, mid-air tricks

— The Tryout —

If you've practiced your cheerleading skills and done your homework, you should have a great tryout. Knowing what the tryout is going to consist of and how to prepare for it is usually tougher than the tryout itself. When you finally walk into the gym, here are some last-minute pointers for a successful tryout:

★ **Smile!** Coaches want happy people on their teams!

★ **Be confident in your abilities.** If you've practiced, you'll be prepared. Even if you don't feel 100 percent self-assured when you walk in, fake it. Before you know it, you *will* start feeling confident and poised.

★ **Take a deep breath and relax before you perform.** This will help to calm you down so that you can let your true abilities shine through.

★ **Wear athletic attire.** Athletic shorts and a T-shirt (fitted, not baggy) are the best clothing items to wear. Avoid wearing shirts that display cheerleading company names, slogans, team names, and such. Many tryouts implement this as a rule so judges won't pre-judge athletes based on what team they've cheered for in the past. You don't want to show up and inadvertently break the rule.

★ *Wear white socks.* It sounds silly, but you don't want to stand out because you're wearing bright blue socks.

★ *Pull your hair back, out of your face.* Wear a bow in your hair for a pulled-together look.

★ *Go easy on the make-up.* Natural is best.

★ *Take off all jewelry.* This is not only safer for you, but demonstrates to the judges that you take responsibility for team safety.

★ *Get to tryouts early.* Arriving late in a panic, and perhaps missing important information, is likely to negatively affect your rating.

★ *Introduce yourself to other athletes.* Be friendly and outgoing, and avoid negative comments about others trying out for the team.

★ *Warm up and stretch.* Make sure you're completely stretched and prepared before performing any skills.

★ *Ask questions.* Don't be afraid to ask if you're not clear on a particular part of the routine/dance/stunt/skill that's being taught.

★ *Listen to the instructions from the judges or coaches.* You need to keep your ears open for your responsibilities during the tryout.

★ *Make eye contact with the judges when performing skills.* Remember, crowd interaction is an important part of cheerleading.

★ *Do your best.* If you make a mistake, keep going rather than stopping in the middle of your routine. Judges are not only interested in your skills, but want to see that you can work through and cover up mistakes.

After the tryout, don't beat yourself up about what you *could* have, or *should* have done better. All you can do now is wait until the list is put up. If you make it, great! Congratulations on becoming a cheerleader for this team! If not, that's okay, too. Read on to find out why.

— If Your Name Isn't on the List . . . —

While you might be tempted to panic if you learn you didn't make the team, don't. Missing the cut doesn't necessarily mean you're a bad cheerleader or aren't a good enough athlete. There are a number of possible external reasons why you didn't make the team (for example, many competitions allow a maximum number of athletes on the floor, thus coaches can only take so many cheerleaders on the team). Even if you didn't make the team because of your level of skill, you can improve your technique with practice.

Many cheerleaders try out more than once before they make a team. It's likely that a few who made the team for which you just tried out didn't make it on the first round either. *But that didn't stop them from trying out again.* If you want to be a cheerleader, don't give up just because your first try wasn't successful. Try again! First, determine what you'll need to do to achieve your goal to be a cheerleader.

First Things First: Review Your Tryout

Take a moment to think about what went wrong. Did you practice too little? Did you forget the cheer that you knew perfectly before tryouts? Has some major event happened in your life that affected your performance? If you feel some temporary issue prevented your demonstrating your real skill, talk to the coach and explain why you don't think you displayed your full talents.

Consider asking the coach to sit down with you for a moment to discuss your tryout and review your score sheet. Although you might feel hurt, avoid coming across as a poor sport and making excuses for why you didn't make the team. You want the coach to remember you as a mature young adult rather than a whiny little kid who doesn't belong on the team for that exact reason.

If you come to the conclusion that your skills just weren't up to par with the candidates who made the team, inquire about lessons or other venues for improving your techniques. Ask the coach whether you can come to practices either to participate inconspicuously or just to watch if they won't allow participation. Find out whether there will be additional tryout dates during the year. Often teams need to pick up a few more athletes after the first semester; you could be just the one the team is looking for.

In addition, although you're disappointed you won't be cheering right away, you'll feel better once you realize that cheerleading offers many more opportunities than just being on a team.

Manage the Team

Being the team manager may not sound as glamorous as cheerleading, but a team manager is an essential part of any cheerleading team. Check out chapter 2 for a detailed list of a manager's responsibilities.

Although you won't have any say in the coaching process or decisions, you will be able to come to all practices and observe the team learning new techniques and skills. Once the coach sees how dedicated you are to the team, you'll have a better shot at making the team the next year.

Assist with Coaching a Junior Team

If you have some previous cheerleading experience, you might want to offer your skills to junior cheerleaders by volunteering at a junior school. If they already have a coach, ask whether you can assist. You'll learn a lot by working with other cheerleaders, even if they are a little younger than

you are. If the school doesn't already have a team, consider starting your own team there. Start out with a good proposal and look for someone to co-coach with you. (It's always easier to start up a team with a helping hand.)

Assist with Coaching a Recreational Program

If coaching a recreational team appeals to you more than coaching a junior team (or if you'd prefer doing something easier than starting up a whole new cheerleading program), contact nearby cheerleading clubs about volunteering. Inquire at recreational facilities such as gymnastics clubs and YMCAs that host cheerleading classes for competitive teams. While you may not be qualified to coach competitive classes, there is often a demand for less intensive, recreational lessons. You could be just the one to start them up!

Volunteer at Competitions

Competitions *always* need volunteers. What better way to learn more about cheerleading than to watch a full day of it? Start by calling up your local cheerleading company (see the list of cheerleading companies in the Resource section at the end of the book) and asking about volunteering at their next event. Most companies will be happy to have your help. You might even be able to arrange some free lessons in exchange for your volunteer work.

While you might feel as though your life is over if you don't make the cheerleading team on your first try, it's not. You will still be able to participate in cheerleading in numerous ways, and you'll be better equipped to succeed at your next tryout.

One final note: Ask the coaches you know how they got their start in cheerleading. Chances are you'll find that more than just a few had to try out twice, and you're likely to get some excellent advice.

Chapter Four

Coaches and Athletes

Making the Most of Cheering

Imagine yourself back in time, in the year 1898. You're on the University of Minnesota campus watching a new game called "football." The crowd's deafening roar rings in your ears. On this brisk November 2, you're in the midst of such excitement that the crowd's energy has you standing on tiptoes cheering along.

But wait! With whom do you cheer? You look around in confusion as the school's many different clubs and teams chant their own cheers in a feverish attempt to drown out one another. The debate team cheers against the chess club while fraternities direct their cheers toward one another. Is anyone watching the game?

Suddenly, a man scrambles down onto the sidelines in front of the crowd and begins to yell: "Rah, Rah, Rah! Sku-u-mar, Hoo-Rah! Hoo-Rah! Varsity! Varsity! Varsity, Minn-e-So-Tah!" The cheer catches the attention of the fans; and before you know it, everyone is breathless and hoarse from cheering along. This man, Johnny Campbell, had just become one of the world's first "cheer leaders."

The first "pep club" had been established around the 1880s at Princeton University when Thomas Peebler organized six men to lead a cheer on the sidelines. His cheer, "Ray, Ray, Ray! TIGER, TIGER, SIS, SIS, SIS! BOOM, BOOM, BOOM! Aaaaah! PRINCETON, PRINCETON, PRINCETON!" was heard throughout the entire football game.

Peebler's "yell" migrated to the University of Minnesota where in 1898 Johnny Campbell jumped out in front of everyone and began his own cheer. It was on this campus that organized cheerleading began its existence. Ever since, cheerleaders have been supporting sports teams.

For one reason or another, some schools or communities lack spirit. At some pep rallies, teachers from the athletic department drone endlessly in monotone voices, practically putting the audience to sleep. Even the players look bored as they're introduced. No band, no entertainment, no cheering . . . nothing exciting happens. Is this a familiar scene at your school? If so, a cheerleading team can have a tremendous impact on increasing spirit. Organizing a team will take a little bit of time and a lot of hard work, but even one performance can accomplish a lot toward boosting the excitement at a pep rally or game. It's a fact that a cheerleading team *does* make a difference in your school and community. As one T-shirt saying goes, "Without cheerleaders, it's just a game." And while the majority of fans come to a sporting event to see the game, some come for the entertainment and excitement these events create. When you get right down to it, without the entertainment and crowd involvement, some sporting events would be pretty dull.

— Pep Rallies, Halftime Routines, and Games —

It's not much fun for fans to go to an event where the athletes' interactions and performances do little to draw enthusiasm from the crowd. Cheerleaders play an important role at games and pep rallies: They keep the crowd pumped up.

What Is a "Pep Rally"?

Pep rallies are designed to bring out the crowd's "pep" (excitement) and enthusiasm for the school or community sports team. Pep rallies are usually scheduled for the day of, or the day before, a big game to increase the players' confidence and to energize the crowd for the upcoming event. Their purpose is to introduce teams and to improve overall school or community spirit and unity.

A typical pep rally consists of the introduction of team players followed by speeches from the coaches and the school principal or dean. Interspersed with these introductions and speeches are crowd-interactive skits and performances from the band, cheerleaders, dancers, and comedians.

What Is "Halftime"?

Football and basketball games always include a break in the middle of the game, between the second and third quarters. Halftime provides an op-portunity for both players and fans to take a break from the game. The break usually runs 15 to 30 minutes, during which time the crowd is entertained with various performances on the field or court. This provides an ideal opportunity for cheerleaders to perform.

Four Ingredients for Effective Pep Rallies and Exciting Games

Good pep rallies and game performances don't just happen. They require planning that typically includes four ingredients: a planning committee, lots of people, good entertainment, and prizes.

1. A PLANNING COMMITTEE

A pep rally committee or a game committee that organizes the event will ensure that everything runs smoothly. Without careful planning and preparation, the event may end up a flop, which will negatively affect the turnout of the following one.

2. LOTS OF PEOPLE

A pep rally isn't effective if only ten people show up, and games aren't much fun without fans either. The best events are big, with lots of people who make a lot of noise. Advertise in the newspapers and put flyers and banners all around town, inviting the entire school and community to attend each rally and game.

3. GOOD ENTERTAINMENT

Make sure your entertainment acts are exciting enough to grab *and* retain the crowd's attention. A marching band, cheerleading routines, singers, comedians, humorous skits, traditions (like fight songs), and crowd-interactive activities provide incentive for fans to turn out for the next pep rally or game.

4. PRIZES

Prizes can be as simple as throwing candy out into the crowd. It's a proven fact that people like get-

---

— TIP —

A pep rally doesn't have to be held in a stadium or in a gymnasium. Many effective pep rallies are run in the form of a parade in which participants march around the campus or along city streets.

ting free stuff and will do just about anything to get it. You'll be amazed at how rowdy crowds can get when you offer a pizza to the loudest group of fans!

— The Role of a Cheerleading Team —

The event is organized, great entertainment acts are lined up, and lots of people are coming. So what exactly do the cheerleaders *do* at events such as games and pep rallies?

At Games

At a football game, the cheerleaders stand on the sidelines (or on the track if there isn't room on the sidelines) and face their fans even while turning their heads to watch the game. At a basketball game, the cheerleaders stand in front of their team's fans, in the out-of-bounds area behind or to the side of the net. During time-outs, the cheerleaders either stay in their positions and perform a pre-arranged segment (for football) or leave their spots and run out on the court to perform (for basketball). For information on the appropriate times to cheer and additional game rules, refer to the section Cheering the Game on page 59.

At Pep Rallies

At pep rallies, cheerleaders don't just lead crowd-interactive cheers, but also perform routines, put on skits, and organize fan competitions between the team introductions and speeches.

— Spirit Ideas —

Because the main goals of a pep rally are to excite the crowd and encourage school spirit and unity, cheerleaders constantly use "spirit ideas" to keep the energy levels soaring. Traditions, interactive games, fight songs, and whatever contributes to increasing the overall spirit of the crowd and the team should be included in planning sporting events. Read on for some ideas you can use before, during, and after the event.

Before the Event

Preparing for the event is just as important as performing at the event. Advertising and organizing beforehand are crucial to ensure that the event runs smoothly.

POSTERS AND BANNERS

Get your school and community all geared up for the coming event by putting up large posters and banners. Advertise all around town, in newspapers, at school, and on local and/or campus radio stations.

Coming onto the Field or Floor

Cheerleaders can bring a great deal of attention to the team by making a dramatic entrance onto

---

C O A C H E S '   C O R N E R

PRE-EVENT CHECKLIST FOR COACHES

★ Do a sound check for all music used for your performances

★ Keep extra copies of your music handy

★ See that everyone has a full uniform, washed and ready to wear

★ Check to be sure everyone has the right shoes and bows

★ Make water and snacks available to the team

★ If it's sunny outside, keep sunscreen close by

★ Make sure the team is clear about when to perform routine(s)

★ Bring a camcorder to videotape the cheerleaders so you can review their performance at your next practice

the field or floor. Here are three ideas for grand entrances.

TEAM TUNNELS

As your sports team comes into the gymnasium or onto the field, have each cheerleader grab a partner and face each other in parallel lines to make a tunnel for the team to run through.

STUNT LINES

Similar to building team tunnels, line up the team in one row and toss up stunts such as Chairs, Hands, or Elevators (see chapter 9) as the sports team runs onto the floor or field. Alternatively, toss up Ripple Baskets (page 257) as the team runs by.

BREAK-THROUGH BANNERS

Before the game or pep rally, paint team banners on large rolls of paper. Have your sports team run through the banners before reaching the floor or the field.

During the Game

Here are some ideas you can use to keep the atmosphere upbeat during the event.

SLING SHOTS

Using a long piece of rubber roping, securely attach a lightweight plastic bowl to the center with duct tape. Use three people (one for each end and the third to pull back on the bowl). Aiming on a 45-degree upward angle, release the bowl and let

---

— TIP —

It's pretty tough to rip through a large, taut sheet of paper. Because it's embarrassing to have your football team run *into* your break-through banner rather than *through* it, you'll want to help them out by making small vertical slits in the banner with a sharp knife so the paper rips open easily.

---

your small prizes (candy, wrapped-up T-shirts, and more) fly into the crowd. Be sure to make the crowd cheer for their prizes first!

FREE PIZZA

Before the game, approach a local pizza store asking for a donation of a few pizzas for the game in exchange for promotion or selling their pizza during halftime. Reward the people who cheer the loudest with pizza.

CROWD CLAPPING

Start off with a slow, steady beat, and increase the speed with each clap until you reach a frenzied pace. This is a great crowd interactive activity that fans easily catch on to and will eventually initiate on their own.

ALTERNATING CROWD CHEERING

Pick a two- or three-syllable word or phrase and break up the crowd into groups, one for each syllable. Divide your team, placing members in front of each crowd section, armed with a sign displaying that group's syllable or word. Teach the crowd to cheer by having each group shout the word/phrase as their sign is raised. Put Elevators (see page 122) up and have the flyer raise the sign so the crowd can see it better. Use words or phrases such as:

★ "GO! FIGHT! WIN!"

★ "BLUE! GOLD!" (Substitute your own colors.)

★ "DE! FENSE!" (Make one sign a big "D" and draw a fence on the other.)

★ "GO BIG BLUE!" (Substitute your own colors.)

★ "LONGFIELD! TIGERS!" (Substitute your own team and mascot.)

FIGHT SONG

A fight song is composed of lyrics and melody written specifically for your school, to be performed by the school band. If your school doesn't have a specific fight song, talk to your music director and choose one to use at games. (You can also choose a recorded song and use it as your team's "theme" song.) Make up a dance or some actions to the song (ones that the crowd can easily catch onto) and perform this same dance every time the song comes on. Soon your fight song will become a spirited tradition!

TUMBLING RUNS

Crowds love tumbling runs! If you have full team tumbling, set up an alternating crisscross of tumblers, one group on each side. If you only have a few tumblers, set up Basket Tosses (see page 223) with the remainder of your team as the others tumble. If your team is at the university or college level, coordinate Basket Toss inverted Tucks, Layouts, or Layout Fulls (see chapter 13 for details) with your floor tumblers.

After the Event

When the game or pep rally is over, you can show support for the team with the following spirit ideas.

CLAP YOUR TEAM OFF THE FIELD OR FLOOR

Whether they win or lose, show your support for your team by clapping them off the field or floor. They may not appear impressed when you do this after they lose, but remember that they're upset about the loss—not upset with you for being supportive of them.

TEAM TUNNELS, STUNT LINES, AND BREAK-THROUGHS

At the end of the pep rally or a winning game, usher your team off the floor or field with a tunnel, stunt line, or another break-through banner. *Warning:* If your team loses, you may want to clap them off the playing grounds instead. It's a good idea to talk to the head coach of the team that you're cheering for to inquire about the preference in the event of a loss.

— Game and Pep Rally Committees —

All sporting events should have an organizing committee, whether it's for a game or a pep rally. Without effective planning and organization, a sporting event can quickly turn into a boring event, even if the team is winning. This committee is responsible for planning the following essential components to a successful sporting occasion.

Master of Ceremonies or Game Announcer

The master of ceremonies (emcee) at a pep rally is responsible for introducing the athletes and each performance. A humorous emcee can often make the difference between a dry pep rally and an upbeat, entertaining one. An emcee helps move the pep rally along according to schedule, while eliminating "dead time" between activities. Maintaining a lively pace during the pep rally is important because fans can quickly become restless.

The game announcer, while having less influence over the pace of the game than the emcee has over a pep rally, shares many of the same responsibilities. The announcer is the direct link between the fans and the game, describing the events that are taking place. The announcer is also responsible for introducing the time-outs, game sponsors, and entertainment acts.

Security

Security is a good idea for large or significant events that may likely have rowdy crowds. The presence of police officers, outside security officers from a security company, or event staff (such as

---

— TIP —

Unless there are lots of crowd interactive games and performances, pep rallies typically run an hour to 90 minutes in length.

college students who work at the game) can ensure that the crowd remains positive and well behaved. While security is less common at pep rallies, it is essential for games that draw a large number of fans. Not only is having security a safeguard against potential problems between home and visitor crowds, but these officials can also prevent game disturbances by removing fans who display unsportsmanlike conduct.

Cheerleaders

Cheerleaders play an important part in both involving and entertaining the crowd. During the game or pep rally, cheerleaders involve fans through the use of cheers/chants and cheer "incorps" (cheers that incorporate stunts). When performing at pep rallies, during time-outs, and halftime shows, cheerleaders take on more of an "entertainment" role, showing off dances, stunting segments, and routines. Cheerleaders make the difference between a quiet crowd and an enthusiastic one!

Mascots

Mascots (people dressed as an animal, creature, or other power symbol such as "Patriot," "Trojan," or "Pirate"—usually representing the team name) are fun to have at games and pep rallies because they entertain the crowd with their outrageous actions and playful attitude. Mascots are especially great additions to sporting events that draw lots of children.

There are also mascot competitions, as well as mascot training camps and videos to help improve their effectiveness in entertaining a crowd.

Volunteers

There is always a need for volunteers at games and pep rallies. Volunteers play a major role in running a smooth sporting event by selling and collecting tickets, holding 50/50 draws (see "50/50 Tickets" on this page), and assisting organizers.

★ ★ ★ ★ ★ ★ ★ ★ ★ ★ ★ ★ ★ ★ ★

50/50 Tickets

Selling "50/50 Tickets" can be a great fundraising activity and add excitement for the crowd. Cheerleaders (or members of another organization) sell these tickets to the crowd, and then someone draws a winning ticket. The holder of the winning ticket receives 50 percent of the ticket sale profits, while the sellers keep the other 50 percent.

★ ★ ★ ★ ★ ★ ★ ★ ★ ★ ★ ★ ★ ★ ★

Volunteers usually wear distinctive shirts so they are easily recognizable and are typically given free tickets for their time and effort.

DJ and Music

Every good sporting event has music! A disc jockey will see that the "dead" times during events—such as time-outs without entertainment and before and after the game when people are coming in and out of the stadium or gymnasium—are filled with music to keep the crowd pumped. A DJ is also essential for dances or cheerleading routines that require music.

Planned Performances

A marching band, singers, dancers, and comedians help to keep the crowd's energy high. While fans enjoy the game, it's always nice to be entertained during the breaks. Unlike games, pep rallies consist mostly of planned performances interspersed with the introduction of players and speeches by the coaches, or the school principal or dean.

Food Vendors

In addition to being a great fundraiser for the school or community, food vendors offer refreshments to the crowd. Fans especially appreciate this during a long game or on a hot day. In turn, the host school can profit by ordering pizza and selling it at home games.

If your school doesn't already have a game committee, or if the committee could use a little help, cheerleading coaches and cheerleaders can be a great addition to this organizing group. A well-organized game committee promotes a larger turnout at games. In turn, a larger number of fans helps build team confidence, increases school or community spirit, and often brings a greater financial return on ticket sales.

Cheerleaders create a noticeable difference in the spirit of the crowd at pep rallies and during games (including during halftime). It's a win-win situation for everyone: Fans are entertained, the team is supported, and the cheerleaders benefit. The opportunity to raise funds, promote the sport of cheerleading, and have fun are all advantages of participating in sporting events. If your team isn't already involved in pep rallies, halftime routines, and games, hurry up and get in on the action!

— Cheering the Game —

Every so often, during the excitement of a game, a football cheerleader will start cheering for defense when offense is on the field. Unfortunately, this little slip-up has the potential to be a cheerleading team's one-way ticket to an irreversibly poor reputation. The best defense against this consequence is simple: Have a meeting prior to each season that focuses on the sport you're cheering for.

Ideally, you'll want the coaches of the teams you're supporting to attend the meeting. They can explain the rules of the game and express their preferences for game cheering. To best support other athletic teams, cheerleaders must respect how these teams want to be cheered. For example, some teams prefer that cheerleaders not cheer them off the field after a humiliating game lost by 50 points; they may rather have you politely clap.

If a meeting with the coach isn't available, recruit the next best authority—an assistant coach, a player, or someone who knows the game inside and out. Make it your responsibility to know the rules of the game, the referee signals, and the most appropriate times to cheer. Remember to watch the game at all times to show interest and to keep track of what's happening (and in case a player inadvertently comes close to running you over!).

The Best (and the Worst) Times to Cheer

While many enjoy watching and cheering along with the cheerleaders, the majority of fans come to games to focus on the athletic contest. Keeping this

---

★ ★

Fundraising Pep Rallies and Games

Games provide huge fundraising potential. There are many ways to raise money for your team, including these:

★ Sell 50/50 tickets

★ Sell tickets for prize draws (ask the community to donate items)

★ Publish and sell game programs

★ Negotiate a portion of ticket sales in exchange for volunteer work at the game or pep rally

★ Run a snack booth

★ Sell pizza or popsicles to fans in the stands

★ Sell team T-shirts, rooter poms, posters, and other team items

Encourage your Game Committee or Pep Rally Committee to scour the community for fundraising possibilities and to brainstorm other ways to involve fans and increase the size of the crowds.

★ ★

> ### — TIP —
> Remember that the rules vary in different leagues and regions so it's important to become familiar with the rules of the specific game you'll be cheering. For example, an American football team has four "downs" in which to advance ten yards while a Canadian football game has only three downs.

in mind, here are lists of the best and worst times to cheer during football and basketball games:

DO CHEER AT FOOTBALL GAMES:

- ★ During a time-out
- ★ When changing of offensive and defensive teams
- ★ Between plays
- ★ After a good or mediocre play
- ★ During "dead" time (when no activity is going on)
- ★ During halftime

DO NOT CHEER, JUMP, OR STUNT:

- ★ During actual plays
- ★ After a bad play
- ★ When a player is hurt
- ★ During official announcements
- ★ When your offensive team is in a huddle close to you or is preparing to play near the opponent's end zone. (If you are cheering loudly close to the team, they'll have difficulty hearing their own plays being called.)

DO CHEER AT BASKETBALL GAMES:

- ★ During the game
- ★ During a time-out
- ★ During "dead" time (when no activity is going on)

- ★ After a good or mediocre play
- ★ During halftime

DO NOT CHEER, JUMP, OR STUNT:

- ★ After a bad play
- ★ When a player is hurt
- ★ During official announcements
- ★ When your team is attempting a free-throw shot
- ★ When the opposing team is attempting a free-throw shot

— Calling the Game —

Designating one person to call the cheers and chants is a very effective way to cheer the game. This person should be skillful, confident, and familiar enough with the game to avoid such mistakes as calling out an offensive cheer when defense is on the field! Callers are also responsible for calling the stunts and pyramid segments as well as any performances during "time-outs."

When calling the game, the caller should yell out the last line of the cheer or chant so that everyone can join in on the next phrase. For example, if your chant is something simple like, "Broncos! Let's do it! Beat those Tigers!" the caller would begin the cheer by yelling "Beat those Tigers!" It's important to remember to start the cheer slowly, as most cheers have a way of speeding up when the team joins in.

Sometimes hearing the caller can be difficult, especially when you're cheering outside or the crowd is rowdy. If possible, situate the caller in the middle of the lineup or use a megaphone so everyone can hear clearly. A megaphone is a valuable prop to ensure that cheers can be heard by other cheerleaders. A good trick is to let your team know ahead of time what cheer is next. This can be done simply by discreetly passing the cheer down the line up (for example: "'Go Broncos!' is next"). A *word of caution:* Avoid setting a specific schedule for calling cheers, which takes away the spontaneity of calling cheers that go with the game and can become boring.

On the other hand, setting a schedule for stunts can be a good idea. The caller just has to say "set" and everyone knows what stunt to perform. This works well because, unlike cheers, stunts aren't necessarily game-specific.

You may want to have two different callers: one for cheers, another for stunts. This takes pressure off the callers by allowing them to concentrate on the most appropriate times to cheer or stunt, and eliminating the confusion of doing both. This is especially a good idea if your caller or team is new to game cheering.

Other teams simply allow anyone to call any cheer at any time, but this method has its problems. It may lead to multiple callings and confusion among team members (with whom do you cheer?). Your best bet is to designate one or two team members who feel confident with both the rules of the game *and* calling the cheers and stunts.

Now that you're armed with the basics of game cheering, you're well on your way to becoming a respected, knowledgeable game-cheering team member. Remember to pay attention to offensive and defensive teams so you can keep this honored status!

— Hitting the Crowd . . . and Keeping Their Respect —

The idea of "hitting the crowd" is used to encourage fans to cheer along and express their excitement over the game or performance. A cheerleader hits the crowd after a cheer or chant at a game, at the end of a stunting sequence, or after any type of performance, such as a competition.

As a cheerleader, your ultimate goal is to get your fans to cheer with you. To do this, you first need to capture their attention. Performing grav-ity-defying stunts, complex pyramids, and fancy cheers usually does the trick. But the best way to get someone to cheer along with you is to pick them out of the crowd, move toward them, look them right in the eye, and yell "CHEER WITH US!" It's a bit of intimidation, but it works. Luckily, this "in-your-face" attitude becomes easier every time you hit the crowd. After a while, it will feel like second nature. But in the meantime, here's your five-step, fool-proof guide:

1. Finish your cheer/chant/stunt/performance and pause a few seconds before moving.

2. After pausing to let the crowd know you've finished, explode forward and move toward the crowd.

3. As you move toward fans, cheer while clapping, hitting a motion, or jumping. Use actual phrases and words, such as these:

> "Let's go Big Blue!"
> "Dragons, #1!"
> "C'mon All-Stars!"
> "You've got it, U of G!"

4. While moving toward the fans and cheering, you hit motions to get more of the crowd's attention, such as a High Punch or Sparkles (see chapter 5 for photographs), the "Come on!" motion, or anything else you like as long as it's big. For added effect, you can incorporate Toe Touches or a walking stunt (such as a Chair) when hitting the crowd. In fact, each cheerleader can do something different; hitting the crowd should be spontaneous.

5. Resist acting *too* crazy, such as gesturing inappropriately or shouting "whoo-hoo." The plan is to encourage the crowd to cheer with you, not discourage them from respecting you. Have fun, but act appropriately.

Prescription for Silent Fans

Some crowds just don't get it. Whether they're embarrassed, shy, or just not interested, they won't

> **— TIP —**
>
> Cheer, but don't "Whoo!" Fans find this incredibly annoying to listen to, especially when a buddy sitting beside them has been "Whoo!"-ing into their ear for the past hour.

cheer along no matter how hard you try. But before you pack up your megaphones, give these crowd-pleasers a try:

1. Use signs.

It could be just that the crowd can't hear you or can't understand what you're saying. Either that or they might be so wrapped up in the game that they keep forgetting when it's time to yell "BLUE!"

2. Add variety to your cheers, stunts, and routines.

While it's definitely a good idea to keep a few traditions, the crowd easily tires of watching the same performances and hearing the same cheers. Remember that a lot of people come just to watch the cheerleaders. Make sure you put on an exciting show every time.

3. Involve your mascot.

Bringing humor and entertainment with every movement, mascots are a great way to bridge the gap between cheerleaders and fans. If you can get fans to interact and have fun with the mascot, you'll watch them slowly but surely warm up to the idea of crowd participation.

4. Look the fans right in the eye and cheer to them.

As soon as they realize you expect them to cheer along, they'll begin to make an effort. Even if they're just mouthing the words to humor you, it's a good start.

5. If this doesn't work, sit right next to them.

It sounds (and looks) a little strange having the team sit in the stands interspersed with the crowd, but fans find it easier to cheer along when someone is yelling beside them.

6. Play fun and interactive cheer games with the crowd.

For example:

CHEERLEADERS: "Hey fans!"

CROWD: "Hey what?"

CHEERLEADERS: "Hey fans!"

CROWD: "Hey what?"

CHEERLEADERS: "We want to see/hear you _____" ("sing the fight song," for example).

The crowd will eventually catch on and begin to initiate the cheers themselves. You have to be patient, though; fans don't pick up on this game immediately. You might want to start with half of the cheerleaders in the crowd to "show them how it's done."

7. Use a slingshot or throw prizes into the crowd.

Candy, T-shirts, and other prizes are always a big hit.

8. If all else fails, order pizza.

Award it to the fans that are cheering the loudest.

Celebration Routines

Fans love traditions. If you want interaction, traditional fight songs, dances, and chants are ways to get it. Don't have any of your own? Then it's time to create some! You need to develop your own "pattern" of celebration. For example, one cheerleading team celebrates by loading Shoulder Stands, then walking around and waving flags to their traditional chant after every touchdown. Another team gets down and performs the same number of push-ups as points. (A *word of caution:* You might want to rethink this celebration routine at games with high scores, like basketball!) Other teams have a special dance or stunt sequence that goes along to the school's fight song. Whatever it is, make it fun and do it after every score. The fans will soon expect it and join in on the fun.

Hitting the crowd isn't easy . . . and it isn't always fun. It's hard to stand there with a big smile on your face when people are ignoring you, pointing at you, or even throwing things at you. Most cheerleaders are fortunate enough to have great crowds, but occasionally they find themselves facing a few ignorant people.

So how would you deal with such negativity? Don't even blink an eye. Beat them at their own game by following these three simple secrets:

1. Act confident
2. Act as though you don't notice
3. Act like you don't care

It's a bit like being teased by a bratty sibling; they quickly lose interest when they don't get a reaction from you. Get out there and act like you own the sidelines. Be proud to show off your hard work. People will soon realize that harassing you is a fruitless activity.

And besides, the joke is really on the ignorant fans; *they*, not you, are the ones who look foolish.

— Top 10 Cheer "Leading" Reminders —

Here, in reverse order, is the list of what I consider the top 10 principles for leading cheers:

10. Avoid Encouraging Distasteful Cheers

It is very important that you *not* join in with fans when they start distasteful cheers, no matter how tempted you are. Showing such poor sportsmanship promotes a negative image of your team, and you will be less respected as athletes if you participate. Remember, you are a *leader*, and the most productive way to support your team is by being positive at all times. Clapping to the rhythm of the questionable cheer *might* be acceptable in

some cases, but be careful not to encourage tasteless cheering from the crowd.

9. Discuss Preferred Cheering Styles with the Team Coach

Clapping your team's entrance or exit, forming a tunnel for them to run through, or lining up stunts as they come onto (or off) the field or court is encouraging when teams have victories to celebrate . . . but should the team lose miserably, athletes may prefer that cheerleaders not show enthusiasm as they leave the field. Find out their preferences before the first game of the season.

8. Keep Your Attention on the Game at All Times

You never know when the quarterback will decide to throw the ball to the receiver standing right beside your lineup. It's unnerving to watch a football player run right for you in an attempt to tackle that receiver. Your best defense is to be aware of the game and refrain from stunting while the play is close by. If you choose to stunt, do so far enough from the action so your Liberty Heel Stretch will be left safely standing during an out-of-bounds tackle.

7. Stand Sideways or Slightly Angled Toward the Game

You'll want to stand in a position that allows you to see the game and gives the crowd a view of your profile rather than your back. Stand in your lineup in neat rows with your hands behind your back or on your hips, at the discretion of your coach. (By the way, now is not the time to re-tie your bow, fix your shoelace, or adjust your bloomers. Not only are these activities distracting, but some are downright rude of you and unpleasant for fans to witness.)

6. Bring Your Own Snacks and Water to the Game

More than likely, watching the game and performing at halftime will occupy all your time during the game, so you can't count on lining up at the concession stand. Especially if the day is hot, you'll need lots of water and high-energy, nutritious snacks to keep you fueled up for the long hours of cheering ahead. *A word of warning:* Bring your own water bottles, as it's unsanitary to share with your teammates.

5. Keep Your Spirits High

Imagine this: You're cheering at your arch rival's brand new stadium, being verbally abused by your opponent's immature freshmen as you stand before a sparse crowd of your fans. It's raining, it's cold, and your team is losing pitifully. You're thinking, "Remind me again why I'm putting myself through this . . ."

No one said cheerleading was easy. It's especially tough to maintain a positive attitude and put on a lively performance when your spirits are down. The truth is, even when you're treated like an annoyance rather than a positive influence, you are still supporting your team and representing your school or community.

And if you think *you* feel bad throughout a humiliating game experience, think about how the players must feel. Then think about how they would feel if *no one* was there to support and cheer for them. You are *needed* as leaders to set an example and keep the spirits high.

4. *Earn* Respect

Yes, you provide fans with a form of entertainment, but you are also an athlete. If you want to be respected and treated as a true athlete, you must act like one, *on and off* the field. The crowd, players, and your school or community do not give out respect freely; *you must earn respect.* Earning respect requires that you:

★ Maintain a sense of professionalism at all times.

★ Stand neatly in your line up unless hitting the crowd, cheering, or stunting.

★ Keep your talk to teammates at a minimum while you're cheering a game.

★ Listen to your caller's instructions for stunts and cheers. You'll all look foolish if everyone is hitting their Basket Tosses except your group.

★ Stay with your team. Avoid going off to talk to your friends while in your game lineup.

★ Show respect for the crowd, players, and your teammates.

★ Ignore rude comments from the crowd.

★ Avoid participating in unsportsmanlike behavior and cheers.

★ Present yourself well by keeping your hair done, bows tied, shoes clean, uniform pressed, and a smile on your face.

3. Make the Visiting Cheerleaders Feel Welcome

As mentioned before, cheerleading is unlike any other sport. Through the common goal of promoting the growth and popularity of the sport, cheerleaders support one another, regardless of what team they're on. If you find yourself feeling animosity toward another team, lose the bad attitude—fast. You'll gain nothing from making enemies, and everything from making friends with other cheerleaders.

Go on over and make the visiting cheerleaders feel welcome by introducing yourself. Show them where the change rooms are and where they can purchase snacks. When it's your turn to go to an away game, it's nice to have some friends there to make you feel welcome.

2. Respect Your Coach

You won't always agree with your coach, but arguing in front of fans and teammates during a game will do you and your team no good. Instead, show respect during games and practices and speak to your coach about your concerns in privacy, at another time and place. By doing so, you will retain the respect of the crowd and of others around you.

ı. Interact with the Crowd and Have Fun!

Cheerleaders often make the mistake of entertaining rather than interacting with the crowd. Remember that you are "cheer-*leaders*," not "cheer-*performers*." For that reason, it's not enough to "perform" a cheer; instead, look people in the eye and get them to cheer along with you. Move right on up to them and get in their faces, or sit beside them if you have to, and they'll soon start to cheer along.

You have been chosen to represent your school or community because of your leadership abilities and enthusiasm. This is something to be proud of! Where else can you stand in front of hundreds or thousands of people and energize them to cheer along with you? Besides, you have front row seats to the game! Smile and have fun doing what you love to do.

PART TWO

Motions, Cheers, Chants, and Jumps

Everything for Cheerleaders to Learn and Coaches to Know

Chapter Five

Motions, Cheers, and Chants

Watching cheerleading would be boring if all cheerleaders did was stand around and yell at the crowd. Choreographed movements spice up cheers and chants, grabbing the attention of a crowd. When twenty athletes move in perfect coordination, people definitely notice!

— Motions —

With the basic hand, arm, and leg positions, the possibilities for creating cheers and chants are endless. Look at the following pictures, paying careful attention to how tight and strong the cheerleader's motions are. Practice these motions, going from one to another taking the shortest route between them. This means quickly "snapping" into the next move, keeping arms tight and straight—no sloppy or limp motions allowed!

Hand Positions

Fists: Keep your fingers squeezed tightly together. Make sure you keep your thumbs wrapped around the *outside* of your fingers. Otherwise, if your hand gets bumped, you could break your thumb. This is the most common hand position for motions.

Clap (see figure 5.1): Cup your hands so that when they are "clapped" together they make a loud sound. Place your hands just under your chin, slightly away from the body. Tuck your elbows in so the only parts moving are your arms slightly coming apart when clapping.

Figure 5.1 *Clap*.

Figure 5.2 *Blade Clap.*

Figure 5.3 *Sparkles.*

Figure 5.4 *Hips.*

Blades: Notice in figure 5.2 the flat, open hands with fingers and thumbs tight together. A common mistake is allowing thumbs to stick out. Make sure you tuck them together with the fingers!

Blade Clap (see figure 5.2): Perform the Blade Clap the same as the clap, but keep your hands flat together when clapped. Blade claps are used more for visual effect rather than to generate sound.

Sparkles (see figure 5.3): For Sparkles, keep your fingers taut and spread apart. You'll usually shake your wrists during this motion so that hands are "sparkling."

Arm Positions

Hips (see figure 5.4): Place your fisted hands on your hips.

Figure 5.5 *High V.*

Figure 5.6 *Low V.*

High V (see figure 5.5): Extend your arms straight and slightly in front of your body (you should be able to see them out of the corners of your eyes while looking straight ahead). Keep fists straight and turn them so that the thumbnails are facing outward. High V is one of the most common cheerleading motions.

Low V (see figure 5.6): Extend your arms downward, straight and slightly in front of the body. Keep fists straight and turn them so thumbnails are facing inward.

T (see figure 5.7): Extend your arms straight out from the body, parallel to the ground. Position them slightly in front of the body so you can see them out of your peripheral vision when looking forward. Keep fists straight and turn them so thumbnails are facing the ground.

Broken T (see figure 5.8): This is a "T" with bent elbows.

Figure 5.7 *T.*

Figure 5.8 *Broken T.*

Figure 5.9 *Touchdown.*

Figure 5.10 *Low Touchdown.*

Touchdown (see figure 5.9): Extend your arms upward and parallel to one another, as close to the head as possible. Turn your wrists so your thumbnails are facing inward.

Low Touchdown (see figure 5.10): Make your arms parallel, extended downward.

High Punch (see figure 5.11): Extend the right arm close to the right ear and turn your wrist so your thumbnail is facing inward. Place your other fist on your left hip. This is also known as a "number one."

Broken High V/Broken Low V (see figure 5.12 for illustration of Broken High V): The Broken High V and Broken Low V are the same as the High and Low V (see figures 5.5 and 5.6 for illustration of regular High V and Low V) but with bent elbows.

Figure 5.11 *High Punch.*

Figure 5.12 *Broken High V.*

Figure 5.13 *Table Top.*

Table Top (see figure 5.13): Keep elbows in to the sides, hands in fists in front of shoulders. Face thumbnails inward.

Right Diagonal/Left Diagonal (see figure 5.14 for illustration of Right Diagonal): Place one arm in a Low V position and the other in a high V position. Switch positions of arms to determine Right Diagonal and Left Diagonal (when your right arm is in the air, it's a Right Diagonal; when your left arm is in the air, it's a Left Diagonal).

Right L/Left L (see figure 5.15 for illustration of Left L): Place one arm in a High Punch, the other in a T position. Switch positions of arms to determine Right L and Left L (when your right arm is in the air, it's a Right L; when your left arm is in the air it's a Left L).

Check Mark (see figure 5.16): Place one arm in a High V with the other bent close to the body.

Figure 5.14 *Right Diagonal.*

Figure 5.15 *Left L.*

Figure 5.16 *Check Mark.*

Figure 5.17 *Clean.*

Figure 5.18 *Lunge.*

Figure 5.19 *Back Lunge.*

Figure 5.20 *Wide.*

Clean (see figure 5.17): Keep arms tight at sides, hands in blade position, and legs together.

Leg Positions

Lunge (see figure 5.18): Keep the front leg bent (women: toes are usually "popped" up; men: entire foot is flat on floor) and the back leg straight. The straight leg classifies the lunge as either "right" or "left."

Back Lunge (see figure 5.19): Keep front leg bent (women: toes are usually "popped" up; men: entire foot is flat on the floor). Your hips should face forward and the other leg should extend straight back. Weight is on the back leg.

Wide (see figure 5.20): Keep your leg stance open, slightly wider than shoulder width apart.

— Motion Drills —

Motion drills are a great way to perfect motions and improve the team's synchronization. Drills that focus on "snapping" motions quickly and perfecting team coordination are most effective. See the Coaches' Corner box below to know what motion drills are in store for you.

— Choreographing Cheers and Chants: For Coaches and Athletes —

Cheers and chants . . . what's the difference? For starters, chants are often short, one or two simple lines that crowds can easily catch on to. They are often used when you have only a few seconds to cheer because they can be stopped easily by calling "last time!" between repetitions.

A cheer, on the other hand, is often longer and somewhat resembles a song in the sense that it has a beginning, middle, and end. Cheers are most often used during longer time-outs, game halftimes, or competitions. They often incorporate stunting and pyramids whereas a chant might only be composed of motions.

These aren't concrete rules for cheers and chants, though. If you feel like adding stunts to a chant, go right ahead. Creativity is the basis of cheering, stunting, and routines. The more creative you are, the more audience appeal your cheers will have and the more chance you have of getting others to cheer with you.

C O A C H E S ' C O R N E R

EFFECTIVE MOTION DRILLS

Use the following motion drills to improve the team's performance.

★ **'Til Everyone Is Perfect:** This is one of the most dreaded motion drills for athletes because by the end their arms feel like they're going to fall off! But it's also a great muscle-strengthening exercise. Call out a motion and wait until everyone is holding a perfect position before calling out the next. Walk around, testing to be sure everyone is holding their motions tight (tensed muscles) and making sure everyone has perfect technique.

★ **Eight Cheerleader Line-Up:** Line eight cheerleaders up across the gym and let each choose a different motion, representing a count from one to eight. Make sure athletes hold this position until the exercise is completed. Then instruct the team to follow each demo at the front to each of the eight counts. Once the team is comfortable with the motions, speed up the counts.

★ **Line Drill:** Have the cheerleaders stand in a straight line, one behind the other, in front of you. As you call out a motion, the cheerleaders' aim is to synchronize their motions with those of everyone else in line. As accuracy improves, speed up the counts.

★ **Circle Up:** Have the cheerleaders stand in a circle, facing one another. Along with the line drill, this is another good exercise to teach cheerleaders to watch one another and move as one team, rather than as individuals.

★ **Coach Says:** Following the "Simon Says" game format, call out motions and other cheerleading techniques.

Follow these guidelines when creating cheers and chants, remembering that the main goal is to get the crowd to cheer along:

CHOREOGRAPHING A CHANT

1. First find a beat, then try humming a tune that has a catchy rhythm.

2. Add words.

3. Add motions that go with the words. (For example: "Tigers" could elicit a claw hand motion or the word "Big!" can be accompanied by a jump with a big outward motion.)

CHOREOGRAPHING A CHEER

1. Find a beat or rhythm.

2. Think of a cheer similar to a song: a beginning, middle, and an end with a common rhythm or a chorus. For example:

   a. Hey Broncos! In the stands yell BLACK c'mon BLACK!

   b. Hey Broncos! All the fans yell RED c'mon RED!

   c. Hey Broncos! Loud as you can yell WHITE c'mon WHITE!

      All together one more time yell BLACK RED and WHITE!

      BRONCOS (pause) LET'S FIGHT!

   d. Yell it! BLACK RED and WHITE!

      BRONCO'S (pause) LET'S FIGHT! (repeat)

3. Put motions to the words. For repetitive verses, use repetitive motions.

4. Incorporate stunts. Here's an effective format for adding stunts to cheers:

   Verse a: motions
   Verse b: transition
   Verse c: stunt
   Verse d: dismount and hit the crowd

Look at the previous cheer. See how it is broken into four different segments, each one using either motions, transitions, stunting, or dismounting and hitting the crowd? Notice how more counts are given to stunting as this segment requires more time to perform and is the most exciting part of a cheer. Be sure to include adequate time to execute the stunt or pyramid safely without feeling you need to rush through it.

Open your cheers or chants with a big explosive motion or stunt (such as a Basket Toss) to grab the crowd's attention right away. With chants, you only have a few seconds to get the crowd to cheer with you so you want to make the opening as impressive as you can.

Another thing to remember when writing cheers and chants is to use phrases that have meaning to your school, such as a line from the school song or a school slogan. It's also fun to use interactive cheers with the crowd or with the mascot. The University of Guelph uses a great cheer with their mascot, the Gryphon, that either the crowd or the cheerleaders can initiate:

HEY GRYPHON! (the mascot makes a "hey what?" motion)

HEY GRYPHON! (he makes another "hey what?" motion)

WE WANNA SEE YOU GET DOWN!

D-O-W-N THAT'S THE WAY WE GET DOWN! (clap)

D-O-W-N THAT'S THE WAY WE GET DOWN! (clap)

While the cheerleaders are cheering, the Gryphon is entertaining the crowd with his crazy "getting down" dance. It's also fun when the crowd initiates the cheer and shouts "Hey cheerleaders! We wanna see you . . ."

Don't Forget Link Words!

Link words are simple words and phrases that you can spontaneously fit in between verses. For example:

"Louder!"
"Cheer with us!"
"Let's go!"
"C'mon!"
"Last time!"

Link words communicate helpful information to the crowd and to the rest of your team. For example, if you don't yell "Last time!" someone in the crowd might still keep on cheering and then feel embarrassed afterward. And if the crowd feels embarrassed, chances are they won't want to cheer with you next time. Or worse yet, some of your fellow cheerleaders might continue cheering and then you'd all feel embarrassed!

However you choreograph your cheers and chants, have fun with your crowd! Involve them in your cheering, and they will *want* to cheer along with you.

— Final Cheer Pointers —

The thrill of being in front of so many people, actually *leading* them, can be nerve-racking at first; but don't let the crowd intimidate you. Have fun with them! You wouldn't be on a cheerleading team if you didn't have what it takes to be a leader. Just remember to take a deep breath and put on a smile. Even if all else goes wrong, a smile will always make things better.

Keep these final pointers in mind while cheering:

VOICE

★ *Cheer together.* Nothing sounds worse than half a team cheering a few seconds apart from the other members. A great way to get your team to work as a cohesive unit is to have everyone clap together to the words before you add motions. This helps team members internalize the rhythm.

★ *Designate a caller to start off the cheer.* This person should cheer loudly enough that the whole team can hear and slowly enough that the crowd can catch on.

★ *Pronounce words clearly.* Avoid sing-song voices that are hard to understand and follow.

★ *Cheer from the diaphragm (stomach), not the throat.* This protects your voice and enables you to cheer louder.

★ *Keep voice pitch lowered.* Cheering in a high voice sounds weak and is hard to understand. It can also damage your vocal cords.

EXECUTION

★ *Use link words.* Don't forget the link words (see sidebar on this page) to help prompt your squad and the crowd on what to do next.

★ *Keep cheers slow.* Cheer slowly enough that the crowd can follow; if they get frustrated, they will stop cheering with you all together.

★ *Use words that reflect good sportsmanship.* Never use rude or swear words. It only reflects poorly on your school and team.

★ *Stay enthusiastic.* Keep your enthusiasm and be genuine about what you're cheering.

★ *Use your voice, face, and body to emphasize words.*

C O A C H E S '   C O R N E R

TEACHING A CHEER

Once you have created a masterpiece, the next step is to teach it to the team. All it takes is four simple steps to teach even the hardest cheer or chant to any age group or level of cheerleaders:

Step One: Show the entire cheer, full out with motions.

Step Two: Teach the words to the cheer, clapping to the words (no motions or stunts). If it is a long cheer, break it up into verses and practice each one before going onto the next.

Step Three: Teach the motions to the first line or so of the cheer. Repeat it until the cheerleaders feel comfortable and then go on, reviewing from the beginning each time.

Step Four: Add your transitions and stunts. Perform the entire cheer: words, motions, transitions, and stunts.

Don't try to teach the entire cheer or chant all at once. You'll frustrate yourself and the cheerleaders. Take it step-by-step, and the cheer segment will come together in no time.

★ *Be creative with your cheers and motions.*

★ *Use signs.* Paint signs with words such as "GO!" or "BLUE!" to prompt the crowd to cheer along during key points of the cheer or chant.

★ *Use sharp, strong motions.* This will make the crowd notice you, and make the cheer more effective.

★ *Add motions.* Motions that complement the words are more fun to watch.

★ *Incorporate your mascot, school colors, or slogans.*

★ *Add jumps, stunts, and formation changes.* This will, without a doubt, keep the crowd's attention.

★ *Use repetitive motions for repetitive verses.*

★ *Be heard.* Raise your voice and hold the last word a little longer than usual when finishing a cheer or chant.

★ *Make an impact.* Hold your last motion for a few seconds when your cheer or chant is done.

★ *Hit the crowd.* When your cheer or chant has ended, hit the crowd.

★ *Smile and have fun!*

— Sample Cheers and Chants —

Here are some sample cheers and chants along with photos to help get you started. In this section you'll also find examples of other cheers and chants for games, events, and competitions.

While reading the following cheers and chants, you'll notice an occasional [X] between words and that some words are **bolded**. Treat each [X] as either a clap or pause, depending on the cheer (in many cheer lists, it is only listed as an X with no brackets, so expect to see it both ways throughout your actual cheering experience). Bolded words should be emphasized.

Chant #1

See figures 5.21 through 5.29 to follow along with this cheer.

Stand
up
For the
Tigers
[X]

Go!
Red
and white
go!

Figure 5.21 *Stand . . .*

Figure 5.22 *up . . .*

Figure 5.23 *for the . . .*

Figure 5.24 *Tigers . . .*

Figure 5.25 *[X].*

Figure 5.26 *Go . . .*

Figure 5.27 *red . . .*

Figure 5.28 *and white . . .*

Figure 5.29 *go . . .*

Chant #2

See figures 5.30 through 5.37 to follow along with this cheer.

Eagles!

[X]

Let's do it

right!

We will

win

to-night!

[X]

Figure 5.30 *Eagles! . . .*

Figure 5.31 *[X].*

Figure 5.32 *let's do it . . .*

Figure 5.33 *right!*

Figure 5.34 *We will . . .*

Figure 5.35 *win . . .*

Figure 5.36 *to-night . . .*

Figure 5.37 *[X].*

How to Perform These Cheers and Chants

When you see an [X], remember to clap or pause. When you see **bolded** words, try making one of the following changes according to what sounds best in the cheer:

★ Emphasize the word by saying it slower than the rest of the cheer

★ Emphasize the word by raising or lowering your voice on that word or group of words

Be creative and experiment with the tempo, rhythm, team colors, team names, pauses, claps, voice pitch, and words. Add your own individuality and school style to create personalized cheer combinations for your team. The best thing about cheering is that you can let your own personality shine through; there is no right or wrong way to do it!

Chants for Any Event

Here are additional sample chants you can adapt for your community, school, or team:

Hey Dragons! [X] You look **so** good!

Go **all the way,** ND! [X][X] Go all the way! [X][X]

Move it! [X][X] Move it! [X][X] **Go Irish go!** [X]

What's [X] your favorite **color,** Gryphons? Red, gold, and white! [X]

Hey! [X] Here we go, ND! **Here we go!** [X][X][X]

We're [X] number one in spirit! Come on fans, let's hear it! [X]

Let's M-O-V-E! **Move** that **ball** for a victory!

W-I-N! [X][X] **Fightin'** Irish, let's win! [X]

1-2-3-4! **Come on,** Eagles, let's score! [X]

Get that ball! Get that ball and GO! GO! GO! [X]

Let's go! [X][X] Let's fight! [X][X] Let's **win,** and do it **to**-night!

Hey Hawks! [X][X] Let's go! Fight! Win! [X][X]

Hey! Let's go! Get ready to fight **to**-night!

Our Braves can't be beat! So Tigers **take a seat!**

Tigers! [X][X] Tigers! [X][X] Yell **F-S-U!** (Yell it!) **F-S-U!**

Falcon fans, let's hear it! [X] **Show** us your spirit!

Irish! [X][X] Irish! [X][X] N-D-H-S!

Go gold! [X][X] Go white! [X][X] Come on, **Braves,** let's fight!

Let's go, Cardinals, let's go! [X][X]

Go! [X] Go Rockets! [X] **Let's all cheer** for the Rockets! [X]

Let's go! [X][X][X] Let's go, Eagles! [X][X][X]

Go! [X] Go! [X] Go Tigers Go! [X]

Football Chants

D-E [X] **F-E** [X] N-S-E! Defense!

D-D-D Defense! Hold **those** Bulldogs! [X]

De-fense hold tight! FIGHT! FIGHT! FIGHT

Six! [X] Six more! [X] Cougar team, let's score! [X]

First and ten! Do it again! **We** want a win!

Tiger team [X] six points more! Come on ND! Raise that score!

Offense! [X] **Take that ball** and GO! GO! GO!

Basketball Chants

Basket! [X][X] Basket! [X][X] Do it again, 'cuz we want a win, so **shoot** it on in!

Hey you! [X][X] Score two! [X][X] **Let's** go, Big Blue! [X][X]

Hands up! [X][X] Defense! [X][X] Hands up! [X][X]

Down to the rim! [X][X] Shoot two and win! [X][X]

Shoot! [X] Shoot it in! [X][X] Fighting Irish, let's win! [X]

Basket! [X][X] Score! [X] **Two points more!** [X]

Shoot for two, Bulldogs! **Shoot for two!**

Hey you! [X][X] Get that ball and **shoot for two!**

Two! [X] Two more! [X] Cougar team, let's score! [X]

We want a basket! [X][X] Go Eagles go! [X]

Basket! [X][X] Basket! [X][X] Go red and white. Let's fight!

Everybody yell M-S-U! C'mon fans, yell "shoot for two"!

Victory! **On the floor! Let's score** [X] two points more!

Offense! [X] Take that ball and **GO! GO! GO!**

— Sample Cheers —

Hey **fans**! [X] Help us out! [X] Make some noise and **shout it out!**

Everybody yell G [X] O! G [X] O!

Everybody yell Fight! Fight!

Everybody yell W-I-N! Yell it now, W-I-N!

Let me hear you say go fight win!

Come on! Go fight win!

⁓

Irish Fans, in the stands

Yell **let's** beat those Tigers!

Let's beat those Tigers!

⁓

Fire it up! [X][X] Fire it up! [X][X]

Hey Patriot fans, **let's get fired up!**

Let's show the Bulldogs how it's done

'Cuz there's a game **to be won!**

Fire it up! [X][X] Fire it up! [X][X]

⁓

Let's hear it **for** the blue! [X][X] BLUE! [X][X]

Let's hear it **for** the white! [X][X] WHITE! [X][X]

P-D-H-S

Fight, **Cardinals** fight!

(repeat)

⁓

Come on **fans,** in the **stands**

Yell Red [X] RED!

Make us proud, say it loud

Yell white [X] WHITE!

All together and **get real loud**

Red **and** white!

Yell it, RED **AND** WHITE!

(repeat)

⁓

Crusader **fans** on this side,

Yell go! GO!

All the **fans** on this side,

Yell fight! FIGHT!

All the **fans** in the middle,

Yell win! WIN!

Crusader **fans,** together **now** yell:

GO FIGHT WIN! GO FIGHT WIN!

⁓

Go Big Green!

Let's hear it for LCS!

Go Big Blue!

Let's hear it **for** the best!

Yell Sherwood! [X] Eagles! [X]

SHERWOOD! [X] EAGLES! [X]

(repeat)

⁓

If **you** want to win,

Yell with all your might!

When we say "go!" you say "fight!"

GO! (FIGHT!) GO! (FIGHT!)

⁓

FI-GHT! Fight Lancers fight!

SC-ORE! Score Lancers score!

Fight **Lancers** fight!

Score **Lancers** score!

⁓

ONE, we are the Gryphons

TWO, a little bit louder

THREE, we still can't hear you!

FOUR, more more more!

(repeat from "ONE")

⌒

Irish fans have spirit!

Shout it out, let's hear it!

We're number one! (back row)

We're number one! (front row)

(repeat, alternating front and back rows)

⌒

Hey **Dragon** fans! Come on, **let's** yell,

Go **big** red!

Yell it: GO **BIG** RED!

Dragon fans! Come on, let's spell it,

R-**E**-D! Yell it, R-**E**-D!

Go **big** red! R-**E**-D!

(repeat)

⌒

Devil spirit!

Come on crowd, let's hear it!

Stand up and scream,

Go Central team!

Let's hear it!

GO CENTRAL TEAM!

⌒

Let's hear it for the Hawks,

Yell **Purple,** gold, and white!

PURPLE, GOLD, AND WHITE!

Yell **fight,** Valleyfield fight!

FIGHT, VALLEYFIELD FIGHT!

Purple, gold, and white,

Fight, Valleyfield fight!

PURPLE, GOLD, AND WHITE!

FIGHT, VALLEYFIELD FIGHT!

(repeat last two lines)

⌒

Red! [X] Say it again! [X] **Red let's go!** [X]

Black! [X] Say it again! [X] **Black let's go!** [X]

Gold! [X] Say it again! [X] **Gold let's go!** [X]

Red, Black, and Gold! [X] **Marauders, let's go!** [X]

(repeat)

⌒

Who [X] are you yelling for?

Mayfield! [X] Hornets! [X]

Stand up and **cheer** once more!

Mayfield! [X] Hornets! [X]

Louder now, let's hear it **for**

Mayfield! [X] Hornets! [X]

(repeat)

⌒

We're not number 5,

Not number 4, number 3, number 2 . . .

We're number **one!**

GO **BIG** BLUE!

⌒

Hey **you!** In the crowd!

If you've got spirit, shout it loud!

GO, **STINGERS** GO!

GO, **STINGERS** GO!

⌒

Hey! [X] Let's hear it! [X] **Lions** are the best!

Hey! We're number one!

P-C-H-S!

Dolphins! [X] It's time to fight!

Everybody **yell** blue and white!

BLUE AND WHITE!

BLUE AND WHITE!

Dolphins! [X] Let's do it again!

Everybody **yell** go fight win!

GO FIGHT WIN!

GO FIGHT WIN!

Jumps

Jumps are an important, and often required, part of cheerleading routines. They demonstrate flexibility, precision, and skill, as well as increase the level of excitement during a performance. In this chapter, you'll find information on the different types of jumps, directions on how to perform them, and practice drills for perfecting them.

— Popular Jumps —

The most popular jump is the Toe Touch, followed by other jumps such as the Front or Side Hurdler, Double Nines, and Around the World.

Toe Touch

Most jumps are typically done to an eight count. This timing gives the athlete enough time to properly execute the technique and provides for a clean finish.

When learning how to do a Toe Touch, a partner can be helpful by standing behind you and lifting you by the waist when you jump. This drill is useful for practicing proper jumping technique and adding height to your jump. The jumper performs each count the same way as a regular Toe Touch.

Figure 6.1 *Assisted Toe Touch, Count One.*

Assisted Toe Touch, Count One (see figure 6.1): Assisting partner grasps the jumper's hips; thumbs pointing upward and palms toward the back of the hips, rather than the sides of the hips. This enables the assisting

Figure 6.2 *Assisted Toe Touch, Count Two.*

Figure 6.3 *Assisted Toe Touch, Count Three.*

Figure 6.4 *Assisted Toe Touch, Count Four.*

partner to hold on to the jumper better and to help the jumper roll the hips at the height of the jump.

Assisted Toe Touch, Count Two (see figure 6.2): Assisting partner follows the jumper upward as the jumper rises on the toes (the jumper should be allowed to rise up alone; the assisting partner shouldn't pull the jumper upward). Jumper rises on the toes, keeping the arms locked out in a High V.

Assisted Toe Touch, Count Three (see figure 6.3): Assisting partner sinks with the jumper. Jumper swings the arms inward and down in front of the body to a crossed position while bending the knees to "wind-up" for the jump.

Assisted Toe Touch, Count Four (see figure 6.4): Assisting partner uses the jumper's momentum to lift the jumper upward. The assisting partner helps the jumper to roll the hips into

Figure 6.5 *Toe Touch, Count One.*

Figure 6.6 *Toe Touch, Count Two.*

the correct jump position by pushing forward against the jumper's seat with the assisting partner's forearms. The assisting partner should try to suspend the jumper as long as possible so that the jumper can get a feel for the correct jump positioning. The assisting partner should then return the jumper to the ground in a controlled manner. The jumper continues the circular motion with the arms, pulling the arms upward into a T and jumps off of the ground into a Toe Touch. (For further explanation of how to do this jump correctly, the jumper should read the following section on the timing for a Toe Touch.)

This is the timing for a Toe Touch starting from a clean position:

Toe Touch, Count One (see figure 6.5): Athlete snaps arms up into a High V.

Toe Touch, Count Two (see figure 6.6): Rising on his or her toes, the athlete keeps arms locked in a High V. There is a tendency for cheerleaders to allow their High V's to widen and their backs to arch on this count. The proper technique is to keep the upper body still while the athlete rises onto the toes.

Toe Touch, Count Three (see figure 6.7): The athlete swings arms inward and down in front to a crossed position while bending the knees. This is the "wind-up" for the jump and should be executed sharply to gain momentum. The athlete should remember to keep the chest and head up during the entire jump.

Toe Touch, Count Four (see figure 6.8): Continuing the circular motion with the arms, the cheerleader pulls upward into a T and jumps off the ground into a Toe Touch. The athlete should use the momentum of

Figure 6.7 *Toe Touch, Count Three.*

Figure 6.8 *Toe Touch, Count Four.*

Figure 6.9 *Toe Touch, Counts Five and Six.*

Figure 6.10 *Toe Touch, Counts Seven and Eight.*

the arms in combination with a powerful jump from the legs to gain height. The athlete rolls the hips underneath the body so shoelaces are facing the back wall, keeping the chest and head up. This position creates the illusion of a hyper-extended jump. Athletes mistakenly try to jump with their legs out to the sides rather than in front of them. A Toe Touch actually requires very little flexibility; hip flexor strength and a powerful jump off the ground are the keys to a good Toe Touch. The athlete's hands can be in Blades or in Fists and should reach for underneath the calves.

Toe Touch, Counts Five and Six (see figure 6.9): The athlete snaps his or her legs back together and lands with knees bent, hands beside knees, and chest up.

Toe Touch, Counts Seven and Eight (see figure 6.10): Standing up into the Clean position on count "seven," the cheerleader remains still for count "eight."

Front and Side Hurdlers

The Front Hurdler (see figures 6.11 and 6.12) is executed with the same timing and technique as the Toe Touch, only the athlete snaps his or her front leg up to the chest, keeping the back leg bent behind the body on count 4. The athlete must swing the arms hard to help lift him or her up into the position. On the jump, the arms should be extended straight in front of the athlete in Blades. A Side Hurdler is executed in the same way except that the torso faces the side, rather than the front.

Around the World

The Around the World is just a front pike jump (legs are brought straight in front of the body at a 90-degree angle or less) that opens up into a Toe Touch. The athlete must have excellent hip flexor strength and control to execute this jump.

Figure 6.11 *The Front Hurdler (side view).*

Figure 6.12 *The Front Hurdler (front view).*

Double Nines

This jump is less common than the others described previously but is still used in some routines.

Using the standard jump counts, the athlete jumps off the ground on count "five." Keeping one arm straight, the athlete bends the other and joins it to the straight arm, making the shape of a nine. The legs do the same. (See figure 6.13.)

— Jump Drills —

There are a number of useful progressions and drills to help athletes perfect their jumps. Here are a few of them.

Straight Jumps

The first thing an athlete must learn is proper timing. This is best done by substituting the actual jump (Toe Touch or Front Hurdler, for example) with a straight jump, keeping arms out to the sides in a T. This also teaches the athlete the importance of using the motion of the arms to gain height on the jump.

Figure 6.13 *Double Nines.*

Tuck Jumps

After proper timing is learned, athletes should substitute a Tuck Jump for the straight jump, keeping the chest up and pulling the knees into the torso. Athletes often mistakenly allow their chests to drop, which lowers the height of the jump.

Frog Jumps

When learning Toe Touches, it's helpful to do "frog jumps" to learn the proper positioning of the hips. Using the standard jump counts, the athlete jumps into a "frog position" (knees are bent and pulled up to the sides while the toes remain relatively close together). Knees should be apart and pulled up to the front of the body. If the legs were extended, athletes would be in a hyperextended Toe Touch. Athletes should tuck their hips underneath the body, allowing the back and shoulders to slightly slouch forward so that the body is in a "C" position. Athletes should keep their chests up during this drill.

Snap-Ups

Athletes begin by lying on the ground with arms above the head and legs together (see figure 6.14). Keeping the legs straight, they snap up into a Toe Touch position (see figure 6.15) and immediately snap back down to the ground. Athletes should practice Snap-Ups in sets of five to start and gradually build up to twenty in a row. This drill builds hip flexor strength and conditions the body to snap up into the jump. Additionally, it helps athletes practice the proper positioning on the ground before attempting it in the air.

Standing One-Leg Snap-Ups

This drill is similar to the previous one, except that athletes begin standing up with their arms out in a "T." One leg at a time, the athlete snaps the working leg up in behind the arm, keeping the leg straight and immediately snapping it back

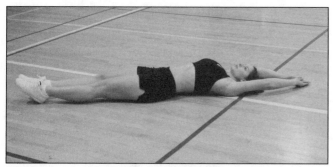

Figure 6.14 *Snap-Ups, beginning position.*

Figure 6.15 *Snap-Ups, ending position.*

down to the original position. One side should be worked at a time, first one and then the other. Again, this drill works on building leg strength and teaching the athlete to snap quickly.

Seated Leg Raises

In this drill, athletes sit on the floor in a straddle and either alternate lifting each leg 6 inches off of the ground (ten times on each side) or lift both at the same time with hands placed in front for support. This drill is great for increasing hip flexor strength.

Repetitive Jumps

While coaches count, athletes perform one jump consecutively after another. This drill builds skill as well as endurance.

Jump drills should be a regular part of every practice, and athletes should practice jumps at home to improve their jumping skills. And, as always, keep in mind that practice will increase your skill level!

PART THREE

Moving Beyond the Basics

Important Stunt Information for Cheerleaders and Coaches

Chapter Seven

Preparing to Stunt

Stunting . . . one of the most exciting parts of cheerleading! Who doesn't love the adrenaline rush of being thrown high into the air? Or how about lifting, tossing, and balancing a flyer into a perfect Liberty? No matter what role you play in the stunting process, nothing beats the feeling of hitting a solid stunt.

Games and performances are much more interesting to watch when cheerleaders build creative pyramids and throw high Basket Tosses. And at competitions, the distinguishing factor between first- and second-place teams is the level of difficulty and execution of the stunts they do. There are endless stunt combinations and pyramids, limited only by creativity and a few guidelines that must be put in place for athletes' safety.

This chapter will begin with sections on the three most important aspects of successful stunting: stunting roles, safety and spotting, and a positive attitude. You might be tempted to rush right to the step-by-step chapters on multiple-base stunting (generally all-girl) and single-base stunting (which includes all-girl as well as co-ed stunts), but it's essential that you first read through each part leading up to the actual stunts. Especially take note of the section on safety and

spotting, and practice the drills provided before you attempt to put flyers in the air.

Above all, stay safe, get creative, and have fun!

— Stunting Roles —

Each athlete has a specific position and role while stunting. Cheerleaders should experiment with different positions, even if participating just to gain an appreciation of the other people's jobs. There are four main positions in stunting:

1. The **flyer,** who you see "flying" through the air, dazzling the crowd with breathtaking tricks and flips.

2. The **base** (or bases, depending on the style of the stunt), who tosses, holds, and supports the weight of the flyer.

3. The **third,** who is not only responsible for the back portion of the stunt, but is there to assist the bases with tossing, holding, and supporting the flyer. The third is sometimes considered a "base" as well since his or her role can be much more than just watching the flyer.

4. The **spot (or fourth),** who is there to "spot" and ensure the safety of the stunt, or to assist with the stunt as necessary.

Remember that although anyone *can* be a flyer, base, or third, certain body types are best suited for each of these roles.

Note: When discussing single basing, the flyers will be referred to as "she," as this is the most common arrangement. However, it's possible for either sex to perform well in all positions.

Flyer

Also known as a "top" or a "climber," flyers are typically smaller in size than the others in the group because they are being tossed into the air. As a flyer, you must:

1. *Keep your body tight.*

Flyers should always stay tight, with shoulders back and knees locked out. In this position you can be tossed up and balanced with ease by your base (or bases). As soon as you allow your back to slouch or your knees to bend, your center of gravity will shift. This makes it very difficult for your bases to compensate for the change of positioning and increases the chances of the stunt coming down. Flyers who relax their bodies instantly feel heavier to the base, making the stunt difficult to stick. Another important body position hint is this: Unless you are standing on one leg or in a stunt that specifically requires that your feet are together, your feet must *always* be shoulder-width apart. Any wider and you'll begin to push your bases out, reducing the stability of the stunt and increasing the chances of it coming down.

2. *Allow your bases to balance for you.*

Letting your bases balance for you is a difficult technique to learn at first because you must stay tight and allow your bases to do the shifting for you, rather than trying to balance yourself. Think of being one entity with your bases, rather than a separate piece, and allow the balancing to come from the bottom.

3. *Look in the direction you want to go.*

If you look up, you're going to stay up. But if you look down, you're going to come down. Always keep your head up and find a stationary point on which to focus. You'll also find that concentrating on one point helps you find your balance and perfect your technique.

4. *Keep tight if you're coming down.*

As a base, nothing is scarier than watching your flyer coming down from a stunt frantically flailing her arms and legs right at you. It's a good way for a base to lose an eye. For the flyer, it's a good way to discourage your bases from wanting to catch you. Stay tight and keep your arms either straight above your head or glued to your sides.

Base

Bases come in all sizes and heights but are physically strong and able to completely support the flyer. All-girl stunting uses two bases, while partner stunts use only one main support. As a base, you must:

1. *Keep tight and stand tall.*

Just as with flyers, you are most effective if you stunt with a straight back and tight midsection. The most common mistake that bases make is arching their backs while stunting. This puts enormous strain on the lower back and also reduces the stability of the stunt. For safe and easy stunting, keep your pelvis tucked under and aligned with your legs, back, shoulders, and neck.

2. *Always look upward at the flyer, keeping your eyes on her hips.*

The movement of flyer's hips is the primary indicator of which direction the flyer's body is about to go—a valuable sign that tells her bases where she's going to land if she happens to be coming down. Bases are responsible for catching the flyer's hips, regardless of how she dismounts (vertically or horizontally).

3. *Minimize movement underneath the stunt.*

While it's a good idea to adjust below a stunt in an attempt to balance it, refrain from shifting during loading of a stunt. Too much movement is liable to disrupt the balance and cause the stunt to come down. While stunting, imagine you are standing in a tube. This will help keep your body aligned and remind you to keep your feet still.

4. Use your legs as your main source of power.

Your quadriceps (great extensor muscles at the front of the thigh) are the primary source of strength while stunting, and must be used first for efficient basing. When sinking in a stunt (for example, before cradling or tossing), concentrate on sinking deeply and using your leg strength to explode upward. This will produce far greater height and increased stunt stability than using only your arms and upper body.

5. Stay close to your other base.

This is especially important when basing extended one-leg stunts, such as Liberties or Cupies. In these types of stunts, bases should be chest-to-chest. When performing other double-base stunts, such as Elevators and Extensions, you should never be more than the flyer's shoulder-width apart.

Third

Also called the "back spot" or "back," the third plays a major role in the success of all-girl stunting, in part because of their typically tall stature. The third is responsible for the back portion of the stunt, constantly following the head/neck/shoulder area of the flyer and watching for any indication that the flyer may be coming down. Thirds are also responsible for calling the timing of the stunts. As a third, you must:

1. Keep physical contact with your flyer at all times.

Hold tightly onto the waist, ankle, or any other body parts you are able to reach in a stunt. Not only does this put you in prime position to save the stunt if it begins to wobble, but it makes your flyer feel much more confident in the air. Keep your eyes focused upward; the third's number one responsibility is protecting and catching the flyer's neck and head.

2. Be a participant in the stunt.

You are of no help to the stunt if all you do is hold onto the flyer. Thirds must work just as hard as

bases to lift up, and keep the flyer in the air. In mid-level stunts, your height will give you an advantage to help alleviate some of the flyer's weight from the bases by pulling upward on the ankles or waist while you hold on.

3. Use your legs and keep tight.

As in the other positions, a third who maintains a tight, strong body rather than a slack body is better equipped to hold a flyer. Focus on using your legs to give added power while loading or dismounting the flyer.

4. Be responsible for calling the stunt.

Thirds call every stunting cue, from the prep to the dismount. This eliminates confusion among the group because everyone is aware that you are the single, consistent source of instructions.

Spot

Standing either in front of, or to the back corner of a stunt, the spot (also called "fourth," "spotter," or "front spot") is responsible for the safety of the members of the group. When needed, the spotter's role typically involves assistance in catching the flyer or providing the base with extra support holding the stunt (see the "More on Spotters" section on page 100 for additional information). Regardless of whether the base needs assistance, partner stunting often involves a spot for safety reasons. When spotting you must:

1. Be ready for the unexpected.

Watch the stunt at all times. Pay attention and don't get distracted. Know where the weakness in the stunt lies and position yourself in that corner. Always be alert and ready to give extra support to the base or to help catch the flyer.

2. Be prepared to assist with the stunt if needed.

Your role as a spot isn't just to catch the flyer, but to stabilize and to provide extra help to the bases. If this means grabbing onto a base's wrist or the flyer's ankles, go ahead and do it! It's better to help the stunt than let it fall.

3. *Avoid reaching into a stunt with your arms.*

If you reach into a stunt, you're risking getting your arms broken. (Unfortunately, it's been known to happen.) If you aren't directly catching the flyer, stand behind the bases and back with your arms held wide to support their bodies. This is a good way to prevent the bases from falling over from the impact of catching the flyer. Whatever you do, watch out for your face, thumbs (another common injury), and arms.

4. *Avoid letting the flyer rely on you.*

If flyers know they can grab for you every time they feel they might come down, they will. Don't allow them to reach downward for you with outstretched arms while they're standing in the stunt. Avoid this by looking up, but not reaching up.

Practice these guidelines for each stunt you perform and eventually these good habits will become second nature. Remember, good technique, not strength, is the key to successful stunts.

MORE ON SPOTTERS

Spotters provide assistance to stunts, acting as an additional safety measure when groups are learning new stunts or performing stunts that are not yet perfected. Spotters should feel confident with spotting the stunt and ready to help bases stabilize the flyer when necessary.

There are two main schools of thought on how spotters should stand: arms up versus arms down.

— TIP —

Regardless of whether they stand with hands up or hands down, too many spotters can make a flyer nervous. Additionally, having too many spotters lessens each spotter's feeling of responsibility toward the stunt. "I thought you were going to catch her" is a common excuse when too many spotters surround the stunt.

Spotters who have their hands up are in closer proximity to the flyer and can provide assistance as soon as she begins to come down. On the other hand, flyers tend to reach for spotters' hands at the slightest wobble rather than try to pull up and stick the stunt. Hands up and touching the stunt allow spotters to detect the possibility of a stunt coming down by "feeling" rather than just "seeing," but hands up may also distract and unnerve the flyer.

A "hands up" versus a "hands down" approach depends on the ability and comfort level of the stunt group. Novice stunters tend to benefit from the "hands up" approach while more advanced groups should be able to stunt comfortably with the "hands down" approach.

Coaches should beware of overprotecting stunt groups with too many spotters. Three spotters standing around a Liberty group that hits a solid Heel Stretch each time is unnecessary and fosters uncertainty in the minds of the stunters. (They might wonder: "Are we so bad that we need all these spotters?") Once a stunt group has proven its ability to stunt safely, spotters should be used only when the group is learning new stunts or working on stunts that have problem areas. A maximum of three spotters (front, back right corner, and back left corner) is usually sufficient.

SAFETY AND SPOTTING

Participating in cheerleading, just like any physical activity, has its risks. But you can prevent most, if not all, accidents and injuries by using proper spotting and technique. Before attempting any stunt, all cheerleaders must understand and have practiced safe spotting. In addition, an experienced coach with first-aid training should always be present.

It is common for new cheerleaders to be anxious when stunting for the first time. Unlike experienced cheerleaders, new ones do not yet have confidence in their own skills or trust in their stunt partners.

How does having confidence and trusting your partners relate to safety? For a flyer, it means

> ### — TIP —
>
> While it's instinctual for people to shy away from falling objects, falling cheerleaders must be caught! Because catching a flyer challenges our natural impulse to run away from a dismount and being tossed in the air makes one automatically flinch, athletes must fight their instincts. Practice the following spotting and safety drills until every member on the team feels comfortable with both catching and being caught.

knowing that if she loses her balance and begins to fall, someone will bring her safely to the ground. For a base, it means knowing that if your flyer begins to teeter out of her Scorpion Liberty, she will fall properly so that you can catch her. When you trust one another, attempting a difficult stunt or a high pyramid becomes easier because you can focus on proper technique rather than worry about your safety.

— Starting Off Right: Pre-Stunting Precautions —

Like any other sport, cheerleading has its hazards, and stunting is definitely one of them. Taking a few preventative measures, however, can do a great deal toward minimizing the risk of injury and increasing the chance of successful stunts.

Make it routine to go through the following five checkpoints each time you're ready to start stunting.

1. Stunt Only in the Presence of an Experienced Coach

An experienced coach will be able to not only ensure your safety while stunting, but will show you the proper stunting technique. You won't want to put all your effort into a stunt only to discover you've been doing it the difficult way. One little tip from an experienced coach could save you hours of unproductive work. More importantly, a coach's expertise could save you and your teammates from injury.

Most schools require a teacher supervisor to be present during cheerleading practice. If this is the case, don't *ever* stunt without a supervisor present. Otherwise, your team will be at risk for assuming all responsibilities and liabilities if an injury happens.

2. Take Off All Jewelry

Earrings can certainly look attractive, but they can be dangerous. As unpleasant as it might be to think about an earring getting ripped out, keep in mind that fingers, hair, and clothing can easily be caught in earrings. Rings, belly rings, and necklaces are also accidents waiting to happen thus are best taken off or taped down. You don't want to have to find out the hard way that serious injuries can occur to both bases and flyers when jewelry hasn't been removed.

3. Fully Understand the Stunt You Attempt

It is a waste of time and effort to attempt a stunt that even one person doesn't understand. Have it demonstrated, watch a video, or break it down step-by-step before you begin. Go through the motions of the stunt with just the bases before adding the flyer to make sure all participants are clear on their specific roles. It's also important to use good spotters who are experienced and able to recognize the weak points of your stunt.

4. Establish a Clear Line of Communication

Make it general practice for the third (the stunter who stands behind the stunt) to be the only one calling stunts. The third is in the best position to see the stunt and to be heard by everyone. Aside from the third (or your coach), no one else should be talking while stunting. Although it's especially tempting to make suggestions to the flyer, this is likely to confuse her, and she probably won't even be able to hear what's being said. If someone in the group decides that the flyer must come down, for whatever reason (for example, you're in danger of losing your right eye!), use the word "down." Never scream or panic; it will only worsen the situation.

5. Commit to the Stunt

It's self-defeating to attempt a stunt before you are mentally prepared for it. Before you begin a stunt, have faith that it will "hit" (be successful). Take a deep breath and envision the stunt hitting perfectly without any wobbles or difficulties. After this visualization, you *will* stick it (hold the position steadily) with success.

Go through this checklist each time you're ready to attempt a stunt. Even if you're experienced and you've done the stunt a million times before, following these reminders is essential for safe, solid stunting.

— Safety Reminders —

Here is a list of important safety reminders—some are discussed in more detail in the following section.

★ Always stunt with an experienced coach present.

★ Take off all jewelry. Tape down rings that cannot be removed.

★ Spit out gum.

★ Tie hair up.

★ Tuck in shirts.

★ Flyers: Pull up and tuck in baggy pant legs. Better yet, wear shorts when stunting.

★ Avoid wearing slippery fabrics. Flyers should be especially cautious in choosing the type of shorts to wear.

★ Warm up first.

★ Rest when you need to.

★ Drink lots of water to stay hydrated.

★ Stay tight (keep elbows/knees straight and flex muscles) when performing drills or executing stunts. This applies to both bases and flyers and serves as a preventative measure against being hit by flailing arms and other body parts.

★ Ask your coach for clarification when you don't understand a stunt or have a question about your responsibilities.

"SLACK"ing Is Accepted!

The acronym SLACK is useful for remembering to practice safe stunting. Review the following five checkpoints before performing a stunt:

"S" IS FOR SPOTTERS

Spotters should be used when performing new stunts, pyramids, transitions, stunts that have trouble hitting 100 percent of the time, or challenging stunts that require spotters for assistance.

"L" IS FOR LIMITS

Know your limits. Don't try an Extension before perfecting an Elevator. Although trying an advanced stunt before completing the progression may seem more exciting, it's unsafe for athletes to

---

C O A C H E S'   C O R N E R

BE PREPARED

Always have an emergency plan in the case of an accident or injury. You should carry all relevant medical information regarding the team at all times.

attempt it, and irresponsible of coaches to allow it. In addition to being familiar with your skill limits, know your physical boundaries. If you're sick, physically exhausted, or overly sore from yesterday's workout, it is not the time to push your limits.

"A" IS FOR ATTITUDE

Athletes: Believe the stunt will stick before you attempt it. *Coaches:* The attitude of your athletes reflects *your* leadership. Believe in your team and encourage them to succeed.

"C" IS FOR CONFIDENCE

Confidence is essential to safe stunting. Flyers must be confident that bases can be trusted to catch them, and bases must be confident that the flyer will execute the stunt to the best of her ability. Both bases and flyers must be confident that each athlete will safely execute the load, stunt, and dismount. Confidence allows athletes to focus on hitting the stunt rather than the possibility of hitting the floor.

"K" IS FOR KNOWLEDGE

Does everyone in the group know exactly what his or her responsibilities are during the stunt? Is everyone familiar with how to perform the stunt correctly? Does the group know which dismount method to use? Can each group member troubleshoot the stunt? For example, if a flyer is leaning back too far, does the group know how to compensate? Knowledge of the stunt is the key to safe stunting.

— Spotting Drills —

Spotting drills are a great place to start building trust. Regardless of the athlete's size, each team member should be able to catch any of his or her teammates. Flyers should practice catching bases and bases should practice coming down from a stunt rather than just bases catching flyers. After doing these spotting drills, everyone can then be confident that each person, regardless of their position, knows how to catch properly.

Bear Hug

The Bear Hug (see figure 7.1) is the position for catching flyers who come out of stunts in a vertical position. Remember these key points:

BASES

★ Tuck your head behind your flyer's back to protect your head.

★ Reach around the flyer's midsection to her opposite hip with your front hand.

★ Reach underneath the flyer's seat with your back hand.

Figure 7.1 *Bear Hug.*

★ Pull the flyer's hip into your shoulder and maintain contact with her as soon as possible out of a stunt.

★ Use the friction of your body against your flyer to slow her down to a soft and safe landing. Resist the gravitational pull of her descent.

FLYER

★ Reach your hands up straight above your head to avoid hitting bases.

★ Keep your legs pulled together and maintain a tight body position. As soon as you bend your knees, you will fall to the ground much more quickly.

★ Keep your head up.

★ Pull up through your chest. Don't let your back slouch or your shoulders slump forward.

Step Off

The Step Off spotting drill teaches flyers to stay tight when coming down from a stunt, and teaches bases to safely bring a flyer down to the ground. The flyer begins standing on a bench or other elevated surface. Using only one base to catch her, she steps off vertically from the bench as if coming down from a stunt (see figure 7.2). The base reaches up to catch the flyer as soon as possible after she steps off (see figure 7.3). Grabbing onto her in a Bear Hug, the base holds on tightly and slowly lowers the flyer down to the ground (see figure 7.4). It's important for the base to bend the knees rather than the back when putting the flyer down. Have each athlete practice both the stepping off (flyer) and catching (base) roles. Gradually raise the height of the platform to increase the level of difficulty.

Lower Down

This is the next progression from the Step Off drill. In this spotting drill, athletes load the flyer

Figure 7.2 *Step Off, Part One.*

up into a stunt and then slowly lower her to ground level. This drill teaches athletes how to safely come down from a specific stunt. It is a particularly effective drill when athletes are learning extended stunts. For example, when learning an Extension, the coach would instruct the team to practice loading the stunt up and then slowly and safely bringing it down without actually hitting the stunt. To bring the flyer down, bases release one hand from her foot and reach upward as high as possible. Keeping the flyer close to their bodies, bases use the "ladder" technique to lower the flyer. That is, bases "climb" up the flyer one arm at a time by reaching one arm above the other to

Figure 7.3 *Step Off, Part Two.*

Figure 7.4 *Step Off, Part Three.*

hold onto the flyer and resist her weight as she descends.

The team would use the same lowering-down technique when learning Liberties. They would load the flyer up to an extended level, then control the flyer down to the ground without stopping in a Liberty. It's better to practice lowering a flyer from a stunt in a drill rather than trying to learn how to catch her safely out of a stunt that doesn't stick.

The "Fall Back" Cradle

To familiarize athletes with the feeling of catching or being caught in a Cradle, start with the simple

---

— TIP —

If the flyer begins to fall from an extended stunt, bases should immediately get her feet underneath her so that she's in an upright position. If this isn't possible, bases must release the flyer's feet and reach for her body. If the bases continue to hold onto her feet as she falls, her head and neck will be the first body parts to land—very dangerous!

"Fall Back" Cradle drill. Athletes should familiarize themselves with holding the flyer in a Cradle Catch before attempting to catch a flyer from a backwards fall. Details on this position are provided on page 128.

The flyer begins by standing backward on the edge of a raised platform that is waist-high or taller (for example, a sturdy table or bleachers). The flyer's bases are positioned on the ground behind her with their arms up, ready to catch the flyer as she falls backward. Spotters should stand ready on each side of the stunt group. Bases' arms should be in a crisscross pattern: Base 1's back arm, Base 2's back arm, Base 1's front arm, Base 2's front arm. The third stands at the back of the stunt, reaching upward to catch the flyer. With arms up, the flyer leans backward and falls into a Cradle, remembering to use upper body strength to catch herself around the bases' shoulders and hold the legs up with the abdominal muscles. The bases should reach up to catch the flyer as high as possible, resisting the flyer's weight on the descent and absorbing the impact with their knees. As the base group becomes comfortable with this height, they should progress to shoulder height. Coaches should be cautious of having athletes practice this drill too much, as it may actually teach the flyer bad habits. That's because in an actual Cradle, flyers shouldn't fall backward but straight down into their own base group. Once flyers and bases feel comfortable with the drill, the base group should progress to dismounting an Elevator into a Cradle.

Willow in the Wind

In this simple trust drill, four bases (thirds and spots included) stand in a circle with the flyer in the middle. The flyer crosses the arms on the chest and keeps the body tight throughout the entire activity. Leaning to one side, the flyer allows herself to fall against one of the bases and be pushed back up toward the center. Staying tight, the momentum from being pushed back up sends the flyer toward another base to be caught and pushed back up again. For the flyer, the basic idea of this drill is to learn to trust the bases and to stay tight in a stunt. For the bases, this drill stresses the

---

C O A C H E S '   C O R N E R

WHAT GOES UP MUST COME DOWN SAFELY

Unfortunately, stunts don't always dismount safely. In the event of a fall, coaches should be prepared.

★ *Be prepared for emergencies.* Have a first-aid kit, medical forms for the team, and an emergency plan on hand in the event of an injury.

★ *Move other athletes away from injured person.* With too many people surrounding him or her, a hurt athlete may become more nervous and upset. Send the team outside the practice area, but do keep at least one other person in the same room. This person can call for help if the situation requires it while you stay with the injured person.

★ *Evaluate the seriousness of the situation.* Is the athlete only startled and upset from the fall, or is he or she actually physically injured? If just startled, let the athlete sit there and rest until he or she feels well enough to get up. If the person is hurt—especially if it is a head, back, or neck injury—do not move the person. Immediately call for help. Do not leave the person alone and do not let him or her try to sit up. Other minor injuries, such as scratches and minor bruises, can be taken care of with basic first aid.

importance of keeping eyes on the flyer at all times and helps to teach them to anticipate the flyer's moves.

— Attitude Is Everything —

The true test of great cheerleaders isn't whether or not they can make a stunt hit with their group. It's whether they can readily work with, and adapt to, one another's timing and rhythm. You need to connect *mentally*, as well as physically with your team members.

Working with someone who hasn't quite mastered this skill can be frustrating, as can working with someone who isn't at your skill level. Keeping a positive attitude and deciding to use this as an opportunity to help strengthen your own skills will make you a better cheerleader. If you don't enjoy sharing your skills and work with others, you might want to rethink your reasons for being a cheerleader. Keeping a positive attitude every time you cheerlead—especially when you feel tired, sick, or just not in the mood to practice—is not easy. If you can keep an upbeat attitude throughout difficulties and negative phases, not only will your stunts stick, but you'll end up being a better cheerleader overall.

To stay positive, you can do a number of things:

Smile!

Keep smiling—*especially* when you don't feel like it. Whether you or someone else is having an off day and just can't seem to make the stunt work, a smile will relieve a lot of built-up frustration and encourage others. It may be just what you need to make that Heel Stretch, Double Full Dismount hit perfectly.

Avoid Criticizing Your Group

The worst thing you can do when things aren't working is criticize your partner(s). Offer suggestions in a way that won't make them feel as though you're attacking their abilities. An easy

way to do this is by using the "sandwich" approach: compliment, suggestion, compliment. For example, "You've got great push off of the shoulders. Your Elevator would be really awesome if you straightened up a little faster. Your cradle looks great!" (*Coaches:* Note that this constructive criticism style is an effective way to correct technique, especially with younger cheerleaders.)

Encourage One Another

Simple words such as "good," "slow down," and "stick it!" work wonders. When you communicate helpfully and encourage your group or partner, you increase the chance of making your stunt work. (Just beware that there isn't too much talking and that everyone isn't talking all at once.) Keep in mind that your flyer probably won't be able to hear everything you say, so keep talk to a minimum. Try this exercise: Agree on a challenging stunt or stunt combination. Do it once without saying a word. The second time, encourage and help one another. You'll notice that your stunt will work better the second time.

Stunt Slowly

Stunting slowly gives your base group control over the stunt. When the stunt moves too quickly, participants don't have enough time think about what they're doing, or to place hands properly or work with one another's rhythm to execute the best possible stunt. Stunting too quickly also means that if a stunt comes down, you'll often fall harder than if the stunt was executed with control. Stunting slowly is beneficial for three main reasons:

1. It's a lot safer.

2. There is time to think about what you're doing and properly position yourselves for the next move.

3. The stunt is controlled and more likely to stick. And when the stunt sticks, a positive attitude is likely to follow!

Work As a Team

Of course you know it's important to work as a team, but do you practice doing it? When the flyer sinks (bends elbows and/or knees to lower herself), do the bases sink also? When the bases extend (straighten the elbows and/or knees), does the flyer extend too? Stunting is not three bases and a flyer working to perform the stunt; it is *becoming* the stunt with your partners. You will achieve your stunting goal by becoming one machine, not by working as separate parts. If you understand that you need to follow one another's rhythms and style when stunting, you can understand the meaning of "working as a team." This is the secret of stunting, but many cheerleaders never really apply this basic principle.

Stunting requires 100 percent effort from all group members. How each participant acts and reacts plays a crucial role in the success of stunts. When you feel frustrated, take 10 seconds to relax and make a conscious effort to turn around your mood. Then try your stunt again, envisioning it hitting perfectly as you perform it. While you may not always be able to control your stunt, you can control the way you react toward it. Your positive attitude will be contagious!

After you've worked on spotting drills and reviewed safe stunting, you're ready to put your skills into action. Recruit a qualified coach, grab some teammates, and have fun learning the stunts in the next chapter!

Chapter Eight

Stunting Basics

Now that you know all the safety precautions and positions of stunting, it's time to start with the basics and work up to more advanced skills. *A reminder:* Perfect the basics before attempting the more advanced stunts and combinations, and always use a qualified spotter when stunting.

— Stunting Techniques —

What is it that makes one team's stunting ability higher than another team's? After safety and spotting, the next most important aspect of stunting is good technique.

People mistakenly think that the success of a stunt depends on how big the base's muscles are. Wrong. Stunting is 10 percent strength and 90 percent proper form. Although strength *does* play a significant role in successful stunting, technique is the bottom line. Poor technique can cause a strong, muscular base to drop the stunt. On the other hand, good technique can help a more slightly built base toss the flyer into a single-base stunt without breaking a sweat.

Proper technique makes learning new stunts fun, fast, and easy. On the other hand, poor technique makes stunting more difficult, resulting in frustration, sloppy-looking stunts, and often injury. Keep in mind the techniques mentioned in this section as you participate in each stunting position, and your stunts should stick every time.

Before moving onto the step-by-step stunting guide, it's useful to define some stunting basics: common terms, grips, and timing.

— Common Stunting Terms —

If you're fairly new to the stunting scene, it can be confusing when you first read the step-by-step stunting section. Even if you've have had experience in stunting, there may be terms you are not familiar with or you might refer to the technique by another name. To make it easier for you, here is a list of the most commonly used stunting language and expressions in this book:

Back hand/arm/leg: The hand, arm, or leg closest to the back/rear of the stunt.

Dip: Bases will often dip in a stunt to initiate the momentum to transition into the next position. Dips are small bends in the knees and are executed in one count. Dips are often used for Pop Downs and for initiating momentum at the beginning of Sponges.

Dismount: The way a stunt is brought back to the ground. The most common dismounts are the

"Pop Down" and "Cradle." The "Walk-Off" is used occasionally as well, and is great for beginners who are just becoming familiar with stunting.

Explode upward: This term is just a fancy way of instructing bases and flyers to push hard and fast, extending or locking out arms and legs as quickly as possible.

Front hand/arm/leg: The hand, arm, or leg closest to the crowd.

Hit a stunt: Synonymous with "sticking a stunt," this term means to execute a stunt with perfection. When a stunt group hits a stunt, there are no wobbles or mistakes.

Hollowed out: In many positions (Elevator, Chair, Liberty), a flyer must be "hollowed out" in order for the stunt to be properly balanced. To "hollow out," the flyer thinks about tightening the abdominals and pulling the belly button into the spine. Shoulders are slightly pulled upward and are rounded forward. Hips are slightly tilted backward and tucked under so that from the side, the flyer's torso appears to be slightly curved into a "C" shape. Most gymnasts are likely familiar with this term. "Hollowing out" is the opposite of "Laying out."

Inside hand/arm/leg: The stunting guidelines commonly refer to the base's inside or outside hand, arm, or leg, which is the one closest to the flyer. For example, the right base's inside arm is the left arm.

Layout: When referring to cradling, the flyer's position is called a Layout and occurs on the upward motion of a straight Cradle or after a trick. The sequence would go something like this: The flyer is tossed up, hits a Toe Touch, snaps into a Layout, and then lands in the Cradle. Laying out creates the appearance of being suspended in the air and is a good preparatory position for landing in a Cradle. It also functions to give the flyer more height by keeping the chest up.

Left base: When facing the crowd in a stunt, the base on the left is referred to as the "left base." This means that if you are in the stands looking at the stunt, the base on your *right* is considered the "left base."

Lift: Not to be confused with the "pop," a lift's main driving force is the muscle strength of the bases lifting the flyer. Unlike a pop, the bases and flyer remain connected at all times. A lift is generally slower and more difficult to perform than a pop. An example of a lift is a Press Up Extension.

Lock out: A flyer is locked out if her knees are completely straight and her body is tight. To lock out, she contracts all of her muscles and keeps her body tight throughout the entire stunt. For example, to perform a Liberty, the flyer must pull up and stay locked out the entire time.

Outside hand/arm/leg: The outside hand, arm, or leg is the one farthest from the flyer. For example, the right base's outside arm is the right arm.

Pop: An explosive motion that uses momentum as its main driving force. A pop from the bases results in the flyer being propelled upward. The pop is a useful motion for dismounts or for loading stunts.

Prep: This short form for the "preparation" position for a stunt is synonymous with the term "load." The most common is the Standard Prep or Standard Load.

Pull up: A common command to a flyer, "pulling up" refers to the straightening and tightening of the body. Being "pulled upward" is a useful mental exercise for a flyer. It helps her to stabilize a stunt by thinking of keeping her posture upright rather than letting her body sink into a slouching, loose position. Pulling up also helps to achieve the illusion of a suspended Cradle, one with lots of height that appears as though the flyer is momentarily still. It's difficult for a stunt to hit without the flyer "pulling up."

Ride: When the flyer pulls up to the very height of the toss before executing a trick.

Right base: When facing the crowd in a stunt, the base on the right is called the "right base." This means that if you are in the stands looking at the stunt, the base on the *left* is considered the right base.

Set: When the base group sets, they are in the "ready" position to begin a stunt.

Sink: The extended version of a dip, a sink is a deep bend in the knees. When sinking to load a stunt or dismount a flyer, the bases primarily use quadriceps strength rather than allowing their upper bodies to slouch. In contrast to the dip, a sink generally takes up two counts rather than only one. Two counts allows for a deeper sink, which leads to more powerful loads and higher tosses (the "slingshot" effect).

Sponge: The process of taking a finished stunt and returning back to the load position. It is just the reverse of loading "up" a stunt, and is frequently used to transition one stunt to another.

Sticks: A stunt that "sticks" is successfully completed without wobbles or unnecessary movements and stays up until you want it to come down). "Stick it!" is an instruction to the stunting group to keep the flyer in the air and successfully perform the stunt.

Stunt: A stunt involves two or more people, with one person being held or supported by another.

Stunting: The process of performing a stunt.

— Grips —

Knowing which hand grip to use in a particular stunt is imperative to the stunt's success *and* the

---

— TIP —

When holding onto a flyer's foot, squeeze tightly. The pressure will help to stabilize the flyer's ankle and prevent the foot from slipping out of the grip.

---

stunters' safety. The most commonly used grips are shown in and described under the following illustrations:

Prep Grip

The bases' hands are ready to catch the flyer's feet. Hands are taut and close together (see figure 8.1).

Natural Grip

The base's front hand is firmly gripping the flyer's toe while the back hand is holding onto the flyer's heel. Fingers are wrapped tightly around the foot,

Figure 8.1 *Prep Grip.*

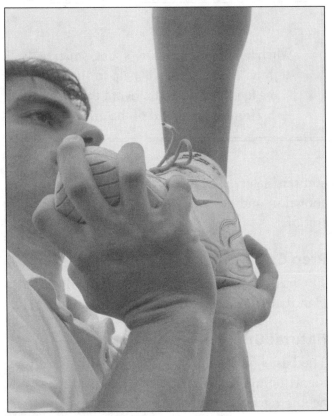

Figure 8.2 *Natural Grip.*

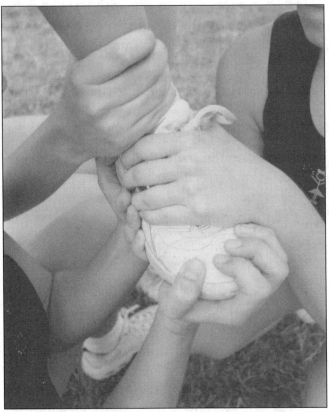

Figure 8.3 *Sandwich Grip.*

Figure 8.4 *Reverse Handshake Grip.*

and wrists are close together to prevent the flyer's foot from slipping through (see figure 8.2).

Sandwich Grip

The main base in the stunt holds the flyer's foot in the same way as a Natural Grip except leaves a space between the wrists. The assisting base places his or her back hand underneath the flyer's arch, in the space between the main base's wrists. The assisting base grips the top of the flyer's foot with the front hand. The third maintains a firm grip on the flyer's ankle (see figure 8.3).

Reverse Handshake Grip

The palms of the flyer and the base connect together and fingers and thumbs are wrapped around each other's hand. In a Reverse Handshake, grip either the base or the flyer's hand is flipped upward, angled downward, or turned over. Alternatively, in a regular handshake both the base and the flyer would be gripping one another's hand with thumbs pointing upward, the way a normal handshake would occur (see figure 8.4).

Hands Grip

The base's palms are holding under the center-back part of the flyer's foot. The last three fingers and thumb are wrapped around the outsides of the flyer's foot while the index finger is extended straight back underneath the flyer's heel. This finger positioning gives greater control to the base by allowing him or her to manipulate the stunt via the flyer's foot. It also prevents the flyer's heel from slipping through the base's hand (see figure 8.5).

Liberty Grip

In a right-foot Liberty, the base's right hand is underneath the flyer's foot in a Hands Grip and the left hand is positioned directly in front of the right

Figure 8.5 *Hands Grip.*

hand, supporting the rest of the flyer's arch and the ball of her foot. The right hand is supporting the majority of the flyer's weight by holding underneath the flyer's arch and heel. The left hand plays an important role in preventing her toes from pointing downward too much (see figure 8.6). Bases should familiarize themselves with this grip by practicing on the ground before putting her in the air. In a left-foot Liberty, the base's left rather than right hand would be toward the back of the flyer's foot.

Basket Grip or Shreddie

Bases hold onto their own left wrists with their right hands. The bases then grab onto their partner's right wrist with their left hand, forming an interlocking platform for the flyer to kneel or stand on (see figure 8.7).

Figure 8.6 *Liberty Grip.*

Figure 8.7 *Basket Grip or Shreddie.*

— Timing Is Everything —

When stunting, timing is everything! Timing can make the difference between sticking a stunt or collapsing, so it's important to make sure everyone is working together and on the same counts. Putting counts to each move in a stunt is imperative to making it stick. Counts also keep the stunt moving at a controlled pace.

Many teams stunt too quickly, allotting only one count per move. When you rush, you aren't able to utilize your full range of motion. As a result, you aren't able to get the maximum power and height from your body. To stunt effectively, you need to use as much of your available resources as you can.

With more time, bases are able to sink deeper. With a deeper sink, it's easier to use legs to power the stunt. This means a bigger explosion with less effort. As all stunters can testify, it's incredibly difficult to perform an intricate stunt combination when things are happening too fast. Without adequate time, the stunt very quickly becomes messy and there's a greater possibility that it will fall. With more counts per move, the stunt stays clean and controlled.

There are many other disadvantages to stunting quickly, besides not being able to use your full power. You don't have full control over the stunt; you don't have enough time to execute the stunt properly; and most importantly, it isn't safe to just throw your flyer around.

Think of stunting as similar to using a slingshot. The deeper and slower you pull it back, the more explosive it is on the release. If you act like this slingshot when performing all of your stunts, stunting will improve. Use a "two-count" timing (pulling back the slingshot) for the most logical part of the stunt. For example, in a Cradle, sink on the counts "three" and "four" and toss your flyer (letting go of the slingshot) on the count "five." You'll be amazed how much easier stunting becomes when you take your time.

This counting procedure makes a world of difference for those executing a stunt. Not only will stunters feel less rushed, but they will feel more in control. Having control is imperative for making a stunt stick and for linking stunts together.

Now that you're familiar with the stunting lingo, grips, and timing, you can read on for step-by-step guidelines that explain how each stunt is executed. You'll find chapters on the two main stunt

---

— TIP —

While you don't want to stunt too quickly, you don't want to stunt too slowly either. Sometimes two counts per move is the appropriate number while other times one count per move is necessary to make the stunt work. Make sure you know which parts of the stunt to speed up and which parts to slow down before you begin the stunt.

types: Multiple-Base Stunting and Single-Base Stunting, as well as chapters on Transitions, Basket Tosses, and Pyramids and Combination Stunts. Each section describes in detail the main stunts executed at each level. You'll also find creative loads, dismounts, and variations for each stunt, along with combination ideas to put them all together.

Because many of the stunts build on one another, it helps to familiarize yourself with all the stunts before you begin. This way, you'll have a solid foundation of stunting and be able to mix and match variations to come up with unique, new ideas of your own. Many basic stunts can be turned into advanced stunts and vice versa just by changing the load, dismount, or height variations.

You should work on perfecting the easier version of loads, dismounts, and stunts before you move on to the next, more difficult one. You'll find it easier to hit the variations the first time when you have solid technique behind you. Also, remember that while certain stunts may appear in your category, they may not all be appropriate for your stunting level or may not comply with your competition or school regulations. Check first before you attempt anything you're not 100 percent sure about.

When you're trying something new, it's important that you always have a qualified coach and spotters to help you out. Make sure everyone is clear on what he or she is doing *before* the stunt is put up. It's nearly impossible to explain a Cradle to the flyer while she's standing in a Liberty!

And remember, these instructions are only guidelines. Change things around, put in more counts, add another base, or invent your own variations. The more creative you are, the better!

Chapter Nine

Multiple-Base Stunting

In multiple-basing, three bases and a flyer are used to load, hit, and dismount stunts. An additional base or spot is occasionally required to perform more challenging stunts. Most multiple-base stunts are performed by, but are not exclusive to, all-girl teams. Athletes on all-girl squads also perform single-base stunts but less frequently than a co-ed team would. Both mixed and ladies stunt groups will find the instructions for single-basing in the next section practical, and will benefit by experimenting with both styles.

— Chicken Position —

The flyer should be in the Chicken position (see figure 9.1) when she jumps into Standard Loads and Basket Tosses.

Figure 9.1 *Chicken position.*

— TIP —

Although female athletes are demonstrating the multiple-based stunts in this section, these moves are not exclusively for all-girl teams; many co-ed teams perform these stunts too. Regardless of what type of team you are on, you will find the tips provided in *both* the multiple-base and single-base sections helpful for stunting.

FLYER bends at the knees and waist, keeping her chest up and slightly arching her back, keeping it relatively straight. Her shoulders, knees, and toes are directly over one another in a straight line. Feet are shoulder width apart or slightly closer together. Arms are strong and out to the sides, supporting her weight when she loads into a stunt. The flyer should never let her seat drop below 90 degrees (that is, below her knees). If it does, her weight will shift and the stunt will not load properly.

— Loads —

You can't hit a stunt without first "loading" it! The load is the way in which a stunt group gets the flyer from the ground and up into the stunt.

Standard Load

The Standard Load (see figures 9.2 and 9.3 for front and side views) is one of the most typical and versatile loads for all-girl stunts. Here are the basics for each participant:

THIRD is holding onto the flyer's waist. Legs are shoulder width apart.

BASES are facing one another and are positioned relatively close together. Elbows are bent and

Figure 9.2 *Standard Load (front view).*

arms are tucked in close to the ribs. Hands grasp the flyer's feet in the Prep Grip. Hips are in line with the shoulders, and backs are straight.

FLYER begins with her hands on the bases' shoulders. Feet are close together. With her weight in her arms, the flyer loads into the bases' hands and holds herself in the Chicken Position.

One-Foot Load

In this load, the bases hold the flyer's foot in a Sandwich Grip rather than a Prep Grip (see figure 9.4).

THIRD crouches behind the flyer and places one hand on the flyer's ankle and the other underneath the middle of the flyer's seat. On the upward motion, the third first pushes under-

Figure 9.3 *Standard Load (side view).*

TIP

Here's an effective way to get the flyer to hold her own weight in her arms: Instruct her to hop into a Standard Load without the bases holding onto her feet. She should be hanging in the Standard Load on her own. This drill forces the flyer to rely on her upper body strength to stay in the Chicken position rather than letting the bases do all the work. Stunts are much easier to perform when the flyer uses her arms to hold her own weight in the load and pushes off from her bases' shoulders on the upward part of the stunt.

---

neath the flyer's seat to help the flyer get her center of gravity overtop of her bases. The third then pulls upward on the flyer's ankle. In the finished stunt, the third continues to hold tightly onto the flyer's ankle with both hands.

Main Base grips the flyer's foot in a Prep Grip and executes the stunt exactly the same as if the flyer had loaded into a Standard Load.

Assisting Base places the back hand underneath the flyer's arch, between the main base's Prep Grip. The front hand holds onto the top of the flyer's foot.

Flyer starts in the same way as the Standard Load except that one foot remains on the ground. On the ground, the flyer stays close to her bases and rises up on the ball of her foot. These two positioning techniques help the flyer keep her center of gravity over the top of the bases. The majority of her weight is still held in her arms.

In a variation of this load, the assisting base can leave her hands at her sides (rather than gripping the flyer's foot) and join in on the stunt only when needed.

Figure 9.4 *One-Foot Load.*

Toss Load

See figure 9.5 for photo of the Toss Load.

Third and **Assisting Base** stand on either side of the flyer. Their front hands are underneath the flyer's armpits and their back hands firmly grasp the flyer's forearms for maximum tossing assistance. At the risk of the flyer being thrown backward or toward one side, the third and assisting base must make sure they put both moderate and equal strength into the toss.

Main Base holds firmly onto the waist and hip area of the flyer with her thumbs pointing upward. This hand positioning helps to keep the elbows in close to the main base's body. Elbows that stick out during the toss eliminate

Figure 9.5 *Toss Load.*

much of the available strength from the arms and upper torso by causing unnecessary energy expenditure from the shoulders. The majority of the strength from the toss comes from the quadriceps. The main base's legs are soft (bent) either equal distance apart or with one foot slightly ahead of the other, and the torso is close to the flyer. The main base follows the movement of the flyer and allows the flyer to sink *on her own*. This is a very im-

> **— TIP —**
>
> If the main base is having trouble getting the hands underneath the flyer's feet in a Toss Hands stunt, have the main base concentrate on dropping the hands as quickly as possibly to the shoulders after the height of the toss, rather than trying to catch the flyer's feet in mid-air.

portant factor in achieving a good, high toss. If the main base pulls the flyer downward for the sink, this is a waste of energy and strength. The main base's strength should take effect on the upward motion *after* the flyer has initiated it by jumping. Quadriceps aid the toss, followed by a shrug of the shoulders, full extension of the arms, and a flick of the wrists. To ensure a straight and powerful toss, the main base's elbows are kept close to the torso until the extension of the arms. Eyes always follow the flyer's hips. The main base catches the flyer's feet as high as possible and either controls the hand down to a shoulder level stunt or continues extending upward for an extended-level stunt. The main base absorbs the flyer's landing with "soft knees" (knees that are neither locked nor overly flexible, but will give slightly under weight) and a tight frame.

FLYER stands straight with her hands firmly grasping the wrists of the main base. Head is up and shoulders are back. The flyer sinks, being careful not to drop her seat below her knees. She then explodes upward using her quadriceps in a powerful, straight jump. Chest, shoulders, and head stay upward, with a focus on keeping them from dropping forward. Throughout the toss, the flyer maintains a tight body position, keeping her head up, shoulders neutral, and body aligned. A good way for flyers to remember this is to think about having a string attached to the center of the chest and pulling upward. At the height of the toss, just before the main base is about to let go, the flyer's hands flick off the main base's wrists (downward, not outward) for added height.

Once in the stunt, the flyer stays tight and hollowed out with her shoulders neutral and back straight.

— TIP —

If the flyer has trouble ending up overtop of
her base, instruct her to lean very slightly
backward into the base before the toss.
Be careful though—if the flyer leans too
far backward, she will be tossed into the
main base rather than above her

Walk Load

See figure 9.6 for photo of the Walk Load.

THIRD is in a squat position on the same side as
the flyer's Walk leg (the leg that loads into the
base's hands). One hand is on the flyer's ankle
and the other is positioned underneath the
flyer's thigh. The third first pushes upward on
the flyer's thigh and then pulls up on the

Figure 9.6 *Walk Load.*

flyer's ankle as the stunt extends. The third
lets go of the flyer's ankle just before the flyer
turns toward the front, and moves to the rear
to continue "thirding" (carrying out the
third's responsibilities in the stunt).

MAIN BASE begins in a squat position with chest
up. Knees are at or above a 90-degree angle.
Any lower and the base will likely fall over
when the flyer loads in. The main base's right
hand is on top of the left hand and held in
close to the chest. Elbows are tucked in and
rest on the knees. The base sinks with the
flyer and drives straight upward, extending the
arms and the legs at the same time. As the
flyer reaches the height of the stunt (base's
arms are extended), the base rotates the right
hand around so the fingers point toward the
back. The base must extend the arms as much
as possible, turning the hands at the height of
the stunt. The left hand reaches for the flyer's
left foot as the flyer turns to face the front and
finishes in the stunt.

ASSISTING BASE holds onto the flyer's waist and
tosses the flyer upward into the stunt. The assisting base then reaches for the front of the
flyer's shins (if possible) to stabilize the stunt
as the flyer comes around toward the front. If
the assisting base cannot reach the flyer's
shins, for example, in an extended stunt, the
assisting base should reach up as high as possible on the flyer to help stabilize the stunt.

FLYER sets by placing her right foot into the main
base's hands and puts her hands on the main
base's shoulders. The flyer is standing on her
left toe with her center of gravity positioned
directly overtop of the main base. When the
flyer is in the correct position, she should be
able to see down the main base's spine. Just as
with the Standard Load, the flyer keeps most
of her weight in her arms. The flyer sinks with
the main base and pushes straight upward off

from the main base's arms. Many flyers make the mistake of pushing *backward*; the stunt will not work if the flyer's center of gravity is not directly over her main base. Keeping her legs close together (about 6 inches apart), the flyer straightens her legs. At the height of the load, the flyer looks over her right shoulder to initiate the 180-degree clockwise turn to the front.

(The photos of the Walk Load on page 121 may also be helpful.)

Standard Load to an Elevator

This is one of those moves where timing is extremely important to the success of the stunt. For this reason, you'll find the instructions to this stunt are broken down according to counts.

Here's an example of slowing down the counts in an elevator:

ON COUNT ONE

This is the same as Count Two (see figure 9.7), except the flyer's feet are flat for Count One.

THIRD firmly grasps the flyer's waist.

BASES set into their positions, waiting for the flyer to jump in.

FLYER places her hands on the base's shoulders.

ON COUNT TWO

See figure 9.7 for photo of Count Two.

THIRD maintains a firm grasp on the flyer's waist.

BASES wait in their positions for the flyer to jump in.

FLYER rises onto the balls of her feet.

ON COUNTS THREE AND FOUR

See figure 9.8 for photo of Counts Three and Four.

Figure 9.7 *Standard Elevator Load, Count Two.*

Figure 9.8 *Standard Elevator Load, Counts Three and Four.*

THIRD follows the movements of the flyer, maintaining a grasp on the flyer's waist.

BASES remain in their positions, waiting for the flyer's feet to land in their hands.

FLYER sinks, ready to jump in on the next count.

ON COUNTS FIVE AND SIX

See figure 9.9 for photo of Counts Five and Six.

THIRD continues to follow the flyer into the Standard Load.

BASES catch the flyer's feet in their hands and sink using their quadriceps.

FLYER holds her weight in her arms, keeping her seat above her knees as the bases sink.

ON COUNTS SEVEN AND EIGHT

See figure 9.10 for photo of Counts Seven and Eight.

THIRD tosses the flyer upward, then reaches for the flyer's ankles and helps control the flyer down into an Elevator.

BASES explode upward, using their quadriceps as the main source of power. Bases simultaneously extend with their arms, driving the flyer upward. Bases' knees and elbows lock out at the same time so that the flyer is actually temporarily in an Extension, then bases slowly lower the flyer into an Elevator, making sure that they move in unison.

Figure 9.9 *Standard Elevator Load, Counts Five and Six.*

Figure 9.10 *Standard Elevator Load, Counts Seven and Eight.*

FLYER pushes off with her arms and extends her legs to achieve the standing position in an Elevator, then stays tight with arms at her sides.

ON COUNT ONE (END)

See figure 9.11 for photo of Count One, the final count.

THIRD holds onto the flyer's ankles and pulls upward, alleviating some of the weight from the bases.

BASES hold each of the flyer's feet against their chests in a Natural Grip. Bases should be careful to keep their backs straight.

FLYER hits a motion and stays tight.

— Dismounts —

Hitting a stunt also requires "dismounting," which is how the flyer gets back on the ground. Here are several common dismount methods.

Walk-Off Dismount

The Walk Off (see figures 9.12 through 9.15) is one of the easiest ways to dismount. It is typically done at the direction of the third or the coach rather than to counts. A Walk-Off should only be done with stunts at shoulder level or below. In the case of an extended stunt, the stunt should be lowered to shoulder level and then walked off.

THIRD maintains a firm grasp on the flyer's ankles, then reaches for the flyer's waist and follows her to the ground, resisting her weight along the way to ensure a soft and safe landing.

Figure 9.11 *Elevator Load, Count One (end).*

Figure 9.12 *Walk Off Dismount (front view).*

Figure 9.13 *Walk-Off Dismount (side view).*

Figure 9.14 *Walk-Off Landing (side view).*

Figure 9.15 *Walk-Off Landing (front view).*

BASES shift the weight of the flyer's foot to the back hand. Bases' front hands reach up to grab onto the flyer's closest outstretched hand in a Reverse Handshake Grip. A good way for a base to remember the proper grip is to reach up as though reading an imaginary watch. As the flyer steps off, bases reach upward with their back hands and grab underneath the flyer's underarms. Bases resist the flyer's weight, slowing her down and ensuring a light landing.

FLYER bends at the waist, shifting her hips slightly backward as she reaches for her bases' hands. To dismount, the flyer steps off of the bases' hands one at a time, keeping both legs straight until the landing. The flyer should land on

---

— TIP —

Whenever possible, stunts should
be walked off the first time, rather
than popped down or cradled.

her toes and absorb the impact by bending her knees.

Assisted Front Tuck Dismount

See figure 9.16 for a photo of Assisted Front Tuck Dismount.

THIRD holds onto the flyer's ankles and tosses the flyer straight upward to allow her hips to rotate above her head. As the flyer is coming down toward the ground in an upright position, the third reaches for the flyer's waist and helps slow down her landing.

BASES reach up to hold onto the flyer's hands, as if preparing for a Walk-Off Dismount. The bases sink together and toss the flyer's feet upward as if performing a Cradle, but continue to hold onto the flyer's hands. The bases catch the flyer as if she was dismounting from a Walk-Off, with the outside hands still holding

Figure 9.16 *Assisted Front Tuck Dismount.*

onto the flyer's hands and inside hands underneath the flyer's underarms to slow her descent. The base's hands maintain contact with the flyer throughout the entire dismount.

FLYER reaches for the bases' hands as if to walk off the stunt. It is very important that she hold onto her bases' hands in a Reverse Handshake Grip. The flyer is tossed upward and allows her hips to come up into a vertical position *before* tucking. If the flyer tucks too low, she will not have enough time to land properly and will risk injuring her ankles and legs. When the flyer's hips are directly above her shoulders, she quickly snaps into a tuck position. Equally as fast, she un-tucks to land in an upright, vertical position, keeping her chest up. The flyer holds onto the bases' hands throughout the entire dismount.

OPTIONAL SPOT stands to the side of the stunt. As the flyer un-tucks, the spot reaches for the flyer's waist and helps to slow the flyer down as she lands.

Check to make sure that the Assisted Front Tuck Dismount is legal under your regulations before attempting it.

Pop Down Dismount

The Pop Down is a good method for dismounting the flyer from lower- to mid-level stunts, such as Thigh Stands or Elevators. In this dismount, the bases pop the flyer straight down from the stunt, assisting her as she lands on her feet. While it is possible to pop down a flyer from an extended stunt, it is safer for the flyer's ankle to be cradled from an extended level, or alternatively, lowered down to shoulder level, and then popped off. To illustrate the importance of using the appropriate number of counts when stunting, the instructions for the Pop Down will be separated according to counts. (See figures 9.17 through 9.20 for photos of the Pop Down Dismount.)

Figure 9.17 *Pop Down Dismount, Counts One and Two.*

ON COUNTS ONE AND TWO

ALL remain in an Elevator position; flyer's arms are in a "High V" (see figure 9.17).

ON COUNT THREE

THIRD dips with the bases, keeping eyes on the flyer's hips (the primary indicator of the direction she's moving toward) and maintains a firm hold on the flyer's ankles.

BASES dip with their legs, keeping their backs straight and eyes focused on the flyer.

FLYER maintains a tight position. It is *very* important that the flyer does not bend her knees or jump out of the stunt.

(Count Three is the same as figure 9.17, but bases and third sink.)

ON COUNT FOUR

THIRD extends the arms and legs in an explosive motion, tossing the flyer upward. The third

Figure 9.18 *Pop Down Dismount, Count Four.*

has to be careful not to throw the flyer's feet forward, but directly upward.

BASES extend arms and legs in unison, tossing the flyer directly above them, keeping their eyes focused on the flyer. While this is a powerful motion, bases are not tossing with the same amount of power used as if they were cradling the flyer.

FLYER stays straight, quickly snapping her arms to her sides without bending the elbows.

ON COUNT FIVE

THIRD reaches up to catch the flyer's waist.

BASES reach for the flyer's underarm with the front hand while the back hand reaches for the flyer's forearm. The bases' job is not just to *catch* the

Figure 9.19 *Pop Down Dismount, Count Five.*

Figure 9.20 *Pop Down Dismount, Count Six.*

flyer, but to use their strength to oppose the downward motion, slowing the flyer down so that her feet do not crash into the ground.

FLYER stays tight the entire time, ensuring that her legs are pulled in together. Her arms reach for her third's wrists. It is important to remember this part, or the bases will not have anything to hold onto.

ON COUNT SIX

FLYER lands on the ground. The ending position is the same as a Toss Load.

— TIP —

If the flyer forgets to reach for her third's wrists and it is not possible to grab underneath her underarms, she should be caught in a Bear Hug, as demonstrated in the stunting drills.

Cradle Dismount

The Cradle is the most widely used method of dismounting a stunt. In contrast to the Pop Down, bases sink for two counts instead of only one. This creates a "slingshot" effect, projecting the flyer much higher than in a Pop Down (see figure 9.21 for the Cradle Catch Position).

CRADLE CATCH POSITION

THIRD holds the flyer underneath the flyer's arms, using the biceps (the large muscle on the front of the upper arm) and forearms to pull the flyer into the third's chest. There shouldn't be any space between the flyer's body and the third's body.

BASES hold the flyer underneath the flyer's lower back and the underside of her thighs with the arms in an alternating crisscross pattern: Base 1's back arm, Base 2's back arm, Base 1's front arm, Base 2's front arm. The bases' backs

Figure 9.21 *Cradle Catch Position.*

should be straight and their elbows should stay above waist level when holding the flyer in a Cradle. Note that the flyer is being held too low if either her seat is below the bases' waists or if there is a space in between the flyer's body and the bases.

FLYER wraps her arms around her bases' upper backs and shoulders. She holds herself up in a piked ("V") position using her upper body strength and abdominal muscles. The flyer should keep her body tight at all times. If the bases were to let go, she would still be left in a piked position.

KEY POINTS TO THE CRADLE DISMOUNT

Before attempting the cradle dismount, athletes should practice the Cradle position on the ground and familiarize themselves with the following key points:

THIRD

★ Keep your eyes on the flyer's head and neck at all times.

★ Reach high. You should be the first one to make contact with the flyer.

★ Reach up in Blades. You can catch in Fists, but avoid tucking your thumbs under your fingers. If your hand gets hit, your thumb could break. Keep your thumbs wrapped around the outside of your fingers.

★ Pull the flyer into your body as you catch.

★ Be careful of the position of your head on the catch. Broken noses are not uncommon for thirds when learning Cradles. The safest place for your head is tilted slightly to the side, but not looking away.

★ Be careful of your flyer's face. Avoid inadvertently hitting her in the head with your hands when she lands by keeping your arms shoulder-width apart.

★ Absorb the catch with your legs.

BASES

★ Watch the flyer's hips at all times.

★ Reach up high for the catch with your arms shoulder-width apart and your hands in Blades.

★ Resist the flyer's weight on the descent rather than allowing her to just fall into your arms.

★ Pull the flyer in close to your body on the catch.

★ Avoid arching underneath the toss and catching the flyer on your chest. Keep your body aligned and absorb the catch with your legs.

★ Keep your back straight during the entire stunt: sink, toss, and catch. Not only does this protect your back from injury, but it protects your face, too. You do not want to end up knocking heads with your base partner on the catch.

★ Catch as high as possible in the Cradle. The flyer's hips should never fall below yours.

★ Stay close to the flyer on the catch. There should never be a space between you and the flyer. If there is, it means that you are not absorbing the catch with your legs and are allowing her to land too low. Low catches are dangerous to bases' backs and increase the risk of injury to the flyer because she could slip through and land on the floor.

★ Keep your legs shoulder-width apart and beside one another. Resist the urge to place one leg in front of the other. A misplaced knee has the potential to seriously injure a flyer should her spine land on it. A knee in the backside does not feel so great either!

★ Do not dump or throw the flyer out of a Cradle. Release her gently with your front arm and turn to face the front.

FLYER

★ Use your upper body strength and your abdominal muscles to hold yourself up in the Cradle. If the bases were to drop their hands, you should remain in a pike, or Cradle position.

★ Catch yourself around the bases' shoulders. Do not try to catch around their backs; you will not be able to hold yourself up this way.

★ Hold yourself high in the Cradle. Keep shoulders tensed, not relaxed.

★ Cradling in an "L" position makes it hard for your bases to catch you. Keep your body in a "V" (piked) position, about 90 degrees or less. Too narrow and you could slip through the Cradle.

★ Point your toes from the time you are tossed to the time you are caught in a Cradle.

SPOTTERS

★ Stand on the weakest side of the stunt in the corner between the third and the base.

★ Keep your eyes on the flyer at all times.

★ Avoid reaching your arms into the stunt. The best way to spot this stunt is to place one hand on

the third's mid-back and the other on the base's mid-back. Help support the catch by keeping the base and the third close together with gentle pressure from each hand. Not only does this serve as a reminder to catch the flyer in a tight Cradle, but it prevents bases or the third from being forced backward from the stunt and leaving the flyer to fend for herself.

THE STRAIGHT CRADLE DISMOUNT

Taking two counts to sink and one count to explode upward, the bases and third use as much power as possible to toss the flyer upward. Bases sometimes find it helpful to think about jumping off the ground on the upward toss. Check the rules and regulations first before encouraging thirds to do this, as sometimes thirds and /or bases are not

Figure 9.22 *Straight Cradle Dismount, Counts Three and Four.*

Figure 9.23 *Straight Cradle Dismount, Counts Five and Six (front view).*

Figure 9.24 *Straight Cradle Dismount, Counts Five and Six (side view).*

allowed to have their heels come off the ground. (See figures 9.22 through 9.25 for the Straight Cradle Dismount Steps.)

FLYER snaps her arms from a High V to the Clean position to get more height as she is tossed upward. Compare this to being on the bottom of a swimming pool with your arms stretched upward. When you pull your arms downward, you are pulled to the top of the pool. The same idea applies to achieving more height in a Cradle by snapping arms from a High V to Clean. When she is tossed, the flyer should imagine that a string is attached to her upper chest and is pulling her upward. The flyer's

Figure 9.25 *Straight Cradle Dismount Catch (Count Seven).*

back should be slightly arched and she should be on a 45-degree angle in the air as opposed to being straight up and down. The flyer is now in the Layout position. Flyers need to be careful that they do not lean backward before the toss or pull backward during the toss. This will reduce the height of the Cradle and cause the stunt to move backward. Flyers should always think "up." She should wait to pike until just before she lands in her bases' arms. Many flyers snap too quickly, reducing height and visual appeal of the Cradle.

THIRD keeps the arms up after the toss, reaching high in either Fists or Blades. The third catches under the armpits of the flyer. On the catch, the third pulls the flyer's upper back into the third's chest, using the biceps (the large muscle on the front of the upper arm) and forearms (lower arms).

BASES keep their arms up after the toss (hands in Blades), ready to catch the flyer in an alternating crisscross pattern: Base 1's back arm, Base 2's back arm, Base 1's front arm, Base 2's front arm. This ensures a safe and secure Cradle for the flyer to land in. The bases' back arms catch the flyer's lower back while their front arms catch the underside of the flyer's thighs. The bases pull the flyer into their chests on the catch. Catching the flyer high in the air is critical. If the flyer is caught too low, the downward momentum may pull the bases toward the ground, risking the flyer hitting the floor.

CRADLE DISMOUNT FROM AN EXTENDED STUNT

The Cradle from an extended stunt (such as Extension or Liberty) occurs with the same counts and similar motions as an Elevator Cradle. The difference is that the bases keep their arms straight and sink only with their knees when cradling from an extended stunt. On the upward motion, the bases flick the flyer off of their hands by snapping their wrists upward for added height. The flyer will not get as much height from an extended stunt as she will in an Elevator, so she must pull her Layout and tricks faster.

DRILL FOR TWISTING CRADLE DISMOUNT

Flyers should perfect a straight Cradle before attempting a twisting Cradle. When flyers are ready for progress, start out with the following drill (see figures 9.26 through 9.28 for the Twisting Cradle Dismount steps):

THIRD stands behind the bases and assists with the catch.

BASES face each other and hold onto one another's forearms. The flyer completes her practice twist and lands against her bases' arms.

FLYER stands in front of her bases with her feet together and arms in a High V. The flyer snaps her arms down to the left side to initiate the momentum for the twist. She rotates 360 degrees on an angled axis and lands in her

Figure 9.26 *Twist Cradle Dismount, Count One.*

Figure 9.27 *Twist Cradle Dismount, Count Two.*

Figure 9.28 *Twist Cradle Dismount, Count Three.*

bases' arms. When executing a twist, it is important for the flyer to rotate on a 45-degree angle rather than straight up and down. This drill is a good way to learn this technique because the flyer has to practice rotating toward her bases.

TWISTING CRADLE DISMOUNT

FLYER begins with arms in a High V. She must wait until the bases toss her upward *before* initiating the twist. A good way for the flyer to remember this is to take a quick breath before beginning to twist. This also helps the flyer to remember to pull up the chest slightly. The flyer should never twist before leaving the bases' hands! To initiate the twist, the flyer looks downward over her left shoulder while simultaneously snapping her arms down and to the left, as practiced in the drill. The flyer should think about dropping her left shoulder while rotating her upper body and lower body *together*. The most common mistake made while twisting is leaving the hips behind

rather than keeping them in line with the shoulders. The flyer should be twisting on a slight angle backward. The flyer stops the twisting action by looking for the front (the head always precedes the body).

BASES can assist the twist by first tossing the flyer upward and then twisting their own feet in the direction of the turn just before the release.

THIRD can assist the twist by tossing *upward* first and then twisting the ankles counterclockwise.

All bases must be careful not to over-twist, or to twist the flyer too early.

Double Twist Dismount

To execute a Double Twist, the flyer pulls the rotation faster than when executing a single twist. To pull the rotation faster, the flyer should snap her arms down and to the side as quickly as possible and remain tight until opening into the Cradle position. The flyer also must remember to snap into a piked position when landing in the Cradle.

TWISTING FROM A HEEL STRETCH

The flyer stays locked out in position as her bases sink. On the upward pop, the flyer drops her Heel Stretch leg, using this momentum to initiate the twist. She brings her standing leg hip up and over in the direction of the twist rather than just letting her Heel Stretch leg drop. This will keep her hips and shoulders aligned as well as put her on the correct axis to twist. A good way for the flyer to remember how to do this is to think of her legs as scissors and snap them together on the pop. The flyer simultaneously pulls her arms downward and to the side as her legs snap together, and at the same time turns her head to look over her shoulder. There will only be minimal pop from the base(s) so the flyer will have to twist quickly to make it around. Again, flyers must wait for the pop upward before dropping the leg for a successful twist. For a Double Twist, the flyer pulls harder and snaps faster.

TWISTING FROM AN ARABESQUE

To twist from an Arabesque, the flyer must drop her leg and arms on the upward motion of the toss before initiating the twist. Her chest must also come up to a vertical position before rotating, or she will twist with her center of gravity forward instead of backward. This risks falling torso first rather than landing in a Cradle.

Here are some key points to remind the flyer who is performing a Twist Cradle:

★ Wait until the toss to twist. Do not jump out of the stunt or rotate immediately out of the toss in anticipation of the twist.

★ Snap your arms down and to the side to initiate the twist. Look over your shoulder at your third.

★ Continue looking around toward the front once you see your third. This will bring you around in a full rotation.

★ Keep your body aligned and twist in one piece rather than letting your upper body and lower

---

Which Way to Twist?

Note that these instructions for twisting cradles have the flyer twisting counterclockwise. Flyers can also twist clockwise, depending on the coach's preference or on which leg is extended in the stunt. For example, a flyer holding her right leg in a Heel Stretch would twist to the right.

---

body twist separately. Do not allow your shoulders to twist without your hips.

★ Keep on trying. If you do not succeed at first, remember that practice makes perfect.

— Multiple-Base Stunts —

The following are stationary stunts (stunts that "hit" and can be held) and transition stunts (stunts that "hit" and immediately return to a load or are continuous movements linking one stationary stunt to another) that can be performed by a multiple-base stunt group. Here you'll also find variations on loading and dismounting each particular stunt.

Thigh Stand

See figure 9.29 for a photo of the Thigh Stand.

THIRD stands behind the flyer, legs shoulder width apart and hands on the flyer's waist. The third keeps her hands on the flyer during the entire stunt. As the flyer jumps into the Thigh Stand, the third helps to lift the flyer upward and places her on the bases' thighs. To dismount, the third resists the flyer's weight as the flyer steps off the bases and onto the ground.

BASES begin in a lunge position; outside legs are straight and inside legs are bent at a 90-degree angle to create a stable platform for the flyer

Figure 9.29 *Thigh Stand.*

to stand on. The bases watch the flyer's feet as she jumps in, making sure that the flyer lands on the correct part of the bases' legs—the "pocket" at the top of the thigh where the leg joins to the hip. When the flyer stands on the pocket (as close to the base's body as possible), she is standing on the most solid part of the lunge. If she stands too low on the thigh, she will feel unstable and fall off. As soon as the flyer jumps in, the bases wrap the inside/back hand around the top of the flyer's knee to help stabilize her and to help keep her legs straight in the stunt. The bases reach the outside/front arm around and hold onto the flyer's shin. To dismount, the bases walk off the flyer by letting go of her shin and reaching up in a Reverse Handshake Grip (fingers pointing toward the back) to help her down. The other hand reaches up under the flyer's armpit and helps to slow her down as she steps off their thighs.

FLYER stands with her feet together and places her hands on the shoulders of her bases. Using the bases' shoulders for support, she jumps into the pockets of her bases' thighs. Standing up, the flyer locks out her knees and puts her arms in a motion. To dismount, the flyer reaches down to grab onto her bases' outside hands in a Reverse Handshake Grip and steps off from the thigh stand.

ONE-FOOT LOAD VARIATION IN A THIGH STAND

THIRD begins by holding onto the flyer's waist and helps lift the flyer into the thigh stand. Maintaining contact with the flyer the entire stunt, the third helps the flyer dismount gently by resisting the flyer's weight as the flyer steps off the thigh stand.

RIGHT BASE begins in a lunge. The flyer's right foot loads onto the right base's thigh. The right base's inside (left) hand is holding onto the top of the flyer's right thigh, close to the knee. The outside (right) hand is holding onto the flyer's right shin for added stability. As the flyer begins standing up into the Thigh Stand, the right base pushes up under the flyer's thigh with the inside elbow and helps the flyer up into position. The dismount is the same as a regular Thigh Stand.

FLYER begins with her right foot already loaded into the right base's thigh pocket. Using her arms to push off of the bases' shoulders, she stands up into a Thigh Stand and locks her

---

— TIP —

The Two-Foot Thigh Stand Load can be used to load a number of different stunts, such as the Straddle Sit, the Chair, and the Flatback. It is also a popular move used to transition between stunts when used as part of a Sponge.

knees out to stabilize the stunt. The flyer must remember to climb lightly by *pushing off* of her left leg to get into the Thigh Stand rather than *stepping up* with her right foot. The result is that there is little weight put onto the right base. The dismount is the same as the Thigh Stand.

POP DOWN DISMOUNT FROM A THIGH STAND

This is a simple, but clean way to dismount a Thigh Stand.

THIRD holds onto the flyer's waist and helps to lower the flyer safely and gently to the ground.

BASES sink together and pop the flyer upward. For the catch, the bases reach up underneath the flyer's underarm with the outside arm and around the flyer's forearm with the inside arm to absorb the landing.

FLYER stays tight on the sink. On the upward motion, the flyer snaps her legs together and reaches for her third's wrists. The flyer lands in an upright position and absorbs the impact by landing on her toes and bending her knees. The flyer must remember to keep her chest up throughout the dismount.

THIGH STAND LIBERTY AND THIGH STAND HEEL STRETCH

The Thigh Stand Liberty or Heel Stretch (also called a Y-Stand or a Y-Scale) is executed in the same way as a One-Foot Load Thigh Stand, except that the flyer does not place her left foot into the left thigh pocket. For a Thigh Stand Liberty, she steps up onto the right base and lifts her left leg into a Liberty stance (see figure 9.30). For a Heel Stretch, she kicks her left leg up into a Heel Stretch (see figure 9.31). The left base may assist the stunt by holding onto the flyer's leg for her. For both stunts, the flyer is left standing on one leg.

THIGH STAND OFFSET

See figure 9.32 for a photo of the Thigh Stand Offset.

Figure 9.30 *Thigh Stand Liberty.*

THIRD holds onto the flyer's waist and loads the flyer into the Offset by lifting her upward as she steps up onto the left base. The third maintains contact with the flyer during the entire stunt and dismount.

RIGHT BASE begins in a lunge and helps the flyer into the stunt from a One-Foot Load, holding tightly onto the flyer's leg to stabilize the stunt (You'll see in figure 9.32 that the right base has her hand on the flyer's knee—this position is inaccurate. It is important to keep your hand on the thigh, just above the knee.)

LEFT BASE stands facing inward with both hands against the chest. The left base grabs onto the flyer's foot in a Natural Grip as the flyer steps up into the Offset.

Figure 9.31 *Thigh Stand Heel Stretch.*

Figure 9.32 *Thigh Stand Offset.*

FLYER loads into the stunt as if performing a Thigh Stand Liberty by placing her right foot into the right base's pocket. She then stands up onto the right base's thigh pocket and places her left foot into the left base's hands (left knee is bent). The majority of the flyer's weight should be on the right base.

Thigh Stand Offset Dismount

★ The flyer can bring her left leg down into a Thigh Stand and Walk Off to dismount.

★ If the flyer dismounts by popping down from the Offset, she must remember to step up and push off from her left leg for additional height.

— TIP —

Here's a good drill for flyers working on the Thigh Stand Liberty/Heel Stretch or Thigh Stand Offset: Have the flyer place her right foot up on a bench or other elevated surface. Instruct her to practice stepping up onto the bench and hitting her position, whether it is a Liberty, Heel Stretch, or Offset. This drill helps with climbing lightly (pushing off from the ground leg) and hitting the proper body position in the stunt. This drill is also useful when flyers are learning to perform extended one-foot stunts.

★　Alternatively, the flyer can also dismount by stepping up on her left leg into an Elevator and then dismount by cradling.

Shoulder Sit

See figure 9.33 for an example of the Shoulder Sit.

TOSS LOAD TO A SHOULDER SIT

MAIN BASE holds onto the flyer's waist and tosses the flyer up and onto the main base's shoulders. The main base must remember to keep the back straight and sink with the legs to lower the torso so that the flyer is able to sit on the main base's shoulders. If the main base bends the head or shoulders forward, this immediately puts the main base at risk for neck and back injuries because it becomes possible for the flyer to land on the main base's neck

Figure 9.33 *Shoulder Sit.*

rather than the shoulders. When the flyer is seated on the main base's shoulders, the main base wraps the hands around the top of the flyer's thighs to stabilize the stunt.

THIRD and **ASSISTING BASE** toss the flyer up and onto the shoulders of the main base from the regular toss position. They must remember to toss upward, and not backward, or the flyer will not have enough height to land on the main base's shoulders.

FLYER jumps upward as the main base tosses her. The flyer pushes down (not outward) off from the main base's wrists for added height. Once on the main base's shoulders, the flyer wraps her toes around the main base's back for a clean appearance and additional support.

WALK UP LOAD TO A SHOULDER SIT

See figure 9.34 for a photo of the Walk Up Load to Shoulder Sit.

THIRD holds onto the flyer's waist and stabilizes the flyer as she climbs onto the main base's shoulders.

MAIN BASE begins in a left lunge position (right knee bent). The main base's left hand reaches across the body to stabilize the flyer's foot. The right arm is tucked up underneath the flyer's thigh and the right hand is just above the flyer's knee. The main base helps the flyer step up into the Shoulder Sit by pushing up with the right elbow in the same way to load a Thigh Stand.

FLYER begins standing behind the main base. She loads into the stunt by placing her right foot in the main base's right pocket and places her hands on the base's shoulders. The flyer steps up, pushing off from the main base's shoulders. The flyer then swings her left leg around and onto the main base's shoulder to complete the Shoulder Sit.

Figure 9.34 *Walk Up Load to Shoulder Sit.*

Figure 9.35 *Grin 'n' Bear It Load to Shoulder Sit.*

GRIN 'N' BEAR IT LOAD TO A SHOULDER SIT

See figure 9.35 for a photo of the Grin 'n' Bear It Load to Shoulder Sit.

THIRD holds the flyer's waist and follows the flyer as she walks forward toward the main base. As the flyer jumps up for the front straddle, the third tosses her upward to gain more height. Maintaining contact with the flyer's waist, the third then assists the main base in tossing the flyer up and around into a Shoulder Sit.

MAIN BASE begins facing the flyer with legs shoulder width apart. When the flyer jumps into the Forward Straddle, the main base catches underneath the flyer's thighs with the right hand crossed over the left, and sinks. The main base's right hand is underneath the flyer's right thigh and the left hand is underneath the flyer's left thigh. On the upward motion, the main base tosses the flyer upward

and over the right shoulder into a Shoulder Sit. The main base must toss the flyer upward *first*, because the flyer needs lots of height to complete the rotation to Shoulder Sit.

FLYER starts facing the main base. Walking forward two steps (right, left), the flyer jumps onto the main base in a straddle position, arms around the main base's neck for support (like in Swing Dancing). On the upward toss, the flyer pushes up off the main base's shoulders with her forearms. The flyer then swings up and around 180 degrees clockwise to land on the main base's shoulders in a Shoulder Sit.

FRONT DISMOUNT FROM A SHOULDER SIT

The flyer holds onto the main base's hands and kicks her legs out straight in front of her as she is popped upward. The main base helps the flyer dismount by pushing upward and extending the arms upward, which gives the flyer more height. The main base continues to hold onto the flyer's hands and helps to slow the flyer down as the flyer makes contact with the floor. Additional bases or spots can help slow the descent by reaching for the flyer's underarms, as in a Walk Off.

REAR DISMOUNT FROM A SHOULDER SIT

The flyer holds onto the main base's hands and brings her legs together as she is popped off behind the base. The difference between the two dismounts lies in the positioning of the main base's arms: If they are on either side of the flyer's legs, this leads to a front dismount; whereas if the main base reaches in the middle, the flyer will dismount to the rear.

Flatback

See figure 9.36 for a photo sample of the Flatback.

Figure 9.36 *Flatback.*

LOAD FROM A CRADLE INTO A FLATBACK

THIRD is holding the flyer in a cradle position. Tossing the flyer upward, the third holds the flyer in a Flatback by supporting underneath her shoulders. In a Flatback, the third is responsible for the majority of the flyer's weight.

BASES hold the flyer in a Cradle position. Sinking deeply, the bases toss the flyer upward. The bases catch underneath the flyer's seat with the back hand and under the flyer's calf with the front hand. If there is a front base holding the flyer's feet, the main bases can support underneath the flyer's seat and her upper thigh.

FLYER begins in a Cradle position with her hands on the bases' back shoulders (the shoulder closest to the rear) as opposed to around their front shoulders in a normal Cradle catch. As the bases toss the flyer upward, she pushes off from their shoulders and tightens up into a horizontal, flat position. The flyer must remain in a tight position (toes pointed) during the entire stunt.

OPTIONAL SPOT holds onto the flyer's ankles. As the flyer is tossed upward into the Flatback, the spot supports the weight of the flyer's feet.

The Flatback can either be tossed to shoulder-level or an extended level.

THIGH STAND LOAD INTO A FLATBACK

THIRD helps the flyer into a Thigh Stand Load with the hands first around the flyer's waist and then on her shoulder blades after the flyer successfully jumps into the load. As the flyer is lifted upward, the third pushes underneath the flyer's upper back and brings the flyer into a Flatback position.

BASES begin in a lunge, ready for the flyer to jump into a Thigh Stand Load. As the flyer loads in, they grab onto the flyer's ankle with the front hand and underneath the flyer's seat with the back hand. As the flyer sinks and pushes off from their shoulders, the bases push upward underneath the flyer's seat and ankles to bring her into a Flatback position.

FLYER loads into a Thigh Stand Load, pushes off of her bases' shoulders and immediately flattens out into a Flatback by lifting her legs up and lowering her upper body.

GROUND UP LOAD INTO A FLATBACK

See figure 9.37 for a photo of the Ground Up Load into a Flatback.

THIRD begins by standing behind the flyer with hands underneath the flyer's shoulder blades (fingertips pointing up). As the flyer is lifted upward, the third gets underneath the flyer's upper back and pushes the flyer up into a Flatback position.

Figure 9.37 *Ground Up Load into a Flatback.*

RIGHT BASE sets with the left hand on the flyer's seat and the right hand around the flyer's ankle. On the upward lift, the right base pushes up underneath the flyer's seat and ankle into a Flatback position.

LEFT BASE crouches along the side of the flyer, holding onto the flyer's outstretched left ankle with the left hand and the flyer's seat with the right. The bases sink together and the left base lifts the flyer upward into a Flatback.

FLYER begins standing upright, with her left foot set in the hands of the left base. The flyer's hands are on either the bases' heads or shoulders. The flyer sinks with the bases and pushes off from their shoulders or heads to help initiate the upward momentum. The flyer immediately tightens up into a Flatback position and remains locked out throughout the rest of the stunt.

FLATBACK LEG RAISE VARIATION

FLYER executes the stunt in the same way as a regular Flatback; but instead of bringing her feet together, her right leg (or left leg) extends upward into a vertical position (at a 90-degree angle from the rest of her body).

Straddle Sit

See figure 9.38 for a photo of the Straddle Sit.

THIRD loads the flyer into a Thigh Stand Load (the flyer's knees are still bent, not straightened). As the bases bring the flyer's feet up into the Straddle position, the third can either place the hands underneath the flyer's seat to provide added support, or continue to hold the flyer's waist.

BASES place the outside hand on the flyer's ankle and the inside hand under the flyer's seat as the flyer jumps into the Thigh Stand Load. On the upward motion, the bases push up under the flyer's seat and calf, extending the arms and positioning the flyer into a Straddle Sit.

Figure 9.38 *Straddle Sit.*

FLYER jumps into a Thigh Stand Load, keeping her knees bent rather than standing up. On the upward motion, she pushes off of her bases' shoulders and extends her legs into a Straddle position.

FLATBACK LOAD INTO A STRADDLE SIT

THIRD is holding the flyer in a Flatback. The bases sink together using their legs and the third pushes the flyer's back upward into a Straddle Sit. The third then places the hands underneath the flyer's seat to stabilize the stunt and provide support to the bases.

BASES are holding the flyer in a Flatback; the back hand is holding underneath the flyer's seat, and the front hand is holding underneath the flyer's ankles. The bases sink together and, on the upward motion, turn their bodies slightly outward, widening the flyer's legs into a Straddle Sit.

FLYER maintains a tight position while being held in a Flatback. On the pop upward, she simultaneously snaps her chest up and widens her legs into a Straddle Sit. The flyer should not try to roll up into the Straddle Sit but rather keep her back straight throughout the entire stunting sequence.

THIGH STAND LOAD INTO A STRADDLE SIT

THIRD assists the flyer into a Thigh Stand Load with hands first holding around the flyer's waist and then underneath the flyer's seat once the flyer jumps in. As the flyer sinks and pushes off of her bases, the third pushes up underneath the flyer's seat and into a Flatback.

BASES load the flyer in the same manner as a Thigh Stand Load to Flatback but take a small step outward on the upward lift to widen the flyer's legs into a Straddle position.

FLYER loads into the stunt as if performing a Thigh Stand Load to a Flatback. Instead of dropping her upper body on the way up, she keeps her chest vertical as she pops up into a Straddle Sit.

STRADDLE SIT DISMOUNT

THIRD continues to hold onto the flyer's waist and slowly lowers the flyer down to a standing position.

BASES bring the flyer's legs together and slowly lower the flyer's feet to the ground.

FLYER brings her legs together and places her hands around her third's wrists for support when being lowered down to the ground.

ALTERNATE STRADDLE SIT DISMOUNT

THIRD continues to hold onto the flyer's waist or underneath the flyer's seat. The base group sinks and tosses the flyer upward, catching her in a Cradle position.

BASES sink together and toss the flyer upward. Arms reach upward and bases catch the flyer in a Cradle position.

FLYER maintains a tight position as the bases sink. On the upward motion, the flyer snaps her legs together and straightens her body into as much of a Layout position as possible. The flyer then snaps into a "V" position in order to be caught in the Cradle position.

For a Cradle variation, the flyer may twist out of the Straddle Hold, remembering to snap her legs together and pull up with her chest.

Shoulder Split

See figure 9.39 for a photo of the Shoulder Split.

THIRD loads the flyer into the first part of a Thigh Stand. The third helps to toss the flyer into a left split. Once the flyer is in the split, the third either places the hands underneath the flyer's thighs to help alleviate the pressure of the split or continues to hold onto the flyer's waist.

RIGHT BASE reaches up with the outside arm and grasps the flyer's hand in a Reverse Handshake Grip. The left hand is turned over (the arm rotates 180 degrees clockwise so that the elbow is pointing upward and the top of the thumb is toward the ground) and grasps the flyer's ankle. This hand position allows the flyer's leg to rotate up into the stunt. On the upward motion, the right base lifts up the flyer's shin onto the back (left) shoulder and turns 90 degrees to the left. The right base continues to hold onto the flyer's hand with the right arm.

Figure 9.39 *Shoulder Split.*

LEFT BASE reaches up with the outside arm and grasps the flyer's hand in a Reverse Handshake Grip. The left base's right hand is holding onto the flyer's ankle in a regular grip. On the upward motion, the left base lifts up the flyer's calf onto the back (right) shoulder and turns 180 degrees to the left. The left base continues to hold onto the flyer's hand with the left arm.

FLYER jumps into a Thigh Stand Load (legs are still bent). The flyer grasps her bases' outreached hands in a Reverse Handshake Grip and, turning to the left, goes up into the left splits.

In this stunt, the flyer has a tendency to roll forward. It is important that the bases maintain a firm grasp on the flyer and that the third holds onto the flyer's waist if necessary.

SHOULDER SPLIT DISMOUNT

To dismount, the bases sink together and pop the flyer upward. The flyer must be popped up high enough that she can snap her legs together and grab onto her third's wrists. The bases catch her under the underarm with the inside hand and continue holding onto the flyer's hand with the outside hands. The stunt should finish in an ending Walk Off position.

Chair
See figure 9.40 for photo of the Chair.

THE FINISHED STUNT

THIRD stands behind the main base, either holding onto the main base's wrist or the flyer's seat for added support.

ASSISTING BASE is generally to the right side of the stunt, holding the flyer's right knee with the right hand and either holding onto the base's wrist or supporting the flyer's seat with her left hand.

MAIN BASE is supporting the flyer's weight by placing the right hand underneath the flyer's tailbone. The right supporting arm is straight and close to the main base's head. The main base's left arm is firmly holding onto the flyer's left ankle and pushing upward for added support.

FLYER is sitting on the base's hand, comparable to sitting on the edge of a table. Her right knee is bent and at waist level while her left leg is straight and extended downward. Toes are pointed. Shoulders are slightly leaning backward and the mid-section is tight. If the flyer sits up straight or arches her back, she will likely fall off her base's hand.

THIGH STAND LOAD INTO A CHAIR
See figure 9.41 for a photo of the Thigh Stand Load into a Chair.

THIRD holds onto the flyer's waist as the flyer jumps into the first part of a Thigh Stand. In one continuous motion, the third lifts up the flyer into a Chair, either holding onto the flyer's seat or the main base's wrist for support.

LEFT BASE is the main base for this stunt and is positioned in a Thigh Stand stance. As the flyer jumps in, the left base grabs onto the flyer's left ankle with the left hand and underneath the flyer's seat with the right hand. The fingers on the right hand should be spread apart to ensure a solid base for the flyer to sit on. Sinking simultaneously as the flyer jumps in, the left base stands up underneath the flyer, extending the right arm directly above the head, allowing the upward momentum to do the majority of the lifting work.

Figure 9.40 *Chair.*

Figure 9.41 *Thigh Stand Load into a Chair.*

RIGHT BASE is the assisting base and is also positioned in a lunge. As the flyer jumps in, the right base grabs the flyer's right knee and either underneath the flyer's seat or onto the main base's wrist with the left hand. Sinking simultaneously as the flyer jumps in, the right base then stands up to support the stunt.

FLYER jumps into a Thigh Stand Load. She pushes upward off from the bases' shoulders and lifts her right knee into a Chair.

TOSS LOAD INTO A CHAIR

Follow the instructions for a Toss with the two bases or one base and the third tossing on either side of the flyer.

MAIN BASE tosses the flyer upward, extending the right arm to catch the flyer's seat and holds onto the flyer's left leg with the left hand.

FLYER is tossed up into a Chair, lifting her right leg near the height of the toss.

GROUND UP LOAD INTO A CHAIR

See figure 9.42 for a photo of the Ground Up Load into a Chair.

THIRD stands behind the flyer and tosses the flyer up into the Chair position.

MAIN BASE crouches on the left side of the flyer, sitting on the right heel (base's left foot is flat on the ground). The main base's right hand is underneath the flyer's seat and the left hand is holding onto the flyer's left ankle. The main base sinks with flyer and the third. On the upward motion, the main base simultaneously extends the right arm into a Chair position while standing up.

ASSISTING BASE crouches in front of the flyer, holding underneath the flyer's left foot. The assisting base lifts the flyer's foot upward for added power as the flyer is tossed into the Chair.

Figure 9.42 *Ground Up Load into a Chair.*

FLYER stands on her right leg with her left knee lifted up. Her left foot is in the hands of the assisting base toe-pitching in front of her. The flyer sinks. Exploding off her back leg and stepping up onto the toe pitch for added assistance, the flyer simultaneously pushes up from the third's wrists and is popped upward. Near the top of the toss, the flyer lifts her right knee into a Chair.

WALK-IN LOAD INTO A CHAIR

See figure 9.43 for a photo of the Walk-In Load into a Chair.

THIRD stands behind the flyer, holding onto the flyer's waist. The third follows the flyer as the flyer walks toward the main base. As the flyer loads into the stunt and is propelled upward, the third tosses upward for added height. The third then moves to the right side of the stunt to either assist in holding the Chair or to spot. (Third is not shown in figure 9.43.)

Figure 9.43 *Walk-In Load into a Chair.*

MAIN BASE is positioned in a right lunge stance (left leg bent). As the flyer walks in and puts her left foot in the base's thigh pocket, the base's right hand reaches under the flyer's seat and the left hand grabs onto the flyer's ankle. The base sinks with the flyer. As the flyer extends upward, the main base pushes up with the right hand, turning it 180 degrees clockwise with the flyer. The left hand pulls up on the flyer's left leg, helping to put the flyer into a Chair.

FLYER is positioned in front of the main base. She takes two steps forward (left, right) and then places her left foot onto the main base's left thigh pocket. Her hands are on the base's shoulders, and she is leaning overtop of the base so that the base's spine is visible. This position aligns the flyer's center of gravity with the base. When the two centers of gravity are aligned, extending the flyer is easy. The flyer sinks with the base. On the upward motion, the flyer pushes *straight* off of the base's shoulders (a common error is pushing backward or over the top of the base). The flyer pushes off of the main base's thigh pocket for added height and turns clockwise to face the front while lifting her right leg.

Elevator

This stunt is often referred to as a "Double Base," "Extension Prep," or "Elevator Prep." See figures 9.44 and 9.45 for full and close-up views of the Elevator.

THE FINISHED STUNT

THIRD holds onto the highest part of the flyer she can reach, usually the thighs. Alternatively, the third can also hold onto the flyer's ankles and pull upward, alleviating some of the weight from the bases.

BASES hold each of the flyer's feet against their chests in a Natural Grip. They should avoid

Figure 9.44 *Elevator.*

Figure 9.45 *Elevator (close-up).*

holding the flyer's foot away from their bodies. Their bodies should remain aligned during the entire stunt (no arching).

FLYER stays in a tight position, ensuring that the knees are straight, the arms are in a motion or in the Clean position, and her gaze is focused on a point slightly above eye level.

STANDARD LOAD INTO AN ELEVATOR

This is explained in the "Loads" section on page 118.

ONE-FOOT LOAD INTO AN ELEVATOR

THIRD executes the stunt as if performing a normal Standard Load.

MAIN BASE sets by holding the flyer's foot in a Prep Grip.

ASSISTING BASE can either place the hands under the main base's hands in a Sandwich Grip or can wait until the flyer's foot comes up to the hands.

FLYER sets by placing one foot in the main base's hands. Load proceeds as usual, but the flyer loads into the Elevator on one leg instead of two.

WALK-IN ONE-FOOT LOAD INTO AN ELEVATOR

A variation on the One-Foot Load, the flyer begins two steps away from the base group. If the flyer is loading with her right foot, she will step forward right, left, and then step into her base's grip. Alternatively, if she is loading with her left foot, she will start the walk with her left foot.

ONE-FOOT, TWO-FOOT LOAD INTO AN ELEVATOR

This load is executed in the same way as the One-Foot Load except that instead of immediately stepping up into the stunt off the right base, the flyer loads her left foot into the waiting left base's Prep Grip before pushing off into the stunt. The right base actually does a double bounce first when the flyer sinks with her foot in the right base's hands, and again when the flyer places her left foot in the left base's hands. This load is a combination of the One-Foot Load and the Standard Load.

GROUND UP LOAD INTO AN ELEVATOR

See figure 9.46 for a photo of the Ground Up Load into an Elevator.

THIRD holds onto either the flyer's waist or thighs. The third sinks with the flyer and bases. On the way up, the third lifts the flyer into the Elevator position.

Figure 9.46 *Ground Up Load into an Elevator.*

BASES begin in a crouched position with the flyer standing on the instep of each base's back foot. Hands are around the flyer's heel and toes. Bases dip together with the flyer and third and then stand up, extending the flyer into an Elevator position.

FLYER stands in an upright position, either holding onto the back's wrists or her bases' heads/shoulders. On the sink, the flyer bends her knees and gives a little jump upward to begin the momentum. Without this help from the flyer, it is difficult for the bases to stand up.

This is a great load for pyramids because this load creates the appearance of a pyramid extending straight from the "ground up."

SHOULDER SIT LOAD INTO AN ELEVATOR

See figure 9.47 for a photo of the Shoulder Sit Load into an Elevator.

THIRD loads the flyer onto the third's shoulders in a Shoulder Sit. The third then places the hands underneath the flyer's thighs. Sinking with the bases, the third pushes upward, popping the flyer into an Elevator position.

BASES help to load the flyer into the Shoulder Sit. Placing their hands underneath the flyer's feet, the bases sink in unison with the third and extend the flyer into an Elevator.

FLYER loads into a Shoulder Sit. Placing her hands on top of the third's head or bases' shoulders, she pushes off with her arms into an Elevator.

SINGLE BACK LOAD INTO AN ELEVATOR

See figure 9.48 for a photo of the Single Back Load into an Elevator.

THIRD starts out holding onto the flyer's waist. There are two main sinks in this load. On the first one, the third assists the flyer in standing up on the right base's back (see figure 9.48). On the second sink, the third holds onto both

Figure 9.47 *Shoulder Sit Load into an Elevator.*

Figure 9.48 *Single Back Load into an Elevator.*

of the flyer's ankles and lifts the flyer up from the main base's back and into an Elevator.

MAIN BASE is leaning over, with elbows resting on upper thighs for support. The main base's lower back is slightly arched to provide a flat surface for the flyer's foot. The main base remains in position on the first sink. On the second sink, the main base sinks with the knees, and on the upward pop, lifts the hips and slightly rounds up the back. This motion helps to give the flyer additional height on the upward pop. Standing up quickly, the main base turns to face the base partner and catches the flyer's foot.

ASSISTING BASE is standing in toward the stunt with hands against the chest, ready to catch the flyer's foot in a Natural Grip. On the first

pop, the assisting base catches the flyer's foot. The assisting base remains in position during the rest of the stunt as the flyer is popped into an Elevator.

FLYER begins by placing her foot on the back of the main base, not stepping anywhere near the spine, but on the strong, flat lower back. It is easiest to begin this stunt standing on the toe of the supporting leg, because the main base's lower back is usually too high for the flyer to stand flatfooted. On the first sink, the flyer stands up on the main base's back and places her other foot into the hands of the assisting base. On the second sink, the flyer dips with her straight leg to initiate the momentum and steps up into the Elevator.

DOUBLE BACK LOAD INTO AN ELEVATOR

See figure 9.49 for a photo of a Double Back Load into an Elevator.

THIRD loads the flyer onto the bases' lower backs. Holding onto the flyer's ankles, the third sinks with the bases. The third is responsible for the majority of the work on this load by lifting the flyer by the ankles (with the help of the bases' initial momentum). The third continues to pull upward on the flyer's ankles until the bases have time to grasp underneath the flyer's feet.

BASES lean over, resting their elbows on the top portion of their thighs for support. Their lower backs are slightly arched to provide a flat surface for the flyer to stand on. On the sink, bases lower their backs, using their quadricep muscles. On the up motion, the bases propel the flyer into the stunt by lifting their hips and rounding out their backs. Turning quickly to face one another, the bases then reach for the flyer's feet, which, if executed properly, should be at least at the chest level.

FLYER prepares to load onto the lower backs of the bases by putting her hands on their upper backs for support. The flyer jumps onto the bases' backs, taking care to place the feet on the flat bone just below the hips and not anywhere near the spine. The flyer can also load onto the base's lower backs one foot at a time by holding onto her third's wrists for support. On the sink, the flyer bends her knees and gives a slight jump to initiate the momentum upward. It is important for the flyer to stay tight on the way up because the stunt is relatively unstable until the bases grab hold of her feet.

HOP 'N' GO LOAD INTO AN ELEVATOR

The base group begins as though they have just caught the flyer from a Walk-Off. The bases' outside hands are holding onto the flyer's hands and their inside hands are holding underneath the flyer's underarms. The third is holding onto the flyer's waist. The base group sinks together from this position and tosses the flyer upward. The bases turn inward in time for the flyer to land in the Standard Load position. Using the flyer's landing into the Standard Load as the sink, the base group immediately tosses her up into an Elevator without pausing in the load.

180-DEGREE TWIST-UP INTO AN ELEVATOR

See figures 9.50 through 9.52 for photos of the 180-Degree Twist-Up into an Elevator.

FRONT SPOT faces the back and, holding onto the flyer's waist, loads the flyer into the stunt. Once the front spot finishes loading the flyer in, the front spot steps aside and assumes the spotting position. It is possible to do this stunt

Figure 9.49 *Double Back Load into an Elevator.*

Figure 9.50 *180-Degree Twist-Up into an Elevator.*

without the extra base, but groups new to this stunt should start with the extra help. (Front spot is not featured in the photos.)

THIRD is facing the flyer. The third crosses the right wrist over the left in preparation for grasping the front of the flyer's shins. As the flyer loads in, the third sinks along with the other bases and helps to propel the flyer upward. It is important to give the flyer lots of height before attempting to twist her toward the front. To turn the flyer to face the front, the third simply uncrosses the wrists.

BASES are set in the usual Standard Load position but cross the right hand overtop of the left in preparation for the flyer to jump in. (This hand position feels strange in the beginning, but it becomes easy after a few practices.) Bases sink with the flyer, popping the flyer

Figure 9.51 *180-Degree Twist-Up, hand positioning.*

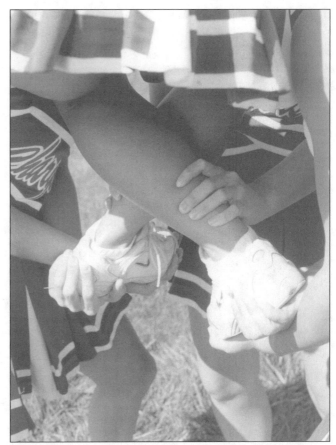

Figure 9.52 *180-Degree Twist-Up (close-up).*

upward with lots of height before attempting to uncross the hands. Without any height, the flyer will not have enough time to complete the twist. At the height of the twist, the bases uncross their hands and lower the flyer into an Elevator.

FLYER starts facing her third. She loads into her bases' hands in a normal Standard Load except that her right foot is crossed over her left. The trick is to land in the bases' hands on the outsides of the feet, not flat-footed. Holding her weight in her arms and keeping her seat up, the flyer pushes off and allows her feet to naturally unwind at the height of the toss, turning her 180 degrees counterclockwise.

FLATBACK LOAD INTO AN ELEVATOR

See figure 9.53 for a photo of the modified Flatback Load into an Elevator.

THIRD holds the flyer in a Flatback position, supporting underneath the flyer's shoulder blades (see figure 9.53). The bases sink deeply and

Figure 9.53 *Flatback Load into an Elevator.*

give a big push upward (not forward) to assist the flyer in standing up. The third stabilizes the flyer in the Elevator by grasping the flyer's thighs as soon as possible after the upward pop.

BASES each support one side of the flyer's seat and use the other hand to hold onto the arch of the flyer's foot (in figure 9.53, the hands are on the flyer's calves—when performing this stunt, bases should put their hands on the arch of the flyer's foot). Giving a deep sink, the bases push the flyer's seat upward and forward while the other hand swings the flyer's foot down into an Elevator position. All bases must sink deeply and push upward with as much power as possible for this stunt to work.

FLYER must stay completely tight during the entire stunt. It is tempting to try to assist the bases by trying to roll upward, but it is impossible to succeed at this load without the flyer remaining tight and still.

EASY FLATBACK LOAD VARIATION FOR AN ELEVATOR

Instead of the flyer keeping her legs straight, the flyer bends at the knees in the Flatback position (see figure 9.54). This makes it easier to pop the flyer up into an Elevator.

360-DEGREE LOAD INTO AN ELEVATOR

In this load, the flyer does a 360-degree rotation clockwise before landing in an Elevator. See figures 9.55 and 9.56 for photos of the load and hands positions of the 360-Degree Load into an Elevator.

THIRD begins as if to execute a Show Extension from a One-Foot Load. The flyer will turn 360 degrees clockwise at the height of the extension. The third assists the rotation by twisting the flyer's ankles clockwise near the height of the stunt. The third must watch the flyer's hips carefully and grab onto the flyer's ankles on the descent to slow her down.

Figure 9.54 *Easy Flatback Load Variation.*

Figure 9.55 *360-Degree Load into an Elevator.*

MAIN BASE (the right base) begins as if to execute a One-Foot Load Show Extension. The back hand is positioned in a normal Prep Grip while the front hand is twisted inward so the fingers are pointing toward her stomach. The main base sinks and drives the flyer upward. Near the height of the extension, the main base untwists the front hand to help initiate the flyer's twist, allowing the flyer's foot to come off of the main base's hands. The main base repositions her hands to allow the flyer's foot to be caught in the Normal Prep Grip while sinking back down into a Standard Load. When timed properly, the flyer should be on the descent after the full 360-degree rotation.

ASSISTING BASE (the left base) executes a One-Foot Load Show Extension, either assisting the flyer's left foot on the ascent in a Prep Grip or holding onto the flyer's supporting (right) foot in a Sandwich Grip. To assist with the rotation, near the height of the stunt the assisting base pushes the flyer's left foot clockwise and together with her right foot. Alternately, the assisting base can hold onto the flyer's foot in a Sandwich Grip and help the main base drive the flyer upward for the

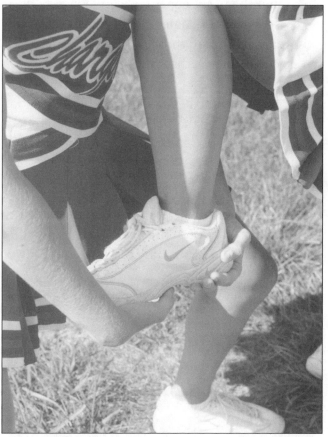

Figure 9.56 *360-Degree Load into an Elevator (close-up).*

360-degree turn. The assisting base must watch the flyer's feet carefully in order to catch the flyer's left foot and bring the flyer down back into the Standard Load.

FLYER begins as though executing a One-Foot Load Show Extension, keeping the majority of her weight on the supporting foot (the one she is going to turn on). Near the height of the Show, she looks over her right shoulder and twists her body to the right. Unlike a Twisting Cradle, the flyer does not look downward over her shoulder, but keeps her head level while looking toward the right. By spotting toward the front (that is, turning her head to look at the front before her body gets there), the flyer is able to stop the rotation at the appropriate time and place her left foot back into the assisting base's hand. The flyer and the main base must coordinate the timing of the twist so that the flyer's upper body and lower body twist at the same time. It is imperative that the flyer pulls upward throughout the entire stunt, especially during the rotation. Her feet should stay relatively close together during the stunt to avoid kicking her bases in the head and to make it easy for the assisting base to catch her foot after the rotation.

FRONT (optional) begins holding onto the flyer's shin. Sinking, the front helps the bases drive the flyer upward for the twist. On the descent, the front grabs onto the flyer's shins, slowing her down and controlling her into the stunt.

There are several ways you can dismount an Elevator:

TO DISMOUNT AN ELEVATOR
★ Walk-Off
★ Assisted Tuck-Off
★ Pop Down
★ Cradle

★ Twist Cradle
★ Trick Cradles (such as Ball-Out or Toe Touch. See the chapter on Basket Toss tricks on page 223 for more information.)

Shoulder Stand

THE FINISHED STUNT
See figure 9.57 for a photo of the Shoulder Stand.

THIRD stands behind the main base and holds onto either the flyer's thighs (if it is possible to reach them) or the flyer's ankles, pulling upward to alleviate some of the weight on the main base's shoulders. (Third is not featured in figure 9.57.)

MAIN BASE is supporting the flyer on the shoulders. Both hands are wrapped around the flyer's calves to stabilize the stunt.

Figure 9.57 *Shoulder Stand.*

FLYER is standing on the main base's shoulders. The flyer helps to stabilize the stunt by turning her feet slightly outward and squeezing inward with her thighs. The flyer remains in a tight, completely locked-out position the entire time.

Note: Although this stunt is shown without additional bases, spotters should *always* be used for this stunt.

GROUND UP LOAD INTO A SHOULDER STAND

See figure 9.58 for a photo of the Ground Up Load into a Shoulder Stand.

MAIN BASE crouches down with the flyer's right foot resting against the main base's right shoulder. It is easiest to crouch down sitting on the right heel, with the left foot flat on the ground. The main base's left and right hands are holding onto the flyer's left and right ankle. On the lift upward, the main base lifts upwards on the flyer's ankles and helps her to stand onto the main base's shoulders. The main base then reaches up to hold onto the back of the flyer's calves and pulls the elbows in for added stability.

ASSISTING BASE stands in front of the flyer, holding the flyer's hands above the assisting base's head. On the upward lift, the assisting base fully extends the arms upward and provides support for the flyer until the flyer is confident enough to let go of the assisting base's hands and stand up straight.

FLYER stands in front of the main base with her right knee bent and her right foot on the main base's right shoulder. Pushing off of the assisting base's hands, the flyer loads up into the Shoulder Stand, releasing the assisting base's hands and standing up when confident.

OPTIONAL SPOT can stand to the right side of the flyer and help push up on the flyer's shin for added assistance in the load.

Figure 9.58 *Ground Up Load into a Shoulder Stand.*

GROUND UP LOAD VARIATION #1 FOR A SHOULDER STAND

ASSISTING BASE stands facing the flyer instead of facing the crowd. The assisting base holds onto the flyer's hands in a Handshake Grip with the right hand crossed over the left. As the flyer stands up into the Shoulder Stand, the assisting base turns 180 degrees to the right and faces the crowd.

GROUND UP LOAD VARIATION #2 FOR A SHOULDER STAND

In this variation, the main base (not the assisting base) is holding onto the flyer's hands and standing in front of the flyer (as shown in figure 9.58). The assisting base crouches behind the flyer and lifts the flyer by her ankles up onto the main base's shoulders as the flyer gives a little jump to initiate the upward momentum. The main base releases the flyer's hands once the flyer is securely standing on the main base's shoulders and is able to stand up straight.

WALK-UP LOAD INTO A SHOULDER STAND

See figure 9.59 for a photo of the Walk-Up Load into a Shoulder Stand.

THIRD stands behind the flyer and helps lift the flyer up into the Shoulder Stand.

MAIN BASE starts in a left lunge, using the right hand to hold onto the flyer's hand and the left hand to stabilize the flyer's left calf. As the flyer steps up and onto the main base's shoulders, the main base stands up and releases the flyer's right hand. The main base then wraps the right hand around the flyer's calf to provide support to the stunt.

FLYER begins with her right foot loaded in the main base's right pocket. Holding the main base's right hand and grasping the third's wrist with her left, the flyer steps up onto the main base's pocket and places her left foot on the main

base's shoulder. The flyer then steps up into the Shoulder Stand by letting go of the main base's hand and placing her right foot on the main base's right shoulder.

As a variation, the base can also hold onto both of the flyer's hands as the flyer climbs up without the assistance of the third.

Offset

In an Offset (see figure 9.60), the flyer positions one foot at the bases' shoulder-level, and the other in an extended position with her knee bent. The trick to a successful Offset is to have the extended base move slightly in front of the flyer, rather than

Figure 9.59 *Walk-Up Load into a Shoulder Stand.*

Figure 9.60 *Offset.*

directly across from the other base. This allows the flyer's knee to be placed in a more natural and comfortable position. Offsets can be loaded with any of the Elevator variations.

Extension

THE FINISHED STUNT

See figure 9.61 for a photo of the Extension.

THIRD is holding tightly onto the flyer's ankles. If the third is unable to reach that high, he or she can hold onto the bases' wrists to provide additional support. The third is looking up at the flyer's head and neck area.

BASES' arms and legs are fully extended and locked out. Shoulders, spine, and pelvis are aligned,

Figure 9.61 *Extension.*

> ### — TIP —
> Flyers should use their leg muscles to pull their feet into a shoulder-width position during Extensions. It is difficult for bases to hold and control an Extension if the flyer's feet are too far apart.

and special attention is paid to keeping the back straight and not arched. All bases are looking up at the flyer's hips.

FLYER is standing tight with her legs no wider than shoulder-width apart. Eyes are focused on a point slightly above eye level.

PRESS-UP EXTENSION LOAD

THIRD loads the flyer into an Elevator. The bases sink together and extend the flyer upward into an Extension. The third holds on tightly to the flyer's ankles and pulls upward to alleviate weight from the bases. If the third is not tall enough to reach the flyer's ankles, she can hold onto the bases' back wrists for support.

BASES load the flyer into an Elevator. The bases sink together and push their arms upward, extending the flyer into an Extension. A common Press-Up mistake is to sink too quickly before extending the flyer upward. The bases must sink for *two counts* and then extend the flyer upward. One count is not enough time for this type of load.

FLYER loads into an Elevator. She stays completely tight and locked out while the bases sink and extend her upward into an Extension. In Extensions, flyers commonly make the mistake of pushing their bases outward because the flyer forgets to pull her legs together on the upward press. The flyer must remember to bring her legs slightly closer than shoulder width apart in an Extension in order for this stunt to stick.

STRAIGHT-UP EXTENSION LOAD

This stunt is just a Press-Up Extension that does not stop at the Elevator level before going up.

THIRD loads the flyer just like an Elevator. Instead of stopping at chest level, the third grabs onto the flyer's ankles as soon as possible and pulls the flyer upward into the extended level.

BASES load and begin the stunt as if to perform a Standard Load to an Elevator. Instead of stopping at chest level, the bases fully extend their arms into an Extension. It is important to extend the arms and the legs *at the same time*. If the bases do not extend simultaneously, they will often get stuck halfway between chest level and the top.

FLYER loads into the Standard Load, pushing extra hard with the arms. The flyer must consciously pull her legs in to shoulder-width or slightly less in order for the Extension to hit. The biggest mistake flyers make in an Extension is to push the bases apart by not controlling the width of their stance.

HOP 'N' GO EXTENSION LOAD

The bases load the flyer up to an Elevator; but instead of stopping at chest level, they sink again at chest level and press the flyer up to an Extension in one continuous motion.

Extensions can also be loaded with other Elevator load variations, such as these:

★ One-Foot Load

★ One-Foot, Two-Foot Load

★ Ground Up Load

★ Shoulder Sit Load

★ Double Back Load

★ Twist-Up Load

★ 360-Degree Load

Single Leg Stunts

Single-leg stunts can be performed either at the shoulder-level (Torch-level) or an extended level (Liberty-level). See figure 9.62 for examples of both levels.

THE FINISHED STUNT

THIRD has a firm grasp on the flyer's ankle. If the third is not tall enough to reach the ankle, he or she can hold onto the base's wrists. If the stunt is at shoulder level, the third can also reach up with one hand and grasp just above the flyer's knee for added support.

MAIN BASE is holding the flyer's foot in a Natural Grip. The flyer's weight is directly overtop of the main base.

Figure 9.62 *Liberty (Liberty-level and Torch-level).*

ASSISTING BASE has a Sandwich Grip on the flyer's foot, back hand underneath the flyer's arch between the hands of the main base, and the front hand on the top of the flyer's foot. The assisting base helps to alleviate the flyer's weight from the main base by pushing up underneath the flyer's arch. In an extended stunt, the assisting base's front hand squeezes the top of the flyer's foot to prevent the flyer's ankle from rolling. In a shoulder-level stunt, the assisting base reaches up and holds onto the flyer's thigh for added stability.

FLYER is standing on one leg with her torso hollowed out. The flyer must stay locked out and tight. An arched back, hips too far forward or backward, or poor posture will cause the stunt to move. Some flyers also find it helpful to keep the toes on their standing foot spread and slightly pulled upward to keep the stunt solid.

OFFSET TO A LIBERTY LOAD

Although this load may appear easier than either of the previous loads, it is actually more difficult because the flyer is fairly unstable while shifting her weight from one side to the other. For this reason, this load is mostly used to introduce the flyer to the feeling of standing on one leg in an extended position and is rarely used in routines.

THIRD is holding onto the flyer's ankles in an Offset. The third sinks with the assisting base and helps to pull the flyer's lower leg up into a Liberty. The third then transfers both hands to the flyer's other ankle as the flyer stands up into the stunt.

MAIN BASE is holding the flyer in an Offset, with arms extended. The main base does not sink with the assisting base, but remains in position as the flyer transfers her weight onto the main base.

FLYER is standing in an Offset. She keeps her standing leg straight as the assisting base sinks. On the upward motion, the flyer transfers her weight onto her other leg and stands up into the stunt.

ONE-FOOT LOAD INTO A SINGLE LEG STUNT

The stunt group executes the load in the same way as loading an Elevator except that the assisting base continues to hold onto the flyer's foot in a Sandwich Grip rather than letting go to grab onto the other foot. This load is commonly used in stunt combinations because of its versatility in transitioning to and from other stunts.

GROUND UP LOAD INTO A SINGLE LEG STUNT

The group begins this load crouching on the ground and holding the flyer's foot in a Sandwich Grip.

THIRD begins crouching to the right side of the flyer, left hand under the flyer's tailbone and right hand firmly grasping the flyer's right ankle. The third sinks with the flyer and the bases. On the lift upward, the third pushes up underneath the flyer's seat, which helps to place the flyer's center of gravity overtop of the bases. The third must push a little faster than the bases in order for the flyer to be able to stand up. If the flyer stands up and the third cannot reach any higher under the flyer's seat, the third places her left hand around the flyer's ankle and, with both hands, pulls upward to finish the stunt.

MAIN BASE begins by crouching down, facing the assisting base. The main base's hands are held close against the chest in a Natural Grip. (It helps to rest the elbows on the thighs for added support.) The flyer starts with her foot in the main base's hands. The main base sinks with the flyer and third. On the lift upward, the main base stands up. For an extended stunt, the main base will lock out the knees and the arms at the same time.

ASSISTING BASE sits on the back heel in a crouch across from the main base. The assisting base holds onto the flyer's foot in a Sandwich Grip. The group sinks together. On the lift upward, the assisting base helps the stunt by pushing up underneath the flyer's arch with the right arm. The assisting base must stay as close as possible to the main base in order for the stunt to stick. The assisting base's left hand squeezes the flyer's instep (top of the foot), or in a shoulder-level stunt holds onto the flyer's thigh for added stability.

FLYER begins by placing her right foot into the hands of the main base. Standing on her left leg, the flyer should be on the ball of her left foot. Her hands are placed either on the bases' shoulders or on the top of the bases' heads. The flyer's center of gravity should be positioned overtop of the main base. The flyer should make sure that her right knee stays directly over her right ankle, with the majority of the flyer's weight on the right leg. The flyer sinks with the bases. On the lift upward, the flyer pushes off from the bases' shoulders (or heads), while simultaneously standing up on the right leg. The flyer should keep her chest up but not arch her back, or the stunt will travel forward. Close to the height of the stunt, the flyer pulls up her left knee to waist level. The flyer's leg should be at a 90-degree angle from her hip. The flyer must remember to pull up throughout the entire stunt.

SPOT stands in front of the stunt with the right hand underneath the flyer's right thigh and the left hand holding onto the flyer's right ankle. On the upward motion the spot lifts up under the flyer's thigh until the flyer stands up. The spot then helps to bring the stunt into position by pulling upward on the flyer's ankle with both hands. When learning this stunt,

spotters should stand in each of the back corners where flyers tend to fall.

SHOULDER SIT TO A LIBERTY LOAD

This load is executed in a similar manner as a Shoulder Sit to Elevator or Extension. Either the base underneath the Shoulder Sit can become the assisting base to the right base or the base underneath the Shoulder Sit can become the main base and hold the stunt in a co-ed Liberty Grip.

FLATBACK LOAD TO A LIBERTY

THIRD loads the flyer into a Flatback, executing the stunt the same manner as loading up into an Elevator but using more power on the upward pop. The third must sink deeply with the legs, keeping the arms locked out if executing the stunt from an extended position. On the upward toss the third must push hard underneath the flyer for the flyer's center of gravity to get overtop her bases. It is also important for the third to grab onto the flyer's ankle and pull upward as soon as possible.

MAIN BASE loads the flyer into a Flatback and holds the flyer's right foot in a Natural Grip. The main base sinks with the other bases. As the flyer is tossed upward and approaches the vertical position, the main base waits a split second before extending the flyer upward into a Liberty. This is similar to the timing of a Ground Up Liberty where the pause allows the flyer's center of gravity to come directly overtop of the main base before the main base extends. In a continuous motion after the pop, the main base presses the flyer up into a Liberty position.

ASSISTING BASE loads the flyer into a Flatback, sinks, then tosses the flyer upward into the stunt. The assisting base transfers the hands to the Sandwich Grip as soon as the flyer is popped upward to help the main base hold the stunt.

FLYER stays tight throughout the entire stunt. It is especially important that the flyer stay locked out near the height of the stunt because this is when it is most difficult for the bases to hit the stunt. A variation of this stunt is to have the flyer pop up into a Heel Stretch from the Flatback load rather than just the Liberty.

Single Leg Variations

The degree of difficulty of a single leg stunt can be increased by varying the position of the flyer's free leg. Variations also add visual appeal to a routine or stunting segment.

HEEL STRETCH

See figure 9.63 for a photo of the Heel Stretch.

FLYER is holding onto her extended left foot with her left arm. The flyer should be grasping the arch of her foot from behind. It is important that the flyer keeps her leg in front of her. Holding it to the side is difficult because the flyer's center of gravity tends to shift in this position. Most flyers tend to fall over when their hips open up like this. In terms of flexibility, it is also more difficult to hold the leg out to the side. When holding the Heel Stretch, the flyer should hollow out and hit a High V with her right arm.

ARABESQUE

See figure 9.64 for photos of the Arabesque.

FLYER leans forward while extending her left leg out behind her. Her chest, shoulders, and head must remain up. The lower back and gluteus muscles are used to keep her leg in the air. There should be a slight arch in the flyer's back and her front hip should be closed, not open (facing forward, not to the side). The Arabesque is usually performed to the side.

SCORPION

See figure 9.65 for photos of the Scorpion.

FLYER must have fairly good flexibility in her back and legs to perform a Scorpion. The flyer

Figure 9.63 *Heel Stretch.*

Figure 9.64 *Arabesque (Liberty-level and Torch-level).*

Figure 9.65 *Scorpion (Liberty-level and Torch-level).*

Figure 9.66 *Scale (Liberty-level and Torch-level).*

holds onto either her ankle or the toe of her front foot and pulls it up toward her head. A Scorpion must be performed with the chest and shoulders up.

SCALE

See figure 9.66 for photos of the Scale.

FLYER extends her free leg backward, similar to an Arabesque. The difference between an Arabesque and a Scale is that the hip is open (turned toward the side), which allows for greater height of the lifted leg. The flyer's front arm holds onto the front shin or knee from behind, with the remaining arm in a High V. This is another variation that is usually performed to the side to show off the flyer's position.

X-SCALE

See figure 9.67 for photos of the X-Scale.

FLYER brings her leg up into a Heel Stretch. Instead of holding it with the same side arm as in a Heel Stretch, she holds onto her X-Scale

Figure 9.67 *X-Scale (Liberty-level and Torch-level).*

with her opposite arm. This variation is also done toward the side.

BOW AND ARROW

FLYER pulls her leg up as if to perform a Heel Stretch. The leg is pulled up toward the front like in a Heel Stretch; but in a Bow and Arrow, the leg is pulled up to the side and held with the opposite arm. The other arm is in a "T" in front of the lifted leg. The flyer must have excellent flexibility to perform this variation. (See page 209 for an example.)

In all Torches and Liberties, the flyer must keep the supporting leg completely straight and locked out.

CORKSCREW

This stunt incorporates an advanced load to a Liberty and both Arabesque and Heel Stretch variations for the flyer. The Corkscrew is just a One-Foot Ground Up Load (as if loading to an Elevator) that rotates 360 degrees clockwise. This is a difficult load because the bases must have complete control over the stunt the entire time, and the flyer must have strong hip flexors to hit her stunts; but this stunt is definitely a crowd stopper.

SPOT crouches in front of the stunt with the flyer's left leg resting on the spot's right shoulder. The spot's hands are positioned around the flyer's ankle or left hand on the ankle, right hand under the calf of the flyer's left leg. As the flyer is lifted upward, the spot pulls upward on the flyer's ankle to alleviate some of the weight from the bases. The spot then follows the bases around 360 degrees clockwise until the spot is no longer needed to complete the stunt.

THIRD crouches with either both hands on the flyer's ankle, or right hand on the flyer's ankle and left hand on the flyer's thigh. The third sinks with the flyer and bases. The third stands on the upward lift, pulling up on the flyer's ankle, and rotates clockwise 360 degrees—until the flyer is in the Heel Stretch position.

MAIN BASE (the right base) begins facing the assisting base in a crouch with the seat resting on the right heel. The main base's left foot is flat on the ground, with the flyer's right foot resting on top in the same position as if to execute a Ground Up Load to an Elevator. The main base's hands are around the flyer's heel and the flyer's toe in a Prep Grip. The main base sinks with the flyer and other bases. On the lift upward, the main base slowly turns 360 degrees, staying close to the assisting base. The upward momentum must remain consistent as the bases press the flyer up into the Heel Stretch.

ASSISTING BASE (the left base) begins in a crouch, facing the main base. The assisting base's right hand is on the instep (top) of the flyer's foot and the left hand is either underneath the flyer's foot or waits until the initial lift to place the hand under the flyer's arch (the latter is easier). Sinking simultaneously with the other bases and flyer, the assisting base remains as close as possible to the main base throughout the entire rotating lift.

FLYER begins standing on her right leg on the main base's foot, with her left leg straight out in front of her and resting on the spot's shoulder. She sinks with her bases and gives a little jump to initiate the momentum, just like the Ground Up Load to an Elevator. As the bases lift up the flyer and begin to turn clockwise, the flyer rotates the left leg's position from straight out in front to an Arabesque. Her body rotates but her left leg stays toward the front until her body is facing the back. At this point she is in an Arabesque. Her arms are out in a T until the full 360 degrees is completed and she is facing the front when she then snaps the Arabesque into a Heel Stretch.

This stunt must be done slowly and with a great deal of control and strength. When done correctly, this stunt looks phenomenal!

TROUBLESHOOTING SINGLE LEG STUNTS

You will encounter some repeated obstacles when trying to master your leg stunts. Following are some of the common ones and some reasons why they might be happening.

Problem #1

The bases stand up in a One-Foot or Ground Up Load but the flyer cannot seem to get overtop of them. There are a number of possible reasons why the flyer's center of gravity is not aligned with her bases:

★ The third may not be giving a hard enough push upward.

★ The flyer's weight may not be over her bent leg. This can be fixed by making sure she is leaning over her bent leg with her knee overtop of or slightly in front of her toes.

★ The flyer may be standing up too late.

★ The bases may be standing up too quickly. Bases should wait one split second after the initial up before standing up to allow the weight of the flyer to transfer directly over top of them.

Problem #2

The flyer gets near the height of the stunt without a problem, but then falls when she reaches it. Some reasons why:

★ The bases could be giving the load too much power. Bases should continue using power and control throughout the stunt but avoid jolting the flyer at the top of the stunt or she will lose her balance and come down.

★ The flyer may not be fully locking out her standing knee. She should straighten her leg in the stunt as soon as possible.

★ The flyer's hip may not be high enough when hitting a Liberty. This problem can be easily fixed by instructing her to pull her knee up as high as possible. She should be consciously lifting her hip up rather than letting it drop.

★ The flyer may not be pulling up in the stunt. If her back is arched, the stunt will likely travel forward. If her shoulders are rounded forward too much, the stunt will likely fall backward. The best way to describe the flyer's proper position is for her to envision that she has just been punched in the stomach; her abs (abdominal muscles) should be pulled in, hips tucked under, and shoulders pulled upward.

Cupie/Awesome

THE FINISHED STUNT

See figure 9.68 for a photo of the Awesome.

THIRD is holding onto either the flyer's ankles (if the third is tall enough), or onto the base's wrists if the third is not able to reach.

MAIN BASE is holding both of the flyer's feet on the extended right hand, fingers spread wide. Left hand is on the hip, in a half–High V or in another motion.

ASSISTING BASE is to the right of the main base, holding the flyer's right toe and heel in both hands in an extended position. The assisting base is responsible for holding the majority of the flyer's weight.

FLYER is in an extended position, squeezing both feet together. In the all-girl version of this stunt, the flyer's weight is generally concentrated on the right foot rather than on both feet evenly so the right base can support most of her weight in a Natural Grip. If this is the case, the flyer should slightly lift up the left hip to help place the majority of her weight on her right foot.

Figure 9.68 *Awesome.*

The difference between a Cupie and an Awesome is in the arm positioning. If the free arm is on the hip, the stunt is called a Cupie; if the free arm is in a half–High V, the stunt is called an Awesome.

GROUND UP LOAD INTO A CUPIE/AWESOME

This load is executed in the same manner as a Ground Up Liberty only the flyer pulls her feet together rather than standing on one leg.

ONE-FOOT ELEVATOR LOAD INTO A CUPIE/AWESOME

The flyer extends straight upward from this load into the stunt by pulling her feet together. The majority of her weight is on the leg that was loaded into the main base.

WALK-IN ONE-FOOT LOAD INTO A CUPIE/AWESOME

This variation is loaded as above except that the flyer takes two steps forward before placing her foot into the main base's hands. The base group sinks as the flyer puts her foot into the main base's hands and extends upward into the stunt. This load can also be done where the base group begins facing the side and turns 90 degrees to the front on the extension.

DOUBLE BACK LOAD INTO A CUPIE/AWESOME

The Cupie/Awesome is loaded in the same way as a Double Back Load to Extension, except the flyer pulls both feet in and keeps the majority of her weight on the assisting base. The third holds most of the weight during the time it takes for the bases to pop up from a crouch to an extended level. A front/spot can be used to help the third pull upward on the flyer's ankles.

Thigh Pop

THIRD loads the flyer into the bases' hands. Instead of stopping at the mid- or extended level, the third continues tossing the flyer upward as high as possible. The flyer is caught in a Cradle.

BASES set in a Standard Load. After the sink, the bases explode upward and throw the flyer upward. The flyer is caught in a Cradle.

FLYER jumps into a Standard Load. She extends upward, pushing off of the bases' shoulders and fully extending the elbows and legs at the same time. The flyer lands in a Cradle.

SPOT helps to increase the height of a Thigh Pop by standing in front of the stunt, holding onto the flyer's ankles and tossing upward with the other bases.

This stunt is performed in one continuous motion from the time the flyer loads into the Standard Load to the time she is caught in the Cradle.

— TIP —

The flyer can land either in a Cradle or in a Standard Load from a Thigh Pop. If she chooses to land in a Standard Load, she should keep her legs relatively close together and her chest pulled up throughout the duration of the stunt.

THIGH POP 180-DEGREE TWIST TO A STANDARD LOAD

Before attempting a 180-degree twist, the base group should be proficient at Thigh Popping the flyer up and catching her in a Standard Load. The Thigh Pop 180-Degree Twist is executed in the same way as a straight Thigh Pop. At the height of the pop, the flyer looks over her shoulder and twists her shoulders and hips simultaneously 180 degrees. She should now face the opposite direction from where she started and land in a Standard Load. The flyer can also land in a Cradle, provided she has enough height to lay out *after* the twist.

THIGH POP 360-DEGREE TWIST

Before attempting the Thigh Pop 360-Degree Twist, the base group should be capable of performing the Thigh Pop 180-Degree Twist. The 360-Degree Twist is executed in the same manner as the 180-Degree Twist, only the flyer completes a full vertical rotation. The flyer must have lots of height from the bases and must twist quickly enough to complete the full turn. The bases can assist the flyer with the rotation by twisting her feet clockwise at the very height of the pop. A front spot holding onto the flyer's shins can be beneficial in adding height to the toss.

Pop Over

This stunt is also referred to as a Leap Frog.

See figures 9.69 through 9.71 for photos of the entire Pop Over stunt.

Figure 9.69 *Prep for Pop Over.*

Figure 9.70 *Pop Over.*

EXTRA BASES stand in front of the main base group in a Standard Load position, ready to catch the feet of the flyer.

FRONT SPOT stands in front of the main base group and holds onto the flyer's hands with extended, straight arms. The front spot must

Figure 9.71 *Pop Over Landing.*

hold the arms close to the ears to ensure that the flyer has enough height to pop over. The wider the spotter's arms are, the closer the flyer's feet will be to the front spot's head and the less room the flyer will have to pop through. When the bases pop the flyer over, the front spot keeps the arms locked out to support the flyer's weight. The front spot keeps the arms tight, letting go to grab the flyer's waist as the flyer approaches the front bases' hands.

MAIN BASES can either pop the flyer over the front spot from an Elevator or from a Standard Load. If they pop her from a Standard Load, they must pop her high enough to clear the front spot's head.

FLYER holds onto the front spot's hands. When she is popped upward, she brings her knees up to her chest. Keeping her arms straight, she pops over the front spot's head. The flyer lets go of the front spot's hands just as she lands in the Standard Load so that she is able to put her hands on the extra bases' shoulders. The flyer must remember to keep her chest and

seat up in the Chicken position. If the flyer allows her chest to drop or her seat to sink below her knees, her center of gravity will not be over the extra bases and she will likely fall to the ground seat first.

Flip Over

See figures 9.72 through 9.74 for photos of the entire Flip Over stunt.

EXTRA BASES stand in front of the main base group and are ready to catch the flyer in a Cradle. The extra bases must stand far enough away from the main base group so that when the flyer lands, her hips are caught in the correct Cradle position. If the extra bases stand too close, they will end up catching the flyer's shoulders and back while her feet and legs crash into the ground.

THIRD tosses the flyer's legs straight upward. The third must toss high enough that the flyer's hips get overtop of her shoulders.

MAIN BASE tosses the flyer's legs upward as if tossing a Cradle.

ASSISTING BASE stands in front of the main base and holds onto the flyer's hands with extended arms. The assisting base must keep her arms straight and continue to hold onto the flyer's hands while she flies overtop and into the Cradle.

FLYER is tossed upward. Instead of tucking, the flyer keeps her legs straight as she is tossed over the bases. Ideally the flyer should hit a Handstand position (shoulders, hips, ankles aligned) in the air and keep her body tight

---

– TIP –

The assisting base is considered the post when the main base tosses the flyer.

Figure 9.72 *Prep for Flip Over.*

Figure 9.73 *Flip Over.*

Figure 9.74 *Flip Over Landing.*

and locked out until landing in the Cradle. The flyer holds onto her assisting base's hands until just before landing in the Cradle when she then catches herself around the extra bases' shoulders. The flyer should keep her arms straight until she catches herself in the Cradle.

This stunt can also be done from a Walk Down position (as if the group was going to execute an Assisted Front Tuck dismount) rather than using the assisting base as the post. Instead of tossing the flyer up and catching her in a vertical position as in the Assisted Front Tuck dismount, bases sink and toss the flyer over into the Cradle of the waiting base group. Alternatively, another spot can act as the post by standing in front of the bases and holding onto the flyer's hands. In this case, the flyer will be tossed over the spot's head by both bases.

Do you think you have it? Let's move on to some more. . . .

Chapter Ten

Multiple-Base Transition Stunts

Transitioning from one stunt to another is important for creating a flow between stunts. Rather than loading a stunt, hitting it, and completely dismounting it, transition stunts serve to link stunts together and add visual appeal.

— Link Stunts —

The Regrab and the Sponge are frequently used to link together a sequence of stunts.

Regrab

A Regrab (also called a Reload or a Retake) is the easiest way to get from a Cradle position back into the Standard Load position or the One-Foot Load and ready to do another stunt.

REGRAB TO STANDARD LOAD

THIRD catches the flyer in a Cradle (see figures 10.2 and 10.3). Absorbing the flyer on the catch, the third immediately tosses the flyer's upper body upward and slightly forward back into the load (see figure 10.4). It is important that the third toss high enough to allow for the flyer's center of gravity to be placed directly over the bases' hands in the load. After the toss upward, the third grabs onto the

flyer's waist and is ready to execute another stunt (see figure 10.5).

BASES catch the flyer in a Cradle (see figures 10.2 and 10.3). Absorbing the flyer on the catch, the bases toss the flyer upward (see figure 10.4). Their hands grab onto the flyer's feet as she rotates into the load (see figure 10.5). The bases' feet stay in one place throughout the Regrab.

FLYER is tossed upward (see figure 10.1) and caught in a Cradle (see figures 10.2 and 10.3). After the catch, she quickly moves her hands to the bases' shoulders closest to her. (In a regular Cradle catch, the flyer wraps her arms around the bases' front shoulders.) On the upward toss from a Cradle, the flyer pushes up and off from the bases' shoulders and rotates her body upright (see figure 10.4). The flyer tucks her feet in underneath her and places them in the hands of the bases. The flyer is then in a load ready to execute another stunt (see figure 10.5).

REGRAB TO ONE-FOOT LOAD

The bases execute the Regrab in the same manner as in the previous stunt, only changing grips from

Figure 10.1 *Twist.*

Figure 10.2 *Cradle.*

Figure 10.3 *Catch.*

Figure 10.4 *Regrab.*

the Prep Grip into the Sandwich Grip. The flyer completes the Regrab by placing one foot into the main base's hands and the other on the ground, ready to load into the next stunt.

The Regrab is an effective stunt for transitioning partner stunts and pyramids. Some ideas include:

1. Elevator + Regrab to Standard Load/One-Foot Load + Elevator

2. Elevator + Regrab to Standard Load/One-Foot Load + Extension

3. Elevator + Regrab to One-Foot Elevator Load + Torch

Figure 10.5 *Standard Prep Position (coming down from Sponge).*

Figure 10.6 *Standard Prep Position (after a Regrab).*

Figure 10.7 *Sponge.*

Figure 10.8 *Standard Prep Position (coming down from Sponge).*

4. Elevator + Regrab to One-Foot Elevator Load + Liberty/Heel Stretch/Cupie or Awesome

Sponge

In addition to the Regrab, the Sponge is another useful transition stunt for partner stunts and pyramids. Think of the Sponge as the reverse of a Load:

In a Sponge, the flyer is brought slowly downward from a stunt into a load.

THIRD begins holding the flyer in a stunt (see figure 10.6). Instead of a big sink used for the preparation for a toss, the bases only give a little dip with their knees to initiate the momentum for the Sponge. The reason for the small dip is to help the bases work together on the same rhythm and to gain a little momentum for the downward motion. The bases follow the flyer on the upward pop and then control her down slowly into a Standard Load (see figure 10.7). From the Standard Load, the bases can then immediately move into another stunt. On the way down, the third places her hands underneath the seat of the flyer to slow her down and to control the momentum.

BASES begin by holding the flyer in a stunt (see figure 10.6). They dip with their knees. When the bases straighten their legs, they simultaneously shrug their shoulders to give the flyer a small, controlled pop upward. The bases change hand positions from a Natural Grip to a Prep Grip during the pop when there is no weight on their hands. This step is important because a Sponge cannot be done effectively if the bases' hands continue to hold the flyer's feet in a Natural Grip. The bases slowly lower the flyer down into a Standard Load by bending their arms and legs at the same time. It is necessary that the bases remember to keep their arms tucked into their sides and to allow them to come down to no more than a 90-degree angle. The bases keep their feet still during the entire stunt. Once in the Standard Load, the bases can continue onto the next stunt in one continuous motion (see figure 10.8).

FLYER begins in a stunt. Keeping her legs straight while the bases sink, the flyer snaps her arms into the Clean position on the slight pop upward. The flyer pulls up with her chest the entire time from the pop until she is in the Standard Load. Pulling up on the downward motion keeps the flyer from falling backward. If the flyer's back becomes rounded, her shoulders fall forward, or her knees bend too soon,

she will descend too quickly and will not be able to get into the Standard Load. (See figure 10.8.)

SPONGE FROM AN EXTENDED STUNT TO SHOULDER LEVEL

This type of Sponge is used to transfer from a one-leg extended stunt (such as a Liberty) into another one-leg extended stunt without coming all the way back down to the ground.

Keeping their arms straight, the bases use their legs to pop the flyer gently upward to initiate the Sponge. Instead of returning down to the original load, the bases bring the flyer's foot to shoulder level and then push the flyer back up to the extended level. Bases must be sure to use their legs, rather than their arms, as the main source of power. Unlike the other Sponges, the bases do not change grips from the extended level to the shoulder level. A variation of this stunt is to make a quarter-turn to face the side on the downward motion of the Sponge and then bring the flyer back up to face the side.

As demonstrated in figures 10.9 through 10.11, a possible Sponge to Mid-Level combination is:

Liberty (see figure 10.9) + Sponge (see figure 10.10) to Mid-Level (quarter turn to the side on the way down) + Arabesque (see figure 10.11)

SPONGE SPLIT

This stunt is explained with the flyer coming down into the right split (right leg forward). The right and left bases would perform opposite roles if she were to sponge to the left.

— TIP —

The flyer pulls her left leg up into the Arabesque (or any other Liberty variation) on the upward motion of the Mid-Level sink.

Figure 10.9 *Liberty.*

Figure 10.10 *Sponge.*

Figure 10.11 *Arabesque.*

THIRD initiates the Sponge as if bringing the flyer back down into the Standard Load. As the flyer descends into a split, the third reaches up under the flyer's thighs and helps to slow her down. The third must remember to sink with the legs. To help the flyer back up into another stunt from the split, the third pushes upward underneath the flyer's thighs and grabs onto the flyer's ankles to stabilize the stunt.

RIGHT BASE begins the Sponge as if to bring the flyer back down into the Standard Load. On the descent, the right base continues to hold onto the flyer's right toe with the right hand and places the left hand underneath the flyer's right thigh to control the flyer down into the splits at shoulder level. The main base is facing the front.

LEFT BASE begins the Sponge as if to bring the flyer back down into the Standard Load. On the descent, the left base turns to the left so that her back is now facing the crowd. The left base continues to hold onto the flyer's left heel with the right hand and places the left hand underneath the flyer's thigh to control the flyer down into the splits at shoulder level. On the upward motion, the left base pushes up on the flyer's front thigh while at the same time pushing the flyer's heel inward and turning to face the front in the new stunt.

FLYER stays tight while the bases gently pop her up to initiate the Sponge. On the descent, she turns to the right into a split position. The flyer can either place her hands on both of the front spot's shoulders or one hand on the third's right shoulder and the other on the front spot's left shoulder for support when coming down into the split. The flyer can also try reaching for the front spot's hands for support on the way down. In this case, the flyer would keep her elbows straight and allow the front spot to absorb the weight. On the upward pop, the flyer pushes off of the spot's shoulders; or if she's holding onto the front spot's hands, she keeps her arms straight and squeezes her legs together into the next stunt. The flyer must also turn her hips to face the front on the upward pop. It is important for the flyer to keep her chest up and her legs straight throughout the stunt.

FRONT SPOT either reaches under the flyer's thighs to help slow her down as she descends, or reaches for the flyer's hands. The front spot then pushes the flyer back upward and helps secure the stunt by holding onto the front of the flyer's shins.

SPONGE SPLIT COMBINATIONS

1. Elevator + Sponge Split + Elevator
2. Elevator + Sponge Split + Extension
3. Elevator + Right Sponge Split + Show Elevator/Extension + Left Sponge Split + Elevator (The motion is continuous between the Right Sponge Split + Show Elevator +

Left Sponge Split and stops only at the final Elevator.)

SPONGE STRADDLE SIT

THIRD executes the Sponge Straddle Sit in the same manner as a Sponge Split, only reaching under the flyer's seat instead of thighs.

BASES pop the flyer up to initiate the Sponge. The bases continue to hold onto the flyer's feet with their front hands. As the flyer comes down, the bases reach up underneath the flyer's seat with their back hands to absorb her weight in the Straddle Sit. Sinking, the bases pop the flyer back up into the next stunt by pushing upward under her seat and bringing her feet back together.

FLYER stays tight until the descent when she sits into a Straddle. If there is a spot for this stunt, the flyer reaches for either the front spot's shoulders or hands for support. On the upward motion, she pushes off from the front spot's shoulders or hands and brings her legs back together into the next stunt. The flyer's legs stay straight throughout the entire stunt.

FRONT SPOT can either reach up for the flyer's hands to help slow her down as she comes into a Straddle, or reach under the flyer's thighs to control her down as the flyer holds onto the front spot's shoulders for support. The front spot then sinks with the other bases and helps to pop the flyer back up into position.

SPONGE STRADDLE SIT COMBINATIONS

1. Elevator + Sponge Straddle Sit + Chair
2. Elevator + Sponge Straddle Sit + Elevator
3. Extension + Sponge Straddle Sit + Elevator
4. Extension + Sponge Straddle Sit + Extension

— Show Stunts —

Show stunts involve momentarily hitting a stunt (for example: a kick, Extension, or Liberty/Liberty variation) and immediately bringing it back down into the load. A Show combination generally involves the showing of a stunt, coming back down to a load, and then coming back up to hit a different stunt. Just like Sponges, the flyer must remember to pull up during the entire stunt, especially during the downward motion. There are an infinite number of creative possibilities with Show stunts. Here are some common combinations:

Show Extension

THIRD begins the stunt as if to hit an Extension; but instead of locking out at the top of the stunt, the third controls the flyer immediately back down into the load position. On the way down, the third spreads the fingers apart and places the hands on the flyer's seat in a Butterfly position (fingers spread apart, hands close together to resemble a butterfly). The third helps to slowly lower the flyer back into the Standard Load or the One-Foot Load position and then uses the arms and legs to push the flyer back up into another stunt.

BASES begin the stunt as if to hit an Extension. Instead of locking out their arms at the height of the stunt, they hit the stunt momentarily and begin to slowly lower the flyer back down into the load position. The bases must have good control of the stunt, making sure that the flyer is brought down relatively slowly. If the flyer is brought down too quickly, her seat will end up below her knees and she will fall backward out of the stunt.

FLYER executes an Extension, hitting the top only momentarily. She then begins descending back into the load. She must pull up the entire stunt, especially when being lowered down. If the flyer does not pull up, she will come down into the load too quickly before the bases are ready. The flyer must remember to prolong the tight and upright position, bending her knees and arms into the load at

the last second and keeping her chest up the entire time.

SHOW EXTENSION TO ANOTHER BASE GROUP

See figure 10.12 for a photo of the Show Extension to another base group.

ADDITIONAL BASE GROUP stands behind the main base group, prepared to catch the flyer in a Cradle.

THIRD loads the flyer into a Show Extension. As the flyer nears the height of the stunt, the third can either move out of the way, letting the other third catch the Cradle, or move backward and catch the Cradle herself.

BASES load the flyer into a Show Extension. The bases show the Extension and keeping their arms straight, follow the flyer into the waiting Cradle. The bases must hold onto the flyer's feet until she lands in the other base group.

FLYER pushes off from her bases and rides the Show Extension with her hands above her

Figure 10.12 *Show Extension to another base group.*

head. At the height of the stunt, the flyer snaps her hands to her sides and lays out, falling backward into the waiting Cradle.

After perfecting the Show Extension to another base group, for a variation the flyer can also twist down into the waiting base group from the Show Extension (see figure 10.13).

Show Liberty

THIRD executes a Liberty (either from a Ground Up Load or a One-Foot Load), allowing the flyer to momentarily hit the Liberty before beginning the descent back down to the original load. The third must remember to slow the flyer down on the descent by pushing upward on the flyer's seat with an extended hand, continuing to hold onto the flyer's ankle with the other. In a Show Liberty, it is easiest for the third to lock out both the extended arm and torso, bending at the legs rather than the elbow.

BASES execute a Show Liberty and are careful not to jolt the flyer at the height of the stunt. The

Figure 10.13 *Twist Down.*

bases slowly lower the flyer back down into the original load in preparation for another stunt.

FLYER executes a Liberty. On the descent, she must remember to pull upward and keep her chest high. Her hands reach down for either the shoulders or the top of the heads of the bases for support. The flyer brings the Liberty leg down beside the supporting leg and remains in an upright, straight position until the last second before bending her supporting leg into the load. The flyer must keep the Liberty leg as close to the supporting leg as possible. If the flyer steps back too far when touching the ground, her center of gravity will shift away from the bases instead of remaining overtop of them. This makes it very difficult to execute another stunt because her base group has to work hard to bring her weight back over the top of the bases.

Show Kick

FLYER stunts the same as in a Show Liberty (see figures 10.14 and 10.15 for the prep and lift), only kicking the Liberty leg straight into a split at the height of the stunt (see figure 10.16). The flyer's hands reach for the kicking foot in Blades. The flyer must remember to kick only as her feet clear the bases. Otherwise, her bases will be the recipients of a swift kick to the head.

Figure 10.14 *Ground Up Prep for Show Kick.*

Figure 10.15 *Lift for Show Kick.*

Figure 10.16 *Show Kick.*

SHOW KICK TO CRADLE
(TO ANOTHER BASE GROUP)

FLYER Show Kicks. Instead of coming down vertically into the load, she drops her leg and falls
into the base group behind her by arching her
back and landing in a Cradle. The bases holding onto the flyer's supporting foot must main-

tain contact with the flyer until she is safely
caught by the other base group.

SHOW KICK SPLIT TO CRADLE
(TO ANOTHER BASE GROUP)

FLYER Show Kicks to Cradle the same way as in
the previous stunt, only she holds onto her leg
while she is falling into the cradle instead of
dropping it cradling down. On a second
bounce in the Cradle catch, she snaps her feet
together in a normal Cradle.

SHOW KICK TO CRADLE
(TO YOUR OWN BASE GROUP)

FLYER executes the Show Kick. On the way down,
the flyer arches and cradles into her own base
group. In order for this stunt to work, the flyer
cannot lean backward like she does in the
Show Kick to Cradle to another base group,
but she must drop her seat directly below her
after the arch into her own base group. The
flyer must also bend her supporting knee as
she comes down into a Cradle rather than

keeping both legs straight. The main base's front hand maintains contact with the flyer's supporting foot during the entire stunt, including when catching the Cradle. This puts the main base in a good position to Regrab the flyer into a One-Foot Load, ready to execute another stunt.

Show 360-Degree to a Standard or One-Foot Load

This stunt is loaded in the same manner as the 360-Degree Load except the flyer comes back down into a Standard Load before hitting another stunt. The third can slow the flyer down by placing his or her extended arms on the flyer's seat in a Butterfly position. During the rotation, the flyer must keep her body aligned and her feet relatively close together. This will help her avoid kicking her bases in the head and will make it easy for the assisting base to catch her other foot.

Show Basket

The stunt is loaded as a normal Basket Toss (see figures 10.17 and 10.18 for load and prep). Instead of tossing the flyer on the upward motion, the flyer is *lifted* into the extended level and left standing on the Basket Grip (see figure 10.19). The

Figure 10.18 *Toss Load for Show Basket.*

Figure 10.19 *Show Basket.*

Figure 10.17 *Prep for Show Basket.*

bases hold this position, then give a slight sink, followed by a small pop upward and slowly lower the flyer back into the load. Using this downward motion as the sink, the bases can then toss the flyer on the upward motion for the Basket Toss. Bases should remember to stand relatively close to one another during this stunt.

360-Degree Log Roll

THIRD begins by holding the flyer in a Cradle position. It is easiest to toss the flyer upward when the third's hands are underneath the flyer's shoulder blades. It can also be done with the third's arms under the flyer's armpits, but the toss tends to be lower. The bases sink together and toss the flyer upward, catching her in a Cradle once she has completed the rotation.

RIGHT BASE sinks with the other bases and tosses the flyer upward from a Cradle position. While tossing the flyer, the right base pulls the arms sharply inward to initiate the flyer's clockwise rotation. The flyer is caught in a Cradle position.

LEFT BASE sinks with the other bases and tosses the flyer upward from a Cradle position. While tossing the flyer, the left base pushes the arms and shoulders quickly toward the right base to initiate the rotation. The flyer rotates toward the left base and away from the right base. The flyer is caught in a Cradle position.

FLYER begins in a Cradle position with her hands on the bases' back shoulders. She pushes upward as she is tossed and hits a Flatback position. At the height of the toss, the flyer drops her left shoulder to help the 360-degree turn. The flyer is caught in a Cradle position.

SPOT plays an important role in the rotation of the flyer. Holding the flyer's feet and facing the third, the spot places the right hand overtop the flyer's feet and onto the side of the flyer's right foot. The spot's left hand is underneath and holding onto the side of the flyer's left foot. The spot tosses the flyer upward, and at the height of the toss gives the flyer's feet a sharp twist to the right to initiate the rotation. The spot must remember to toss the flyer upward before twisting her feet. If her feet are twisted too early, she will not be high enough to complete the rotation.

— Rotating and Moving Stunts —

Rotating and moving stunts are a great way to transition from one stunt to another. Here are some examples to get your own imagination going.

Example #1: From an Elevator, a group sponges down to a Standard Load, travels to a new position, and then pops back up into another stunt, such as an Extension.

Example #2: With the base group facing sideways, the flyer walks into a One-Foot Load Extension, pulling her feet together so it appears that she is hitting a Cupie. As she's ascending, the group turns to face the front as the main base holds onto the flyer's feet with one hand and hits a motion with the other (hand on hip, arm in High V, arm in muscles, and so on).

Example #3: Facing the front, the group executes a Show Kick. They touch down, do a quarter turn to the side (using a double bounce on the ground if necessary; once for the initial touch down, once to the side) and come back up into an Arabesque. The group then rotates 180 degrees while the flyer is in an Arabesque, and the flyer dismounts in a twist.

You can find more Intermediate, Advanced, and Elite stunting combinations to try at the end of this section that incorporate the multiple-base stunts you've learned in previous sections.

While the majority of multiple-base stunts are performed by all-girl teams, it is acceptable for both all-girl and co-ed teams to make use of multiple bases to perform stunts. Starting with the beginning of each stunting section, athletes should perfect each basic stunt before attempting to move on to more challenging levels. For example, an Elevator should be perfected before base groups attempt an Extension. This progression promotes both safe stunting and proper stunting technique, two essential components to successful stunts.

Teams should keep this guideline in mind when learning the multiple-base stunts in this section and the single-base stunts found in the step-by-step instructions provided in the next chapter.

Chapter Eleven

Single-Base Stunting

Both all-girl and co-ed teams will find it practical as well as enjoyable to experiment with both single-basing and multiple-basing styles. Single-base stunting employs many of the same techniques as multiple-base stunting; deep sinks, tight bodies, and center of gravity alignment are critical to successful stunts. Since there is only one base in single-base stunting, it's even more important that the flyers stay directly over top of their base and remain tight throughout the stunt. In some instances, the instructions for single-base stunts are either the same or similar to multiple-base stunts. Please refer to details provided in chapter 9 on multiple basing.

— Loads for Co-Ed Single-Base Stunting —

The following loads can be used when performing single-base stunts. You may also find information on loads in the multiple-base stunting section helpful. *Note:* Because the majority of single-base stunts are performed by co-ed teams, the main base will be referred to as "he" in this section even though female bases are also capable of performing this position.

Toss Load

The Toss Load is one of the most common ways to load single-base stunts. A toss can be to shoulder level (for example, to Chair or Hands), or to an extended level (for example, Liberty or Cupie).

To execute a toss to the Hands position, count to eight, following the steps that go along with the count:

ON COUNT ONE

BASE holds firmly onto the waist and hip area of the flyer with thumbs pointing upward (see figure 11.1). This hand positioning helps keep the main base's elbows in close to his body. Elbows that stick out eliminate much of the available strength from the arms and upper torso by causing unnecessary energy expenditure from the shoulders. The main base is standing close to the flyer with soft (bent) knees, with feet either equal distance apart or with one foot slightly ahead of the other.

FLYER stands straight with her hands firmly grasping onto the wrists of the base (see figure 11.1). Her head is up and her shoulders are back. The flyer should lean slightly backward

Figure 11.1 *Prep for Toss.*

Figure 11.2 *Toss.*

into her base to help ensure she is tossed directly over the base, and not too far in front of him.

SPOT stands to the right of the base and flyer. The spot's right arm is underneath the flyer's right underarm and his left arm firmly grasps the flyer's forearm for maximum tossing assistance. The spot should be careful not to toss with too much force (spot not shown in photos).

ON COUNT TWO

BASE maintains position.

FLYER rises on her toes.

SPOT follows the flyer.

ON COUNT THREE

BASE follows the movement of the flyer, allowing her to sink *on her own*. This is essential for achieving a good toss. If the base pulls the flyer downward on the sink, he will be wasting energy and strength.

SPOT continues to follow the flyer downward.

Figure 11.3 *Toss Hands.*

ON COUNT FOUR

BASE begins to use his strength to toss the flyer on the upward motion *after* the flyer has initiated it by jumping (see figure 11.2). Quadriceps aid the toss, followed by a shrug of the shoulders, full extension of the arms, and a flick of the wrists. The elbows are kept close to the ribs until the extension of the arms to ensure a straight and powerful toss. The base should think about tossing the flyer straight up, rather than overtop of him. The base's eyes should always follow the flyer.

FLYER explodes from her quadriceps in a powerful, straight jump. Her chest, shoulders, and head stay upward, with a focus on keeping them from dropping forward. Her legs straighten from the jump. At the height of the base's toss, her hands flick downward (not outward) off the base's wrists for added height.

SPOT adds height to the toss by tossing the flyer on the up motion. The spot must ensure that there is not excessive strength put into the toss or the flyer will be thrown to one side.

ON COUNT FIVE

BASE reaches for the flyer's feet as quickly as possible and either controls the flyer down into a shoulder-level stunt or uses the momentum to continue upward into an extended stunt (see figure 11.3). The base absorbs the flyer's landing with soft knees and a tight frame.

FLYER maintains a tight body position, keeping her head up and shoulders neutral (see figure 11.3). Her hands are in Blades at her sides.

SPOT is looking up at the stunt, ready to assist the base if the stunt becomes wobbly.

ON COUNTS SIX, SEVEN, AND EIGHT

BASE maintains his position. He may find it helpful to adjust his grip on the flyer's feet with little pops to alter hand positions for a better grip in Hands.

— TIP —

When standing in a stunt, the flyer must stay off her heels. If she leans too far forward on her toes, bases can often bring the stunt down with ease anyway. If she leans too far backward on her toes, it becomes difficult for the base to safely bring her down.

TOSS STAR UP

As the flyer is tossed upward, she snaps her feet out into a star position (like a Star Jump), quickly pulling them back in before landing in the stunt. The base should toss the flyer high enough so that she snaps her legs out above his head. The flyer's feet must come back together quickly in order for the base to be able to execute the extended stunt.

Figure 11.4 *Toss Star Up.*

(See figure 11.4.) This variation is often used to toss the flyer to a Cupie.

TOSS TUCK UP

The flyer jumps upward to initiate the toss and immediately snaps her knees into a Tuck position. As she reaches the base's shoulder height, she un-tucks and stands up and into the stunt. (See figure 11.5.) A Tuck Up Toss to Heel Stretch is a popular combination.

REWIND

BASE holds onto the flyer with his hands on the small of her back and his fingers wrapped around her hips (see figure 11.6). The base tosses the flyer upward and, as the flyer begins to tuck, pushes up underneath her hips to assist with her inverted rotation (see figure 11.7). As the flyer un-tucks, the base catches her feet and straightens his arm into a Cupie (see figures 11.8 and 11.9).

FLYER begins with her hands out to the sides in preparation for a back tuck (see figure 11.6). Jumping upward on the toss, the flyer pulls her arms straight up to set for a tuck. As she is tossed upward, she quickly snaps her legs into her chest to initiate the rotation (see figure 11.7). She should rotate above the base's head as the base gives the flyer the final pop upward. The flyer quickly un-tucks her legs out of the rotation and stands up into the Cupie, remembering to pull her chest up (see figures

Figure 11.5 *Toss Tuck Up.*

Figure 11.6 *Prep for Rewind.*

Figure 11.7 *Rewind.*

Figure 11.8 *Up to Cupie.*

11.8 and 11.9). The flyer must keep her head aligned with her body on the tuck and not tilted backward as in a back-handspring.

Walk Load

BASE begins in a squat position with his chest up (see figure 11.10). Knees are at or above a 90-degree angle (any lower angle will likely cause the base to fall over when the flyer loads in). His right hand is overtop of his left, and both are held relatively close to his body. Some bases prefer to rest their elbows on their knees. The base sinks with the flyer and drives straight upward, extending the arms and the legs at the same time (see figure 11.11). As the flyer reaches the height of the stunt (base's

Figure 11.9 *Cupie.*

Figure 11.10 *Prep for Walk Load.*

Figure 11.11 *Walk Load Lift.*

arms are extended), the base turns his right hand around so that his fingers are now facing the back. The left hand reaches for the flyer's left foot as she turns to face the front. The base must extend his arms as much as possible, turning the flyer at the top so that she is facing the front on the way down to the Hands position (see figure 11.12). When executing a Walk Extension/Liberty/Cupie and so on, the base continues extending instead of lowering his arms.

FLYER sets by placing her right foot into the base's hands and puts her arms on the base's shoulders (see figure 11.10). The flyer is standing on her left toe with her center of gravity positioned directly over the base. When the flyer is in the correct position, she should be able to see down the base's spine. The flyer keeps most of her weight in her arms, pushing upward and into the stunt. Many flyers make the mistake of pushing *backward* rather than upward, but the Walk will not work if the flyer's center of gravity is not directly over her base. Keeping her legs close together (about 6 inches apart), the flyer straightens her legs as she pushes off from her base's shoulders (see figure 11.11). At the height of the Walk, the flyer looks over her right shoulder to initiate the 180-degree clockwise turn to the front (see figure 11.12). The flyer must stay tight during the entire load in order to successfully hit a stunt.

Load Variations

There are several variations you can use to load single-base stunts.

Also called a Retake, this load is performed in the same manner as the Walk Load except that the flyer loads in with two feet instead of one (see figure 11.13). This load is frequently used to supply transition from one stunt to another. The flyer can also load in from the ground in a One-Foot,

Figure 11.12 *The Height of the Walk.*

Figure 11.13 *Two-Foot Walk Load.*

the pop. The flyer is now in a Two-Foot Load. Her weight is in her arms and her chest is up. On the upward pop, she pushes off from the base's shoulders and turns 180 degrees to face the front.

The following variations can be used to execute an extended toss stunt, such as a Liberty or a Cupie.

WALK LOAD REVERSE TO HANDS

This stunt is also referred to as a "Half-In, Half-Out."

BASE loads the flyer as if to execute a Walk stunt, only he brings her to shoulder level facing the back rather than turning her 180 degrees to the front (see figure 11.14). The base must place his left hand over his right (rather than the other way around for a regular Walk Load) to make this stunt successful. Once in Hands, the base adjusts his hands so that his fingers are wrapped around the outsides of the flyer's feet. The base then sinks and pops the flyer up 180 degrees to the front (see figure 11.15). He

Two-Foot Load (one foot in on the first bounce, two on the second bounce).

BASE sets for a Walk Load, except his hands are slightly wider apart to accommodate both of the flyer's feet. He sinks as the flyer puts her first foot in, and sinks once again as she places the other foot into the base's hands. On the upward motion, the base pops the flyer upward and into Hands. The main difference between this load and the Walk Load is that the Two-Foot Load is more of an upward pop motion than a lift motion. The Two-Foot Load is great for linking stunts together.

FLYER places her right foot into the base's hands. She sinks, placing her other foot into the base's hands, and sinks again in preparation of

Figure 11.14 *Walk Load Reverse to Hands.*

Figure 11.15 *180-Degree Pop to Walk Load.*

Figure 11.16 *Walk Load Hands.*

catches her feet in Hands on the descent (see figure 11.16).

Flyer walks into a Walk Load but instead of turning 180 degrees clockwise to face the front, she lands in Hands facing the back (see figure 11.14). On the 180-degree pop to the right, she pulls her feet in slightly (preventing them from becoming too wide) and looks over her right shoulder to initiate the turn (see figure 11.15). She stays tight throughout the duration of the stunt.

Assisted 270-Degree Toe Pitch

The 270-Degree Toe Pitch is a variation of the Toe Pitch Load (see chapter 9).

Spot stands to the left of the main base, facing the main base's left arm (see figure 11.17). The spot tosses the flyer upward and helps to initiate her clockwise turn up to Hands (see figure 11.18).

Figure 11.17 *Prep for 270-Degree Toe Pitch.*

Figure 11.18 *Toss to 270-Degree Toe Pitch.*

Figure 11.19 *Toss into Arabesque.*

BASE begins facing the front in a Walk Load. The base's right hand is twisted inward and holding the flyer's toes so that his fingers are pointing toward his stomach. His left hand is holding onto the flyer's heel in a regular Prep Grip (see figure 11.17). As the base toe pitches the flyer up and into the stunt, he untwists his right hand to initiate her 270-degree clockwise rotation (see figure 11.18). A popular variation is to toss the flyer 360 degrees into an Arabesque rather than rotating her just 270 degrees and hitting a stunt facing the front (see figure 11.19).

FLYER begins facing the right, with her right foot into the base's hands (see figure 11.17). Her hands are holding onto the spot's wrists.

┌─────────────────────────────────┐
│   — **TIP** —   │
│   │
│   This stunt can also be turned │
│   into an Assisted 180-Degree   │
│   Toe Pitch by having the spot   │
│   face the base (the spot's back │
│   should be to the crowd). The   │
│   stunt should be executed as a │
│   Walk Load with the exception   │
│   of the flyer flicking off from │
│   her spot rather than pushing   │
│   off from her base's shoulders. │
└─────────────────────────────────┘

The flyer sinks with her bases and is tossed upward, rotating 270 degrees clockwise to face the front (see figure 11.18) where she performs an Arabesque (see figure 11.19). The flyer must remember to flick off from her spot's wrists as she steps up off her main base's hands.

PRESS UP

BASE loads the flyer into Hands. He sinks deeply (see figure 11.20) and presses the flyer into an extended stunt, straightening his arms and legs at the same time, locking out his elbows at the top. It's important for the base to keep his shoulders and arms pulled in against his ears to avoid over-stressing the shoulders and back. Additionally, this makes it easier to hold the stunt. In the extended stunt, the base continues to look up at the flyer (see figure 11.21).

FLYER is tossed upward and immediately locks out (see figure 11.20). On the upward press, the flyer pulls her feet slightly closer together to make it easier for the base to hold the extended stunt (see figure 11.21).

Figure 11.20 *Press-Up Sink.*

Figure 11.21 *Liberty.*

TOSS 'N' GO

In this load the base tosses the flyer, catches her in Hands, sinks, and immediately presses her up to an extended-level stunt without pausing. The stunt is executed in one continuous, fluid motion.

BASE tosses the flyer up to Hands. As the base catches her, he sinks and presses her up into the extended stunt. Unlike the Press Up, there is no pause at Hands level, but rather a continuous movement, linking the two stunts.

FLYER stays locked out the entire stunt, remembering to pull her feet together as the base presses her up into an extension.

SHOULDER SIT LOAD

BASE loads the flyer into a Shoulder Sit and places his hands underneath her feet (see figure 11.22). The base's fingers are facing toward the front and his elbows are in to the sides. The base sinks and, on the upward pop, moves his hands up to the Hands position with the fingers now facing the back. The base must give the flyer enough height so that the base can change hand positions.

FLYER loads onto the base in a Shoulder Sit (see figure 11.22). Instead of wrapping her feet around the base's back, she keeps her knees at 90 degrees and places her feet into his hands. The flyer's hands are on top of the base's head. On the upward pop, she pushes off from his head and straightens her legs into the Hands position.

CHAIR LOAD

BASE tosses the flyer into a Chair, placing the left hand underneath the flyer's left foot (see figure 11.23). The base sinks and pops the flyer upward, reaching for her right foot to complete the transition to Hands.

FLYER is tossed into a Chair (see figure 11.23). As the base pops her upward, she straightens her right knee and stands up into Hands.

Figure 11.22 *Shoulder Sit Load.*

Figure 11.23 *Chair Load.*

SINGLE BACK LOAD

SPOT helps the flyer onto the base's back and holds onto her ankles (see figure 11.24). As the flyer is popped upward, the spot lifts her ankles up and into the Hands position.

BASE leans over and rests his elbows on his thighs, making sure that his lower back is flat enough for the flyer to stand on (see figure 11.24). The base sinks and pops the flyer off his back by lifting his hips and rolling up into a standing position. The base catches the flyer's feet in the Hands position.

FLYER is loaded onto the base's lower back (see figure 11.24). As the base sinks, she bends her knees and gives a little jump on the pop, which helps initiate the upward motion. The flyer stays locked out as she lands in the Hands position.

Figure 11.24 *Single Back Load.*

Figure 11.25 *180-Degree Toss Over.*

180-DEGREE TOSS OVER LOAD

SPOT stands facing the back and on the left-hand side of the base. He tosses the flyer up and 180 degrees over to the base. (See figure 11.25.)

BASE begins facing the front. The base watches the flyer's feet, catching them in Hands as she rotates toward the front (see figure 11.25).

FLYER begins in front of the spot. He tosses her upward and to her left into the waiting hands of her main base. She helps to initiate the rotation by looking for the front while simultaneously twisting her shoulders and hips to the left (see figure 11.25).

J-UP

Also known as the "Peg-Leg Load," this is a harder variation of the Assisted 270-Degree Toe Pitch.

SPOT begins facing to the right, directly behind the flyer (see figure 11.26). The spot sinks with the base and tosses the flyer upward, remembering to toss her so that her center of gravity is placed over the base (see figure 11.27).

Figure 11.26 *Prep for J-Up Toss.*

Figure 11.27 *J-Up Toss.*

Figure 11.28 *J-Up Liberty.*

BASE begins holding onto the flyer's right heel with his right hand, fingers pointing downward. His left hand is underneath the flyer's right thigh (see figure 11.26). The base sinks in unison with the spot and pushes up underneath the flyer's thigh to position her center of gravity overtop him (see figure 11.27). On her ascent, the base pushes up underneath her right foot and into a Liberty (see figure 11.28). This stunt is referred to as a "J-Up" because the main base has to scoop the flyer's right foot down and then up in the shape of a "J" to complete the stunt. He does this so that her weight is positioned close to his body and the stunt can be executed smoothly and with ease.

> ### — TIP —
>
> An easier version of this load can be done by eliminating the 270-degree rotation and instead J-ing the flyer 90 degrees to the front into the stunt. To do this, the base must turn his right hand over with fingers pointing downward and elbow sticking up. His palm should be closer to the flyer's toes than to her heel. Think of it as loading the stunt (either Hands or an extended stunt) up from the side while keeping the flyer's right leg straight.

Figure 11.29 *Handstand Load.*

FLYER begins facing the right with her right leg extended outward and resting in the base's hand (see figure 11.26). She must keep her leg locked out during the entire load in order for the stunt to hit. The flyer sinks with her bases and flicks off from the spot's wrists (see figure 11.27). Turning 270 degrees clockwise to face the front, the flyer is tossed into a Liberty (see figure 11.28).

HANDSTAND LOAD

SPOT stands to the right of the flyer (see figure 11.29). If the base requires assistance to lift the entire load, the spot will place his right hand underneath the flyer's waist and his left hand either on the flyer's feet or around the base's wrist for support. The spot sinks with the base and the flyer. On the upward motion, the spot lifts up the flyer's waist and pushes up underneath her feet into a Liberty. If the base requires help only on the upward motion, the spot places his left hand on the flyer's seat and his right hand around her ankle and helps to push up into the stunt (see figure 11.31).

BASE places his left arm around the front of the flyer's waist and places his right hand on the flyer's feet in a Cupie Grip (see figure 11.29). The base sinks with the flyer, lifting the flyer

Figure 11.30 *Handstand Lift.*

Figure 11.31 *Handstand Press-Up.*

Figure 11.32 *Cupie.*

by pulling up underneath her waist (see figure 11.30). The base simultaneously rotates his right hand underneath the flyer's feet into an upright position (see figure 11.31) and presses the flyer up into a Cupie (see figure 11.32).

FLYER starts in a Handstand position with her feet together and her knees slightly bent (see figure 11.29). The flyer pushes upward with her arms and tucks her body in as the base pulls her up into an upright position (see figures 11.30 and 11.31). She then stands up into the stunt (see figure 11.32).

BALL AND CHAIN

BASE begins crouched down with his elbows in tight to his sides (see figure 11.33). He holds onto the flyer's feet with his left hand underneath his right. His fingers should be facing away from his body. To initiate the upward momentum, the base rocks backward into an upright position, making sure that the flyer is pulled in close to his torso (see figure 11.34). Using his legs as the main source of power, the base stands up, rotating his hand into the Cupie Grip once the flyer is at eye-level (see figure 11.35), and pushes her upward into a Cupie (see figure 11.36). The base must have good form to execute this stunt with success. The key is to get the flyer's hips into an upright position before attempting to press her up.

FLYER begins lying on her back, knees bent into her chest. Her arms are clasped around her base's neck, and her feet are in the base's hands (see figure 11.33). As the base rocks backward, the flyer pulls herself into her base with her arms (see figure 11.34). On the upward press, the flyer changes arm positions so that her hands can push off from the base's shoulders. She straightens her legs, and near the height of the extension rotates clockwise into the Cupie (see figures 11.35 and 11.36).

Figure 11.33 *Ball and Chain, Step One (prep).*

Figure 11.34 *Ball and Chain, Step Two.*

Figure 11.35 *Ball and Chain, Step Three.*

Figure 11.36 *Ball and Chain, Step Four.*

The Ball and Chain can also be used to load a Liberty.

— All-Girl Single-Base Stunting —

Although it's much more common for single-base stunting to be performed by co-ed stunt groups, single-base stunting is performed by all-female groups as well. Here are three loads that all-girl groups typically use when performing single-base stunts.

Toss Load into All-Girl Single-Base Stunt

An all-girl single-base stunt can be loaded in the same way as a co-ed Toss Load. The third and the assisting base help the main base toss the flyer upward in the same way as they would in a Toss Shoulder Sit. Once the flyer is in the Hands position (see page 187 for details on the Hands stunt), the third stands behind the main base and helps to stabilize the flyer. The assisting base generally stands to the right side of the stunt. (See figure 11.37 for positioning.)

Figure 11.37 *Toss Load into All-Girl Single-Base Stunt.*

Toe Pitch Load into All-Girl Single-Base Stunt

This load is done in the same manner as the Toss Load except that the assisting base crouches down in front of the flyer and lifts up her foot during the toss rather than tossing underneath her arm. The main base and the third toss the flyer as usual. The flyer places her foot on the assisting base's hands and pushes off from them as she is tossed into the stunt. (See figure 11.38 for positioning.)

Standard Load into All-Girl Single-Base Stunt

FLYER starts in the Standard Load (refer to figure 9.2 on page 118) and is popped upward. While the flyer is near the height of the pop, the main base turns underneath her and changes hand positions from the Prep Grip to the Hands Grip to end up facing the front in a single-base stunt. (See figure 11.39.)

Figure 11.38 *Toe Pitch Load into All-Girl Single-Base Stunt.*

Figure 11.39 *Hands.*

Sponge, Shoulder-Sit Load into All-Girl Single-Base Stunt

This load is a great transition move from multiple basing to single basing and looks awesome when it is performed by all the base groups at the same time. This stunt is performed in one continuous motion as the flyer moves from an Elevator to a Shoulder Sit and back up to a single-base stunt.

THIRD loads the flyer into an Elevator. The base group sponges the flyer into a Shoulder Sit on the main base. The third holds onto the flyer's ankles and, on the upward motion, pulls the flyer into a single-base stunt position. The third continues to pull up on the flyer's ankles to alleviate some of the weight from the main base or reaches up and holds onto the flyer's ankles to stabilize the stunt.

ASSISTING BASE loads the flyer into an Elevator. The bases dip to prepare for a Sponge Shoulder Sit and give the flyer a little pop to initiate the Sponge. On the descent, the assisting base helps to slow down the flyer into a Shoulder Sit. Once the flyer is in a Shoulder Sit, the assisting base stays to the right side of the stunt and helps the main base pop the Shoulder Sit into the single-base stunt.

MAIN BASE loads the flyer into an Elevator. The bases dip to prepare for a Sponge Shoulder Sit and give the flyer a little pop to initiate the sponge. On the pop upward, the main base turns to face the front and positions herself underneath the flyer's center of gravity. As the main base turns, the back hand releases the flyer's foot and grabs onto the flyer's opposite foot. The main base's front hand maintains contact with the flyer's foot throughout the entire stunt. As the flyer sits on the main base's shoulders in a Shoulder Sit, the main base's hands lower down to waist level, fingers facing the front. From this position, the main base sinks and pops the flyer up into a single-base stunt.

FLYER loads into an elevator. She pulls up as the bases sponge her down into a Shoulder Sit. As the flyer lowers onto the main base's shoulders, she puts her hands on the top of the main base's head for support. On the way back up into the single-base stunt, the flyer pushes off from the main base's head and stands up. The flyer must remember to pull her feet inward while she is being popped up, or it can become difficult for the main base to control the stunt.

ELEVATOR, SPONGE, SHOULDER-SIT LOAD VARIATION

Once you have mastered the Elevator, Sponge, Shoulder-Sit Load to a single-base stunt, you can change the sequence so that it looks like this:

Show Elevator/Extension + Shoulder Sit + Single Base

The combination should be executed without pauses, unlike the first load, during which the base group stops at the Elevator before moving onto the Shoulder Sit.

As with all stunting, it is not just the result that is important; how you get there is critical as well. Variations and combinations are more impressive than just single stunts performed on their own. Once you have mastered the basic stunts and dismounts, try linking two or more of them together by using the transition moves just discussed.

— Dismounts —

There are two basic types of dismounts from single-base stunts: Pop Downs and Cradles.

Pop Down Dismount

The flyer can be popped down from either an extended stunt or a stunt at Hands level (shoulder level). Flyers are always popped down from stunts such as Chairs, Shoulder Sits, Shoulder Stands, and Hands.

BASE dips in the stunt (see figure 11.40). He tosses the flyer upward—rising onto his toes, shrugging his shoulders, and flicking his wrists for maximum height (see figure 11.41). The base's arms should fully extend before reaching for his flyer's waist (see figure 11.42). The base resists the flyer's descent (see figure 11.43) so that the flyer gently touches the ground (see figure 11.44).

FLYER continues to stay locked out as her base dips (see figure 11.40). On the upward motion, she

Figure 11.40 *Pop-Down Sink.*

Figure 11.41 *Pop-Down Toss.*

Figure 11.42 *Pop-Down Catch One.*

Figure 11.43 *Pop-Down Catch Two.*

Figure 11.44 *Pop-Down Catch Three.*

pulls up through her chest and stays tight. If her arms are in a motion, she snaps them down to her sides as she is tossed (see figure 11.41). Reaching for her base's wrists, (see figure 11.43) she keeps her chest up on the descent and bends her knees on the landing (see figure 11.44).

Cradle Dismount

SPOT stands to the right of the base and steps in to catch the flyer.

BASE tosses the flyer upward, flicking his wrists at the top for added height (see figure 11.45). Turning to face the right, the base keeps his arms up, ready to catch the flyer in a Cradle. On her descent into the catch, he pulls her into his torso and absorbs her landing with his knees (see figures 11.46 and 11.47).

Figure 11.45 *Cradle.*

Figure 11.46 *Cradle Catch (rear view).*

FLYER keeps her legs straight as the base dips. She pulls upward on the toss, snapping her arms down to her sides and lays out (see figure 11.45). Rather than catching herself with one arm around the spot's shoulders and the other around the base's shoulders as in a Multiple-Base Cradle, she wraps both arms around to her main base's shoulders (see figures 11.46 and 11.47).

Figure 11.47 *Cradle Catch (front view).*

★ ★ ★ ★ ★ ★ ★ ★ ★ ★ ★ ★ ★ ★ ★ ★ ★

Cradle Rules

Be sure to read the previous multiple-basing chapters for the full instructions on Twist Cradles as well as for additional Cradle tips and pointers. Note that twisting dismounts exceeding two rotations are prohibited.

★ ★ ★ ★ ★ ★ ★ ★ ★ ★ ★ ★ ★ ★ ★ ★ ★

Figure 11.48 *Twist Cradle Dismount.*

Twist Cradle Dismount

BASE tosses the flyer upward (see figure 11.48) and catches her in a Cradle.

FLYER twists from a single-base stunt the same way as twisting from a multiple-base stunt (see figure 11.48).

— Co-Ed Single-Base Stunts —

The Basket Toss chapter also contains information on trick Cradles. The following are stationary single-base stunts (stunts that "hit" and can be held for a period of time before dismounting).

Side Shoulder Sit

BASE stands behind the flyer and tosses her upward and slightly to the right to avoid being kicked when she tucks her knees up.

Maintaining contact with her waist the entire time, the base sets the flyer onto his right shoulder. He wraps his right arm around her upper legs for stability (see figure 11.49). To dismount, the base reaches in front of the flyer and holds onto her hips. The base sinks and lifts her down to the ground.

FLYER is tossed upward. As she approaches shoulder level, she tucks, brings her knees up, and sits on her base's shoulder (see figure 11.49). To dismount, she holds onto his wrists and keeps her chest up for the landing.

Shoulder Sit

You can use a variety of loads and dismounts with the Shoulder Sit (see figure 11.50), including the following:

Toss Loads

Walk Up Load

Grin 'n' Bear It + Shoulder Sit

Front Dismount

Rear Dismount

Figure 11.49 *Side Shoulder Sit.*

Figure 11.50 *Shoulder Sit.*

Refer to the multiple-basing Shoulder Sit section for details.

Shoulder Stand

You can use a variety of loads and dismounts with the Shoulder Stand (see figure 11.51), including the following:

Toss Load

Ground Up Load

Walk Up Load

The flyer is popped down from a Shoulder Stand. Refer to the multiple-basing Shoulder Stand section for details.

Hands

BASE holds onto the flyer's feet in a Hands Grip and keeps his arms close to his body (see figure 11.52). The base's feet, hips, and shoulders are

Figure 11.51 *Shoulder Stand.*

Figure 11.52 *Hands.*

aligned and his back is straight. The base should always be looking up at his flyer.

FLYER stands pulled up and locked out in the stunt, fixing her eyes on a point straight ahead (see figure 11.52).

TO LOAD HANDS

Toss Load

Walk Load

The most common and most practical dismount from Hands is a Pop Down. While it is possible to Cradle from Hands, a Pop Down is recommended instead.

Extension

BASE holds onto the flyer's feet in a Hands Grip and keeps his shoulders close to his ears. It is important that the base keep his body aligned while performing extended stunts. The wrists must be directly over the shoulders, which must be directly over the hips, which are over top of the knees and ankles. This alignment ensures that the *entire* body is supporting the weight of the flyer, not just one body part. Many bases make the mistake of holding their arms away from their ears, which places excessive stress on the shoulders. The other mistake bases make is arching the back while stunting, which places an enormous amount of stress on the lower back. This poor technique makes it much harder to hold the stunt. In addition, both habits are dangerous for the base and also put the flyer at risk for coming down during the stunt. The base looks up at his flyer throughout the entire stunt. (See figure 11.53.)

Figure 11.53 *Extension.*

FLYER stands pulled up and locked out in the Extension. It is important that the flyer keep her feet no wider than shoulder width. She should squeeze her inner thigh muscles together in an Extension to keep her legs at the appropriate width. Her head should be looking up and her gaze focused on a point straight ahead. (See figure 11.53.)

LOADS FOR AN EXTENSION

★ *Press Up:* The base should sink deeply with his legs and straighten his arms and legs at the same time, remembering to squeeze his arms against his ears.

★ *Toss 'n' Go:* This load is just a Press Up executed in one fluid motion.

★ *Shoulder Sit Load:* This load is executed in the same manner as a Shoulder Sit to Hands except the base continues to extend the flyer upward into an Extension.

★ *Walk Load:* This is the same as the Walk Load for Hands except the base keeps his arms extended at the height of the stunt rather than bringing the flyer's feet down to shoulder level. The base's arms and legs should lock out at the same time.

★ *Toss Load:* Both the base and the flyer must work harder than a Toss Hands to get the height needed for an Extension. Rather than bringing his arms down to shoulder height, the base uses the upward momentum to continue bringing the flyer up to an Extension.

Either a Pop Down or Cradle are appropriate dismounts from an Extension although the flyer typically wouldn't pull a trick from a Cradle; that is, she would do a straight Cradle without variation. (Please see chapter 13 on Basket Tosses for more information on tricks.)

Liberty

SPOT can stand in one of two positions: (1) to the right side of the base holding onto either the flyer's ankle or overtop of the base's hands *or* (2) behind the base and holding onto either the flyer's ankle or squeezing the base's arms together and up, holding onto his wrists (spot is not featured in figure 11.54).

BASE's arms are extended and locked out, holding the flyer in a Liberty. The only difference between holding an Extension and holding a Liberty is that the base supports the flyer on one leg and holds onto her foot in a Liberty Grip. The base should lift his shoulders upward when holding a Liberty, squeezing his shoulders against his ears. (See figure 11.54.)

FLYER stands locked out in a Liberty position (see figure 11.54).

TO LOAD A LIBERTY

★ *Press Up:*

SPOT stands to the right of the base. On the extension upward, he can either hold onto the flyer's ankle and lift upward (if the

Figure 11.54 *Liberty.*

spot is tall enough) or place his hands on the flyer's right foot in a Natural Grip.

BASE loads the flyer into Hands. The base sinks and extends his arms upward. Near the height of the extension, the base squeezes both shoulders and arms together. The base removes his left hand from the flyer's left foot as the flyer pulls her leg up into a Liberty. Placing his left hand on the ball of the flyer's right foot, the base's right hand is supporting the flyer's heel and arch in a Liberty Grip. The flyer is most stable when the base squeezes her foot.

FLYER is tossed into Hands. Keeping the knees locked out and the body tight, the flyer is extended upward. The flyer must wait until close to the top of the extension to pull her left foot up, rather than snapping it up as soon as she feels the base extend upward.

★ *Toss 'n' Go:* This load is executed to the same timing as a Toss 'n' Go Extension, only the flyer is put up into a Liberty.

★ *Shoulder Sit Load:* This load is executed in the same manner as a Shoulder Sit to Extension, except that the Flyer stands up into a Liberty. Bases, remember to use your legs!

★ *Assisted Step Up:*

SPOT stands behind the main base. As the main base pops the flyer behind him to the spot, the spot catches her and sinks for the toss. The spot tosses the flyer up into a Reverse Torch (a shoulder-level Liberty). The spot is holding onto the flyer's opposite foot (not her Liberty foot). Sinking with the base, the spot pops the flyer up into a Liberty on the main base.

BASE pops the flyer down behind him. Placing his hands in a Liberty Grip, the base rests his hands on his right shoulder, ready for the flyer's right foot. The spot loads the flyer into the base's hands. Sinking with the spot, the base uses the upward momentum from the spot's toss to press the flyer up into a Liberty. If this method is a little difficult at first, an alternative method is for the base to begin with the arms extended straight above his head, waiting for the flyer to step up into a Liberty.

FLYER is popped down to the spot, rather than being caught by her own base. Using the downward motion of the catch as the sink for the toss, she is then tossed into a Reverse Torch (opposite foot is standing on the spot's hands, not the Liberty foot). The flyer places her Liberty foot into the base's hands. Keeping her reverse leg straight, the flyer is tossed upward and into the Liberty.

★ *Walk Load:* The Walk Liberty is executed in the same way as a Walk Extension except that the flyer remains standing on one foot, pulling up her left knee at the height of the stunt.

★ *Walk Load Reverse Offset to Liberty:*

BASE loads the flyer into a Reverse Hands. Lifting her right foot with his left arm, the base adjusts his grip so that his fingers face inward and to the right. His hand should be closer to the front of the flyer's foot rather than on her heel. This feels awkward at first, but the left hand has to be in this position to accommodate the flyer's rotation forward. The base's right hand is at shoulder level. The base sinks and keeping his left arm straight, pops the flyer's right foot upward. As the flyer turns toward the front, the base's right hand joins the left in a Liberty Grip. (See figures 11.55 and 11.56.)

FLYER begins facing the back in an Offset (right leg is bent). On the upward motion,

Figure 11.55 *Walk Load Reverse Offset to Liberty.*

Figure 11.56 *Liberty.*

she steps up onto her right leg while turn-ing 180 degrees clockwise to face the front in a Liberty. It is important that the flyer lifts her own leg while stepping up, rather than expecting the base to push it upward for her. (See figures 11.55 and 11.56.)

★ *Toss Load:* Instead of catching one foot in each hand, the base brings both hands together in a Liberty Grip and catches the flyer's right foot. Using the upward momentum from the toss, he continues to extend his arms upward and keeps his shoulders close to his ears as he locks out into a Liberty.

★ *Toss to Heel Stretch:*

  BASE tosses the flyer upward to an extended level. The base should hold her foot in a tight grip and be aware that flyers tend to roll their foot slightly to compensate for the weight of the extended leg.

  FLYER is tossed upward and catches her foot in a Heel Stretch at the same time her base

catches her standing foot from the toss. Timing is crucial in Toss stunts.

★ *Toss to Arabesque:*

  BASE tosses the flyer upward into an extended Liberty position. Instead of placing his hands in the regular Liberty Grip, his right hand holds onto the flyer's arch, fingers turned inward, rather than toward the back as with the Liberty Grip. His left hand is placed directly underneath the right hand, fingers facing inward and hold-ing underneath his right hand or grasping onto his wrist for added support. This hand position accommodates the flyer's 90-degree turn to the side. The base re-mains facing the front. (See figure 11.60.)

FLYER is tossed up into an Arabesque, turning 90 degrees to the side *after* passing the base's shoulder height. The flyer keeps her legs fairly close together until the height of the extension. As she hits the top of the stunt, she *then* extends her leg behind her into an Arabesque. If the flyer extends her leg too soon, she will cut the height of the toss prematurely and risk kicking her base in the face. The flyer is now facing the right side, while the base remains facing the front. (See figure 11.60.)

FLYER VARIATIONS

See figures 11.57 through 11.63 for photos of different flyer variations.

Cupie/Awesome

The Cupie is held with the shoulder pulled upward and tightly against the ear. The opposite arm

(continues on page 210)

Figure 11.57 *Heel Stretch.*

Figure 11.58 *Scale.*

Figure 11.59 *X-Scale.*

Figure 11.60 *Arabesque.*

Figure 11.61 *Scorpion.*

Figure 11.62 *Bow and Arrow.*

Figure 11.63 *Cupie.*

(continued from page 208)

is on the base's hip. In an Awesome, the base's hand is held in a Half–High V. In either version, if the supporting arm is held away from the head, the flyer's weight is being supported by the base's shoulder rather than by the base's entire body. This is both harder for the base and uncomfortable to hold. Any extended stunt can generally be held twice as long if the flyer's weight is positioned directly over top of the base.

The Cupie/Awesome can be loaded in several ways, including:

★ *Press Up:* The base should adjust his hand into a Cupie/Awesome Grip (flyer's foot resting on the outside portion of the fingers and palm) at shoulder level rather than trying to adjust the hand position as the base is extending his arm into the stunt.

★ *Toss 'n' Go:* This load is executed in the same way as a Toss 'n' Go Liberty except the flyer is put into a Cupie or Awesome.

★ *Toss Load:* As with all Toss stunts, the base must fully extend his arms and legs on the toss. This ensures that the flyer achieves the maximum possible height from the stunt. The base must watch the flyer's feet the whole time, as hand placement in a Cupie/Awesome is especially important.

★ *Walk Load:* The base must remember to use his legs as the main source of power, extending his arms and legs at the same time to execute this load.

★ *Single Back Load:* The Single Back Load is executed in the same way as a Single Back Load to Hands except that the base extends right up into an extended stunt. The spot holds onto both of the flyer's ankles and, keeping them together, lifts the flyer up to the base's hand and assists on the extension.

Cupie Variations

TICK TOCK

BASE begins holding the flyer in an Awesome with his left arm. The base's right arm is in a High V,

Figure 11.64 *Tick-Tock, Step One.*

ready to switch positions with the left arm (see figure 11.64). The base gives a little sink and, on the upward pop, quickly alternates arms (see figure 11.65) so that the right hand is now holding the Awesome. The left arm is now in the "High V" motion (see figure 11.66). The base must be careful not to pop the flyer too high; the idea is to pop her just high enough so that he will have time to change hands.

─ **TIP** ─

Here's a challenging variation of the Tick Tock Cupie: The flyer starts in a one-leg stunt such as a Liberty. Instead of the base switching the supporting arm on the Tick Tock pop, the flyer quickly switches her standing leg. This version of the Tick Tock is usually done with the base supporting the flyer with both hands.

Figure 11.65 *Tick-Tock, Step Two.*

Figure 11.66 *Tick-Tock, Step Three.*

FLYER remains locked out during the entire stunt (see figures 11.64 through 11.66).

DOUBLE CUPIE

In this stunt, one base is holding two flyers in a Cupie; one on each hand.

Ground Up Load to Double Cupie

TWO SPOTS assist the load by standing on either side of the base. Holding onto one flyer's waist, each spot tosses a flyer upward and onto the main base's hands as the main base stands up. Once in position, one spot will often stand directly behind the base holding underneath the base's hands or on the base's wrists for added support. Alternatively, each spot can remain on either side of the main base, assisting where necessary on the upward press. Additional spotters should be standing behind the main base.

BASE begins in a squat with both hands positioned over his shoulders and holding onto the inside foot of each flyer. As the spots toss the flyers, the base stands up, either to Hands and then pressing the flyers up into a Double Cupie, or straight up to a Double Cupie.

FLYERS stand on either side of the base with their inside foot (the one closest to the main base's body) set in the base's waiting hand. The flyers are tossed upward onto the base's hands and pull their feet together in a Cupie. To balance, the flyers can either hold onto one another's waist or shoulders.

Knee Load to Double Cupie

TWO SPOTS stand in front of the main base, facing him. Each spot tosses a flyer up from the front onto their shoulders (the flyers are kneeling on the spots' inside shoulders), and the spots place their hands underneath the flyers' shins. Sinking with the main base, the spots push the flyers upward and into the Double Cupie position. Additionally spotters should be standing behind the main base.

BASE begins standing behind the flyers. When the flyers are loaded onto the spots' shoulders, the base places his hands on the flyers' feet in a Cupie grasp. Sinking with the spots, the base waits for them to initiate the upward motion and then presses the flyers into a Double Cupie.

FLYERS begin standing in front of the base, facing their spot. Holding onto the spot's outside shoulder for support, the flyers are tossed up onto their spot's inside shoulder. Kneeling, the flyers wrap their inside arms around one an-other's waist or shoulders for stability. Their outside arms can be placed on their spotter's head for stability. Sinking slightly, the flyers push off from their spots' heads and stand up into a Double Cupie.

To Dismount a Double Cupie

To dismount a Double Cupie, the base can either pop the flyers down to the waiting spots (with the help of a spotter standing behind), or the flyers can fall off the back and into a Cradle of the waiting spots.

Now that we've covered stationary stunts, move on to the following chapter to learn transition stunts, which will help you link your stationary stunts together.

Single-Base Transition Stunts

Co-ed, single-base transition stunts are useful for linking together stationary stunts (such as a Heel Stretch) and serve to add creativity and difficulty to a routine.

— Toss Load —

The Toss Load is the simplest transition from one stunt to another. As the flyer is popped down from a stunt, her landing is used as the sink for the next stunt. For example, a flyer popped down to the floor from Hands immediately is tossed back up into another stunt without pausing at the bottom. The result is one continuous, smooth transition from one stunt to another.

Traveling Toss Load

This is a great way to transition into a new formation and leads right into a new stunt (as the base puts the flyer down into a new position, they both sink for the toss).

BASE sinks with the flyer as if to toss her up into a stunt, but instead lifts her up and moves her to a different area of the floor.

FLYER sinks with the base. On the upward lift, the flyer maintains a tight grasp on the base's wrists and locks out her body.

Cradle to Toss Load

BASE catches the flyer in a Cradle and, after absorbing her landing with his legs, pops her up and into a Toss Load. The base turns 90 degrees to face the front while popping the flyer upward so that both partners are now facing the front and ready to execute the next stunt. The base maintains contact on the flyer's waist with the right hand the entire time.

FLYER pushes off from her base's shoulders and immediately reaches for his wrists as she lands in a Toss Load. The flyer is facing the front the entire time.

360-Degree Log Roll to Toss Load

BASE catches the flyer (see figure 12.1) and pops her upward and slightly forward while quickly rolling his arms forward. This arm movement initiates the flyer's rotation (see figure 12.2). (This motion is similar to a Log Roll in a multiple-base stunt but without a second base.) Watching the flyer's hips the entire time, the base reaches for the flyer's waist as she completes the rotation. The base simultaneously turns 90 degrees to face the front so that both partners are ready to execute the next stunt (see figure 12.3).

Figure 12.1 *360-Degree Log Roll Catch.*

Figure 12.2 *360-Degree Log Roll.*

Figure 12.3 *360-Degree Toss Prep.*

FLYER is caught in a Cradle (see figure 12.1). Holding her weight in her arms, the flyer pushes off from the base's shoulders and rotates toward the base (see figure 12.2). The flyer's hands snap down to her sides. After completing the rotation, she reaches for her base's wrists (see figure 12.3).

— Walk Load —

You've learned the Walk Load, but there are several variations of this that are used to transition between stunts.

Reverse Walk Load

The Reverse Walk Load is one of the most useful ways to link stunts together. This transition can be compared to a Sponge in multiple-base stunting: the stunt, load, stunt combination. In order to be effective, this stunt must be done with control and without rushing.

BASE dips in Hands and gives the flyer a slight pop upward. The pop allows the base to change hand positions from Hands (fingers pointing to the back) to the Walk position (fingers pointing the front). Turning his hands inward as the flyer rotates 180 degrees to face him, the base lowers the flyer down into a Walk Load. The base maintains contact with the flyer's right foot the entire time (except during the pop). He uses the touch down as the sink to come back up to another stunt. The base must always watch the flyer's right foot and use his legs (rather than his back) to control the stunt down.

FLYER stays locked out as her base dips. On the upward pop, she rotates 180 degrees clockwise to face her base. Pulling up, the flyer bends her right knee and places her hands on the base's shoulders to support her weight in a Walk Load position. During the transition, the flyer must keep her center of gravity close to the base and keep it directly over top the base as much as possible. She is lowered into a Walk Load, sinks on the touch down, and pushes back up into the next stunt.

Two-Foot Walk Load

Also called a Double Take or a Retake, this is both a useful transition move as well as a load.

— Regrab —

The Regrab transition is used to link the Cradle catch to the load of another stunt or directly to another stunt (for example, Regrab to Hands, below).

Regrab to Hands

SPOT is optional. If a spot is used, he assists with catching the Cradle and helps to pop the flyer up into Hands.

BASE catches the flyer in a Cradle. On the second bounce, he grabs onto the flyer's left foot with his left hand, fingers pointing upward (see figure 12.4). She is then popped up into Hands while turning to face the front.

FLYER catches herself in a Cradle, placing both hands around the base's shoulders. The flyer must hold herself up by keeping the majority of her weight in her arms; the base will not be able to hold much of her weight as he changes hand/arm positions. On the second bounce, the flyer bends her left knee and places her left foot into the base's left hand. (See figure

Figure 12.4 *Regrab to Hands.*

12.4.) She pushes off from his shoulders and stands up into Hands. Note that this transition can be performed with only one bounce.

Regrab to Liberty

BASE must reach for the flyer's right foot with his left hand, rather than her left foot to Regrab to a right-foot Liberty. The base pops the flyer upward. As she begins to stand upright (her center of gravity should be over her knees), his right hand joins the left and pushes upward on her right foot into a Liberty.

FLYER begins in a Cradle, supporting the majority of her weight with her arms. On the first bounce, the flyer changes positions so that both of her knees are bent and her hips are positioned upright rather than in a Cradle. She continues to support her weight with her arms until the pop upward, when she pushes off from her base's shoulders and stands into a Liberty.

— Sponge from a Co-Ed Extended Stunt to Shoulder Level —

This move is used to transition from a one-leg extended stunt into another one-leg extended stunt without returning all the way back down to the ground. It is just the reverse of an "–'n' Go" stunt.

BASE begins holding the flyer in an extended stunt. Keeping his arms straight, he uses his legs to gently pop the flyer upward to initiate the Sponge. On the downward motion, the base's arms and legs bend at the same time to control the flyer's foot down to shoulder level. At this point, the base's legs should be bent. Using the downward momentum as a sink, the base then pushes the flyer back up into another extended stunt. It's important that the base does not stop once the flyer is at shoulder level but continues the stunt in one fluid motion. This move is similar to a "–'n' Go" stunt (such as Toss 'n' Go) in that the stunt flows together without stopping at each stage.

FLYER stays tight during the entire stunt, keeping her supporting leg straight.

Figure 12.5 *Sponge Variation, Step One.*

Sponge Variation: Liberty, Sponge, Heel Stretch

BASE begins holding the flyer in an opposite Liberty (that is, she stands on the opposite foot from the one she usually performs her stunts on) (see figure 12.5). As the base sponges and brings the flyer down to shoulder level, he reaches for her opposite foot (see figure 12.6). Sinking, he presses her back up into a Heel Stretch on the opposite leg from the one she used for her Liberty (see figure 12.7). Depending on the athletes' preferences, this stunt can also be done with the base crossing his hands at shoulder level.

FLYER keeps her supporting leg straight and crosses her free foot in front of her as she is brought down to shoulder level (see figure 12.6).

Figure 12.6 *Sponge Variation, Step Two.*

Figure 12.7 *Sponge Variation, Step Three.*

Figure 12.8 *Show 360-Degree, Step One.*

Transferring her weight to her free foot, she lifts her other leg up into a Heel Stretch on the upward motion as she is pressed back up into the extended stunt (see figure 12.7). The flyer must keep her Heel Stretch leg straight.

— Show 360-Degree —

SPOT tosses the flyer upward (see figure 12.9). On her descent, he reaches for her waist to slow her down.

BASE begins in a Walk Load (see figure 12.8). The base toe pitches the flyer upward, allowing her foot to leave his hands to allow for her 360-degree vertical rotation (see figure 12.9). As she comes around to face him, he reaches for her foot and lowers her down into a Walk Load.

FLYER is tossed up overtop of her base (see figure 12.9). At the height of the toss, she rotates 360 degrees clockwise. She returns to the

Figure 12.9 *Show 360-Degree Step Two.*

ground in a Walk Load, either reaching for her base's shoulders or for her spot's wrists.

— Grin 'n' Bear It Combinations —

This straddle stunt is also referred to as a Humptie.

Combination #1: Walk Load Toss Up + Grin 'n' Bear It

BASE begins in the Walk Load (see figure 12.10). He tosses the flyer directly upward as high as possible (the base is essentially toe-pitching the flyer) (see figure 12.11). As she comes down in a Straddle, the base scoops under her thighs and holds onto her waist (see figure 12.12). It is important that the base make contact with the flyer as soon as possible, resisting her weight on the descent to ensure a secure Cradle.

FLYER loads into a Walk Load (see figure 12.10) (she can take two steps toward her base before loading into her hands for added power). She pushes directly upward off the base's shoulders

Figure 12.10 *Combo One: Walk Load Toss Up + Grin 'n' Bear It, Step One.*

Figure 12.11 *Combo One: Walk Load Toss Up + Grin 'n' Bear It, Step Two.*

Figure 12.12 *Combo One: Walk Load Toss Up + Grin 'n' Bear It, Step Three.*

as he toe-pitches her (see figure 12.11). At the height of the toss, the flyer snaps her feet into her chest and then out into a Straddle. This move is different from a Tuck X-Out trick because the flyer does not have enough time to lay out or straighten her body horizontally before landing in the Straddle. The flyer is caught on the base in a Straddle position, supporting herself with her arms, which are clasped around her base's neck and shoulders (see figure 12.12).

Combination #2: Cradle + Grin 'n' Bear It

BASE begins holding the flyer in a Cradle. The base sinks and tosses her upward, ensuring that she has enough height to turn toward her base and Straddle without kicking him. The base catches the flyer in a Straddle position, absorbing the catch with his knees rather than bending forward with his back.

FLYER holds her own weight in her arms in the Cradle. The base tosses her upward and she pushes off of his shoulders and slightly toward him. As the flyer turns to face her base, she straddles her legs into a Grin 'n' Bear It, being careful not to kick him in the face. The flyer should wait until the height of the toss (when she clears her base's head) to straddle. As she descends, she reaches around the base's neck and shoulders to catch herself.

Combination #3: Cradle + Tuck In + Grin 'n' Bear It

This stunt is done exactly as described in Combination #2 except that the flyer tucks her knees to her chest and rotates horizontally toward her base before kicking her legs out into a Straddle. As with the straight-legged variation, the flyer must have lots of height to perform this stunt.

Combination #4: Cradle + 270 Degrees + Grin 'n' Bear It

BASE begins holding the flyer in Hands. Sinking, the base tosses the flyer upward and slightly to the side to initiate her clockwise rotation. As the flyer comes around, the base catches her in a Straddle.

FLYER begins in a Cradle, supporting her weight with her arms. As she is popped upward, she pushes up off of her base's shoulders and to the side (away from the base). Tucking her knees into her chest, the flyer rotates clockwise 270 degrees. When the flyer is facing her base's shoulder, she opens into a Straddle, slightly leaning backward to avoid kicking her partner in the head. (The flyer finishes her last airborne 45 degrees in a Straddle). She lands in a Grin 'n' Bear It, catching herself with her arms around her base's neck.

Combination #5: Hands + Toss Up 180 Degrees + Grin 'n' Bear It

BASE begins holding the flyer in Hands (see figure 12.13). Sinking deeply with his legs, he tosses

Figure 12.13 *Combo Five: Hands + Toss Up 180 Degrees + Grin 'n' Bear It, Step One.*

Figure 12.14 *Combo Five: Hands + Toss Up 180 Degrees + Grin 'n' Bear It, Step Two.*

Figure 12.15 *Combo Five: Hands + Toss Up 180 Degrees + Grin 'n' Bear It, Step Three.*

the flyer upward counterclockwise 180 degrees (see figure 12.14) and catches her in a Grin 'n' Bear It (see figure 12.15).

FLYER is tossed upward and rotates counterclockwise 180 degrees (see figure 12.14). The flyer remains in a vertical position as she turns 180 degrees to face her base. On her descent, she snaps her legs into a Straddle and catches herself with her arms around the base's neck and shoulders (see figure 12.15).

Combination #6: Toss Star Up + 180 Degrees Switch Split + Grin 'n' Bear It

BASE tosses the flyer upward. As the flyer turns to face the base and descends, the base catches the flyer in a Straddle position. The base must toss the flyer high enough to complete her switch splits and land in a Grin 'n' Bear It.

FLYER is tossed upward as if to perform a Star Toss Up stunt. As she flicks off from the base's wrists and brings her legs up into a star position (legs wide), she turns to the left into a narrow left split to initiate her rotation. ("Narrow" split meaning that the flyer's legs aren't in a full 90-degree angle, but are at a half 45-degree angle split from the body.) She then quickly switches her legs from the narrow left split into a narrow right split. Coming down from the toss, the flyer turns her hips to face her base and lands in a Straddle position.

Upside-Down Swing Combination

BASE begins holding the flyer in a Cradle (see figure 12.16). In the Cradle, the base twists toward the left to build momentum. He then twists to the right, allowing the flyer's legs to swing to the front and around his back (see figure 12.17). The base's right arm maintains contact with the flyer's lower back to control her movement. He may have to lean slightly forward as the flyer's legs wrap around his back. The base reaches behind the flyer's legs

Figure 12.16 *Upside-Down Swing Combo, Step One.*

Figure 12.17 *Upside-Down Swing Combo, Step Two.*

Figure 12.18 *Upside-Down Swing Combo, Step Three.*

Figure 12.19 *Upside-Down Swing Combo, Step Four.*

and underneath her knees with his left arm. The flyer is now in a horizontal position across the base's back; the base is holding her around her lower back and around her knees (see figure 12.18). Using the flyer's momentum to continue the swing, the base lets go of her lower back (see figure 12.19) and brings his left arm around toward the front (see figure 12.20). As the flyer's upper body snaps up into a piked position, the base catches underneath her lower back (see figure 12.21). She is now back in a cradle position (see figure 12.22). The stunt is done in one continuous and fluid motion, using momentum to execute the stunt quickly. If done too slowly, it is much harder for both the flyer and the base to execute. Additionally, a slower version is not as visually effective as a fast one.

Figure 12.20 *Upside-Down Swing Combo, Step Five.*

Figure 12.21 *Upside-Down Swing Combo, Step Six.*

Figure 12.22 *Upside-Down Swing Combo, Step Seven.*

FLYER begins in a Cradle position (see figure 12.16). Keeping tight, her legs swing outward

and around the base's back (see figure 12.17). The flyer continues to hold onto the base's neck until she is swung around his back where she then slides her legs around his torso (see figure 12.18). As the base lets go of her upper body, the flyer's upper body swings downward (see figure 12.19). The flyer is now hanging upside-down from the base's left arm (see figure 12.20). As the base pulls the flyer to the front, the flyer bends at the waist (see figure 12.21) and snaps up into a Cradle (see figure 12.22).

This stunt should be practiced on a mat while the partners are learning Swing transitions.

Now that you've learned multiple-base, single-base, and transition stunts, let's move on to one of my favorite stunts performed by both co-ed and all-girl teams: the Basket Toss.

Basket Tosses and Tricks

In Baskets, flyers really do fly. These stunts add true meaning to the word "flyer." Basket Tosses add variety and excitement to a routine; with proper technique, flyers can hit incredible heights.

To begin, bases join their hands together to form the Basket Toss Grip. Each base holds onto his own left wrist and then, with his free hand, grasps his partner's right wrist. This makes a strong, interlocking platform for the flyer to stand on and be thrown from (refer to figure 8.7 on page 114).

— Standard Basket Tosses —

There are many trick variations for Basket Tosses, but let's start with the basics.

Loads for Basket Tosses

In a One-Foot Load, both the bases and the flyer have more time to adjust positioning before throwing the basket. A Two-Foot Load can also be used, depending on the team's preference. Teams should try both sets of timing to see what works best with their personal style.

To Set the Basket

THIRD crouches to the right of the flyer with his right hand under the bases' hands and his left hand around the left side of the flyer's waist.

BASES are standing relatively close to one another and form a Basket Toss Grip with their hands (see figure 13.1 and 13.2). Their backs are straight, heads up, and arms loose. If the arms are completely tight and straightened, it will feel uncomfortable to support the flyer in the load as well as be more difficult to toss the flyer to maximum height. Bending with the knees, the bases are ready for the flyer to load in.

FLYER begins by facing the front with her right foot in the Basket Toss Grip, slightly to the right side to allow room for the left foot if setting in a One-Foot Load (see figure 13.1). The flyer is standing on the toes of her left leg. The flyer's arms are on the bases' shoulders and her weight is over top of the bases (the flyer is holding most of her weight in her arms). Head and chest are up. If the flyer is going to use a Two-Foot Load (see figure 13.2), she stands with her hands on her bases' shoulders, ready to jump on top of the Basket Toss Grip.

TURBO (ADDITIONAL SPOT) stands in front of the stunt, with both hands underneath the Basket Toss Grip, thumbs wrapped around the sides for added support (spot not shown in photos).

Figure 13.1 *One-Foot Basket Toss Load.*

Figure 13.2 *Two-Foot Basket Toss Load.*

Counts for a One-Foot Load Basket Toss

ON COUNTS ONE AND TWO

All stunters remain in their load positions.

ON COUNTS THREE AND FOUR

All stunters sink downward. The motion must be fluid, not jerky.

ON COUNTS FIVE AND SIX

THIRD puts her left hand underneath the Basket Grip as the flyer loads into the stunt with her left foot. This sink is bigger and longer than the first one.

BASES sink together, keeping their arms and shoulders fairly loose.

FLYER places her left foot in the Shreddie. The flyer must remain still and allow the bases to sink for her rather than allowing her knees and hips to bend further. The flyer keeps her weight directly over the bases. Her seat must also remain above 90 degrees and her head and chest up, or she will be tossed backward instead of upward.

TURBO stands in front of the flyer, with hands underneath the bases' Basket Toss Grip and sinks with the other bases.

ON COUNT SEVEN

THIRD and TURBO explode upward, stepping right up underneath the stunt. The third and the turbo must be careful not to push the flyer backward or forward, only upward.

BASES explode upward, tightening the arms, shoulders, and torso. The bases' shoulders shrug upward. Simultaneously, their legs straighten as their arms toss the flyer up between them and fully extend. At the height of the arm extension, all bases (thirds and turbos as well) flick their wrists upward to add additional height to the Basket Toss.

FLYER pushes straight up off of her bases' shoulders as they begin the toss. When her feet are at the bases' shoulder level, she straightens her legs and pushes off from the Basket Toss Grip. The toss happens very quickly; the flyer must explode off from the bases just as rapidly as they toss her. The flyer must keep her chest and eyes up (see figure 13.3) or the toss will go backward. The flyer is caught in a Cradle.

In a Two-Foot Load Basket Toss, the group would use the same counts as if loading an Elevator, starting with the flyer's two feet on the ground.

Troubleshooting Basket Tosses

If you have difficulty hitting your Basket Tosses, the following hints should help you diagnose and solve the problem.

THE FLYER GOES BACKWARD INSTEAD OF UP

★ The flyer's seat may be sinking past 90 degrees. When this happens, the flyer pushes herself backward because her center of gravity isn't positioned directly above her bases.

★ The flyer may be placing her weight on her heels rather than her toes.

— TIP —

Bases' feet must remain on the ground when tossing Baskets.

★ The flyer may be pulling backward rather than up (the flyer is leaning backward in an attempt to hit the Layout position). This can be fixed by having the flyer pull upward through her chest rather than leading backward with her shoulders.

★ The turbo may be pushing the flyer backward instead of upward. This can be easily solved by having the turbo step right up underneath the flyer on the toss.

THE FLYER GOES SIDEWAYS

★ One base may be overthrowing the other. Ensure that both bases are tossing upward and with equal strength.

★ The flyer's hips may be twisting to one side. The flyer should keep her body aligned and facing forward to prevent this.

★ The flyer may be pushing off from the Basket Toss Grip to one side rather than upward. This could be due to either a difference in height or in arm strength of the bases.

THE FLYER ISN'T GETTING ANY HEIGHT

★ The flyer may be jumping out of the toss. The flyer must remain tight while the bases sink and then explode upward at the last second.

★ The flyer may not be holding all of her weight in her arms. Have the flyer practice holding herself up without the bases holding onto her feet. Remind her to push with her arms, rather than with her feet.

★ The flyer's feet could be coming apart, allowing the bases to toss right through them.

★ The flyer may be pushing off too slowly, or the flyer and bases may be pushing at different times. Bases and flyers have to explode upward together on Count Seven.

★ The flyer may not be riding the toss to the top before cradling. A good trick is to have the flyer snap into her piked position (or her trick) one second after she initially feels she should. This slight delay should be enough to put the flyer much higher in the air. The Cradle snap into the piked position should occur on the way down, not at the very top or while still flying upward. Additionally, the flyer should remember to pull up through her chest.

★   The bases may not be fully extending the arms and flicking the wrists at the height of the toss. The flyer shouldn't be released until the elbows have fully extended and the flyer has left the hands. The toss shouldn't stop until it's physically impossible to extend any farther.

★   Bases may be standing up or throwing too slowly. Explode upward on the same count as the flyer (Count Seven).

★   The bases' arms could be too far away from their bodies. Bases should think about being in a narrow upright tube; their grips must stay close to their bodies during both the sink and toss.

★   The bases' legs may be too far apart. After the first sink (in a one-foot Basket Toss Load), bases should bring their feet closer together to narrow their stance. This makes bases taller and thus able to throw higher.

★   The third is crucial in a Basket Toss. Thirds need to get their hands right underneath the grip after the flyer is safely loaded into the stunt and push upward along with the bases.

— Tricks —

Tricks are used to add variety and difficulty to the Cradle dismount of a stunt. They can also be performed at the height of a Basket Toss. Not all tricks can be performed out of both; some tricks can only be done out of a Basket Toss because a lot of height is required to execute them.

Most tricks involve the flyer hitting four distinct positions:

— TIP —

All Basket Tosses require three catchers. At the collegiate level, dismounts from single-base stunts may only require one or two catchers.

1. The straight ride
2. The actual trick
3. The layout following the trick
4. The pike for the catch

The flyer must keep her body tight and snap quickly between these positions. A great way for flyers to become accustomed to their body positioning in the air is to practice first on a gymnastics trampoline or while lying down on the floor.

How to Perform Tricks

Because the flyer is airborne in a toss, tricks are never stationary. Since tricks are performed in constant motion, it is hard to capture the entire movement in only one picture. To make things clearer, under each trick you'll find a description of the trick and a sequence of basic trick positions. Using the basic positions as a guide, follow each move to complete the trick. It's a good idea to have the flyer practice the sequence of moves lying down on the ground or on a trampoline before she's actually thrown in the air. Note that all tricks begin with a Straight Ride (arms can be up or Clean) and end with a Pike so the flyer can be caught in a Cradle.

BASIC TRICK POSITIONS

See figures 13.3 through 13.11 for photos of Basic Trick Positions.

Basic Trick Position #1: Straight Ride

Basic Trick Position #2: Layout

Basic Trick Position #3: Toe Touch

(continues on page 228)

Figure 13.3 *Straight Ride.*

Figure 13.4 *Layout.*

Figure 13.5 *Toe Touch.*

Figure 13.6 *Ball.*

Figure 13.7 *Bottle Rocket.*

(continued from page 226)

Basic Trick Position #4: Ball

Basic Trick Position #5: Bottle Rocket

Basic Trick Position #6: Pike
The Pike is the same as the Bottle Rocket shown in figure 13.7, but both legs are extended upward, rather than just one.

Basic Trick Position #7: X-Out

Basic Trick Position #8: Vertical Twist

Basic Trick Position #9: Front Stall

Upright Basket Toss Tricks

The following Basket Toss tricks are all done in an upright position (that is, no inversion). The numbers next to each trick in the following combinations indicate the basic trick position number.

Figure 13.8 *X-Out (front view).*

Figure 13.9 *X-Out (view from underneath).*

TOE TOUCH

Straight Ride (1) + Toe Touch (3) + Layout (2) + Pike (6)

FLYER rides to the full height of the toss. On the instant the "up" motion turns into the "down" motion, the flyer snaps her feet up into a Toe Touch, remembering to roll her hips under.

Figure 13.10 *Vertical Twist.*

Her arms are out in a "T" motion, reaching for underneath the calves. Her back should be in a curved "C" position to allow for maximum hyperextension of the Toe Touch. The flyer must make sure her weight is not forward in the Toe Touch. After the flyer hits the Toe Touch, she snaps her arms and legs together and lays back in a tight Layout position. After hitting the Layout position, the flyer then snaps into a Pike for the catch.

DOUBLE TOE TOUCH

Straight Ride (1) + Toe Touch (3) + Toe Touch (3) + Layout (2) + Pike (6)

FLYER must time the Toe Touches so that the second Toe Touch occurs at the beginning of the "down" motion. The flyer must have strong hip flexors and lots of height to successfully perform a Double Toe Touch.

Figure 13.11 *Front Stall.*

AROUND THE WORLD

Straight Ride (1) + Pike + Toe Touch (3) + Layout (2) + Pike (6)

FLYER rides upward and snaps into a Pike position a split second before reaching the height of the toss. As the height is reached, the flyer snaps her legs open into a Toe Touch and then snaps them downward together. The Pike, Split, and Snap are done in one fluid motion so the flyer appears to be making a circle with her legs.

TOE TOUCH, FULL TWIST

Straight Ride (1) + Toe Touch (3) + Vertical Twist (8) + Pike (6)

FLYER executes the Toe Touch just before the height of the toss so that when she straightens out and initiates the twist, it is on the "down" motion. Alternatively, the flyer can twist on the way up, hitting her Toe Touch on the "down" motion.

BOTTLE ROCKET

Straight Ride (1) + Bottle Rocket (5) + Layout (2) + Pike (6)

FLYER is tossed upward and simultaneously brings one leg straight up into a vertical split that hits at the height of the toss. Arms reach for the foot up in the air. It is important for the flyer not to allow her bottom leg to bend or come forward. After the height of the toss, she snaps her leg down to Layout and Cradle.

SCISSOR KICK

Straight Ride (1) + Bottle Rocket (5) + Bottle Rocket with other leg (5) + Pike (6)

FLYER is tossed upward and kicks one leg into a vertical split, as in a Bottle Rocket. Immediately after the first split, the flyer switches legs and snaps the other leg up into the opposite side vertical split.

BALL OUT

Straight Ride (1) + Ball (4) + Layout (2) + Pike (6)

FLYER rides the toss to the top of the toss, pulling the knees into the chest. At the height of the toss, she shoots her legs outward so that she is relatively parallel to the ground (horizontal layout position). Her arms are at her sides and toes are pointed. It is important that the flyer *does not* tilt her head back at any time during this trick. If she does, she risks flipping over backward.

X-OUT

Straight Ride (1) + Ball (4) + X-Out (7A) + Pike (6)

FLYER executes the trick exactly as Ball Out except she shoots the legs and arms out into a horizontal "X" position instead of a horizontal Layout position.

BALL OUT BOTTLE ROCKET

Straight Ride (1) + Ball (4) + Bottle Rocket (5) + Pike (6)

FLYER executes the trick just as a Ball Out, only she snaps her legs out into a Vertical Split position instead of a horizontal "X" or Layout position.

PIKE OPEN

Straight Ride (1) + Pike (6) + Layout (2) or X-Out (7A) + Pike (6)

FLYER rides the toss while pulling her legs and arms into a vertical Pike position. At the top, the flyer straightens her waist and shoots her legs and arms into a horizontal Layout position. This trick can also be done as a Pike Open X-Out, with the flyer straightening her waist and shooting her legs and arms into an X-position.

180-DEGREE FRONT STALL 180-DEGREE

Straight Ride (1) + 1/2 of a Vertical Twist (8) + Front Stall (9) + 1/2 of a Horizontal Twist + Pike (6)

FLYER rides the Basket Toss, turning 180 degrees just before reaching the top. When she hits the top, she leans forward into a Front Stall. Her back should be arched, chest up, feet together, and arms in a "T" motion. After hitting the Front Stall, she turns another 180 degrees horizontally and lands into a Cradle, facing the same direction that she was initially tossed. The flyer must pull her arms inward from the Front Stall to help initiate the last half twist.

The Front Stall is often referred to as a Swan Dive.

FRONT STALL 720-DEGREE TWIST
Straight Ride (1) + Front Stall (9) + 2 Horizontal Twists + Pike (6)

FLYER rides the toss, hitting the front stall at the height of the toss; then twists 720 degrees, landing in a cradle position facing the back wall.

Inverted Basket Toss Tricks

In almost all federations and competition rules, it is illegal for teams below the collegiate level to perform inverted tricks. Before attempting any of these inverted Basket Toss tricks, the flyer should feel comfortable doing them on the ground or on a trampoline. Two of the most important skills in performing an inverted trick are being familiar with your body positioning in the air and knowing how to compensate for variables that can change with each time you do a trick, such as over- or under-rotations.

This doesn't mean that a flyer needs to be a national gymnast to perform these tricks, but she does have to have near-perfect body control and familiarity with body positioning in the air. It is important to remember that these two conditions are primarily a result of gymnastics training and

---

— TIP —

Flyers may not exceed one flipping rotation (hips over head) or two twisting rotations in a Basket Toss. Double Layout Full Twists are acceptable because the flyer's hips only rotate once over her head and she does not exceed two twists. Tricks such as Double Back Tucks are prohibited in nearly all federations and organizations because they are fairly dangerous to perform.

---

lots of practice. If a flyer can't do a back tuck on the trampoline, she shouldn't be allowed to attempt one in a Basket Toss, for both her safety and the safety of her bases.

INVERTED TRICK POSITIONS

See figures 13.12 through 13.22 for photos of Inverted Trick Positions.

Note: "Layouts" (hips over head rotations) will be referred to as "Inverted Layouts" to avoid confusing this move with the horizontal "Layout" position that the flyer must hit before being caught in a Cradle.

Inverted Trick Position #1: Back Tuck
Figure 13.12 shows the Back Tuck itself in motion. See page 233 for the entire Back Tuck sequence.

Inverted Trick Position #2: Straighten Out

Inverted Trick Position #3: Inverted Layout

Inverted Trick Position #4: Layout Full Twist

Inverted Trick Position #5: Inverted Pike

COURTESY OF PHOTO SPORT.

Figure 13.12 *Back Tuck.*

Figure 13.13 *Straighten Out.*

Figure 13.14 *Inverted Layout.*

Figure 13.15 *Layout Full Twist.*

Figure 13.16 *Inverted Pike.*

Take a Hint

Flyers should be extra careful not to throw their heads back while performing an inverted stunt. This motion could cause a flyer to go backward instead of upward, cutting her height and increasing the possibility of a dangerous catch. Flyers should concentrate on keeping the head in line with the spine and initiating the rotation with the hips rather than the head.

Figure 13.17 *Back Tuck Sequence, Step One.*

Figure 13.18 *Back Tuck Sequence, Step Two.*

INVERTED BACK TUCK
Straight Ride (1) + Back Tuck (10) + Straighten Out (11) + Pike (6)

FLYER pushes straight off from the bases and rides the Basket to the top. The flyer sets by snapping her arms up to her ears (see figure 13.17) and initiates the rotation by bringing her knees up to her chest (see figure 13.18). The flyer must roll her hips up and think about bringing them overtop of her shoulders (see figure 13.19). The flyer un-tucks slightly

Figure 13.19 *Back Tuck Sequence, Step Three.*

earlier than she would when performing the move on the floor (she would start to un-tuck at Step Four; figure 13.20) and straightens her body. The flyer should try to keep her body straight for as long as possible (see figure

Figure 13.20 *Back Tuck Sequence, Step Four.*

Figure 13.21 *Back Tuck Sequence, Step Five.*

Figure 13.22 *Back Tuck Sequence, Step Six.*

13.21). This creates that "floating" look in the air. The flyer then snaps her chest up, bringing her legs into the Pike position (see figure 13.22). The rotational momentum of the Back Tuck will bring her body into the appropriate Cradle position.

INVERTED BACK TUCK X-OUT
Straight Ride (1) + Back Tuck (10) + X-Out (8B) + Straighten Out (11) + Pike (6)

FLYER executes a Back Tuck. The flyer un-tucks slightly earlier than in a regular Back Tuck. The flyer stalls in the "X" position for slightly longer; from just after halfway through her tuck to just before landing in a Cradle. This means that her third will be able to see the "X" from the time she is upside down and until the last second before the Cradle, when she snaps her legs together in a "V."

INVERTED LAYOUT
Straight Ride (1) + Inverted Layout (12) + Straighten Out (11) + Pike (6)

— **TIP** —

A good tip for the flyer is to untuck as she sees her third. She should then immediately pull her chest up in order to land in the Cradle rather than trying to bend at the waist to get her legs underneath her.

FLYER executes the Basket Toss Layout with the same basic mechanics used to perform a Layout on the ground. The flyer rides the Basket to the top, snapping her arms up for the set, and then pulls her arms downward as she brings her hips upward to initiate the inverted Layout. It's important that the flyer pulls her chest up and spot for the front to bring herself back into an upright position for the catch. The flyer must stall in a Layout for as long as possible, but snap her legs into a Pike with enough time to be caught in the Cradle.

INVERTED TOE TOUCH LAYOUT

Straight Ride (1) + Toe Touch (3) + Inverted Layout (12) + Front Stall (9) + Pike (6)

FLYER is tossed upward and hits at Toe Touch on the way up. Near the height of the toss, the flyer inverts backward, pulling her legs together and snapping her hands to her sides in an Inverted Layout. This trick can also be thought of as an upside-down Toe Touch. As the flyer rotates around toward the front, she hits a Front Stall position and quickly snaps her legs into a Cradle position before being caught by her bases.

INVERTED LAYOUT STEP-OUT

Straight Ride (1) + Inverted Layout (12) + Right or Left Split + Straighten Out (11) + Pike (6)

FLYER performs this trick in the same manner as a Layout except that she "steps out" at the height of the trick. The flyer snaps her legs into either a right or left split and then brings them back together to land in the Cradle.

INVERTED LAYOUT FULL TWIST

Straight Ride (1) + Inverted Layout Full Twist (13) + Straighten Out (11) + Pike (6)

FLYER executes the Layout Full in the same way as the Layout, but snaps her hands down to the left (or right) to initiate the twist (see figure 13.15) This movement is similar to the motion of twisting in a vertical position, except that she also rotates with her hips over her head. The flyer must be careful not to twist too early. If she does, she likely won't have enough time to complete the twist. If a flyer finds that she is short on time, the best thing to do is quickly pull her chest up and snap her hip flexors into a Pike position for the Cradle. She should *not* bend her knees in this situation. Bending the knees doesn't help any more than snapping the hips under, and it doesn't look as clean.

INVERTED LAYOUT DOUBLE FULL

Straight Ride (1) + Inverted Layout Full Double Twist (13) + Straighten Out (11) + Pike (6)

FLYER performs the trick in the same way as a Layout Full Twist except she pulls harder and faster to complete both twists.

INVERTED PIKE

Straight Ride (1) + Inverted Pike (14) + Straighten Out (11) + Pike (6)

FLYER hits a Pike position at the height of the toss. Opening up at her waist, the flyer straightens into a Layout position to continue the inversion. She completes the rotation and lands in a Cradle. The Pike Inverted Basket Toss is similar to the Layout, except that the flyer bends at the waist and then straightens rather than maintains a straight body the entire way through. (See figure 13.16.)

INVERTED PIKE STEP-OUT

Straight Ride (1) + Inverted Pike (14) + Right or Left Split + Straighten Out (11) + Pike (6)

FLYER hits a Pike, splitting her legs as she lays back and continues the inversion. For both the Inverted Pike and the Inverted Pike Step Out tricks, the flyer's arms reach up to her toes at the Pike position and then snap downward to her sides as she straightens out.

180-DEGREE FRONT STALL FRONT TUCK

Straight Ride (1) + 1/2 of a Vertical Twist (8) + Front Stall (9) + Front Tuck + Pike (6)

FLYER rides the Basket, turning 180 degrees and hitting a Front Stall at the top. The flyer then front tucks *with her legs straight* and keeping her arms in a "T," lands in a Cradle.

180-Degree Front Stall Front Variation

Straight Ride (1) + 1/2 of a Vertical Twist (8) + Front Stall (9) with one leg dropped down + 1/2 Twist or 1 1/2 Twist + Pike (6)

FLYER rides the Basket just like a 180-Degree Front Stall front tuck but drops one leg in the Front Stall position, perpendicular to her body. She then snaps her legs together and rotates 180 degrees (or 540 degrees) horizontally into a Cradle. As with hitting any Front Stall, the flyer must pull her chest into an upright position and use her arms to initiate the twist.

— Gauntlets —

Gauntlets are Basket Tosses from one base group to another. When first attempting Gauntlets, the spotters should position themselves in the spaces between the "tossing" base group and the "catching" base group. If the flyer isn't tossed far enough to the second base group, the spotters can become catchers. Spotters should be used every time a new base group attempts a Gauntlet, whether or not the flyer has previously performed a Gauntlet, to ensure that she is safely caught.

Front Gauntlet

Straight Ride (1) forward + Front Stall (9) + Front Tuck + Pike (6)

The tossing base group is positioned behind the catching base group; the distance between the two groups will depend on the flyer's trick and on the height and length of the toss.

FLYER is tossed forward into a Front Stall position. Her head and chest are up and arms are in a "T" position. Her back should be slightly arched. On the downward motion of the toss forward, the flyer performs a Front Tuck, *keeping her legs straight* in preparation for landing in the Cradle of the catching bases. Unlike a regular Front Tuck, the flyer keeps her arms open during the rotation, which puts her in the right position to catch her bases.

Sideways Gauntlets

Sideways Gauntlets can be performed in three main ways:

SIDEWAYS GAUNTLET #1: TUCK STAR OUT

Straight Ride (1) forward + 1/4 of a Vertical Twist (8) + Star Position + 1/4 of a Vertical Twist (8) in the same direction as before + Pike (6)

The tossing base group begins facing the catching base group. As with the Front Gauntlet, the distance between the two groups will depend on the individual toss of each base group.

FLYER is tossed forward and to the catching base group. As she pushes off the tossing base group, she turns her body 90 degrees to face the front and snaps her body into a "star" position. As she approaches the catching base group, she turns her body another 90 degrees in the same direction as before. She is now facing her tossing base group. The flyer snaps into a Cradle position and is caught by the second group.

SIDEWAYS GAUNTLET #2: BOTTLE ROCKET
Straight Ride (1) backwards + Bottle Rocket (5) + Layout (2) + Pike (6)

Both base groups begin facing the same side (for example, the right wall).

FLYER is tossed backward from the tossing group; on the ascent, she snaps one leg up into a Bottle Rocket position. On the descent, the flyer lays out and snaps into a Cradle position as she is caught by the catching group. The flyer's body does not change directions during this type of Gauntlet.

SIDEWAYS GAUNTLET #3: BALL OUT
Straight Ride (1) sideways or backwards + 1/4 of a Vertical Twist (8) if tossed sideways + Ball (4) + Layout (2) + Pike (6)

This variation is performed exactly as in the Bottle Rocket (see page 230), only the flyer tucks her legs in and opens into a straight, laid-out position. It is even more visually appealing if the flyer exaggerates her layout and arches her back on the descent.

As with all other stunts, a qualified coach should be present when groups practice Basket Tosses.

Your knowledge of Loads, Dismounts, Stationary and Transition Stunts, and Basket Tosses will all be put to good use in the next section: Pyramids.

Pyramids and Stunt Combinations

Two stunts are always better than one. And five interacting, connecting stunts are always better than two. If you think the crowd is impressed watching your Heel Stretch Fulls, wait until you see their reaction when you perform an Inside Heel Stretch pyramid with twisting dismounts.

What most fans don't realize is that while pyramids look exceedingly difficult, they're really only a group of individual stunts connected together. A pyramid is just one big mega-stunt where the possibilities of creative loads, unique transitions, and innovative dismounts are endless.

— When to Build Mega-Stunts —

★ At games: after a great play, after scoring, or during halftime

★ During pep rallies

★ During competition routines (Don't even think about leaving them out of your routine!)

★ Whenever you want to draw attention to the team

— Pyramid Glossary —

The following terms are used frequently when discussing pyramids:

Inside Skill: Inside Hitch Pyramid, Inside Heel Stretch Pyramid, Inside Arabesque Pyramid. These three pyramids have one thing in common: The flyers on either side of the center flyer are using the leg closest to the middle to perform the skill.

Outside Skill: Outside Hitch Pyramid, Outside Heel Stretch Pyramid, Outside Arabesque Pyramid. In each of these pyramids, the flyers on either side of the center flyer are using their outside leg; the one farthest from the middle. In an outside skill, the flyers are standing on their inside leg.

One-and-a-Half High: Shoulder Sit, chest level Straddle Sit, Chair, Thigh Stand. A one-and-a-half–high skill is the height of one person plus half of the other.

Two High: Elevator, Shoulder Stand, Extension, Liberty, Cupie/Awesome. A two-high skill consists of the height of two people. A stunt is denoted as "two high" regardless of whether the skill is at chest level or at an extended level.

Two-and-a-Half High: A two-and-a-half–high skill consists of a two-high stunt plus half the height of another flyer. This means that there are three levels: a base, a mid-base, and a top

— **TIP** —

Most rules and regulations require that two-and-a-half–high pyramids have a specific spotter for each flyer on the third level, both in the front and in the back of the pyramid.

flyer. In most varsity competitions, two-and-a-half–high pyramids are illegal; check the regulations before you put one into your routine. They are, however, legal for college/university level teams.

High Skill: High Chair, High Liberty, High Awesome. These are two-and-a-half–high pyramids that are built by loading the mid-base into a Thigh Stand. The top flyer is then loaded onto the mid-base in a partner stunt (usually an extended stunt).

Pyramid Pointers

If you want to score five stars from the judges, your pyramids must be solid, controlled, and visually pleasing. These first two conditions rely on the team's skills. The choreography of a pyramid, however, is a factor that any team, regardless of skill, can use to boost artistic scores. The way the pyramid is loaded, transitioned, and dismounted is just as important as hitting the pyramid. Here are some pointers to make your pyramids interesting and reliable.

USE VARIOUS LOADS

Avoid using the same old Toss or Standard Load whenever possible; it's been done a million times before. Twist Ups, 360-Degree Loads, Ground Up Loads, Basket Toss Loads, and other creative mounts will grab the crowd's attention much faster than a common load.

USE CREATIVITY WHEN CONNECTING FLYERS

There are numerous ways to connect flyers in a pyramid—joining arms; holding feet in hitches or Heel Stretches; or by resting feet on shoulders, stomachs, arms, or backs. Experiment with new ways to connect your flyers to one another. This connection could be the difference between a bunch of mediocre stunts and an awesome pyramid. When designing two-and-a-half–high pyramids, get creative with how your flyers link—on the mid-base's pockets, on the lower back, or on the arm at waist level. The possibilities end only where your imagination does.

USE TRANSITIONS TO LINK PYRAMIDS

If two stunts are better than one, two pyramids rather than just one will make your routine ten times more visually effective. (While you're up there, you might as well do another one, right?) Sponges, Regrabs, and Show stunts are perfect for transitioning from one pyramid to the next.

EXPERIMENT WITH DIFFERENT TIMING

Rather than choreograph synchronized timing throughout the pyramid, use timing techniques such as ripples (see chapter 15) and alternating loads to add variety and visual appeal to the pyramid segment. For example, if flyers load up together for the first pyramid, choreograph different timing for each group to transition into the next pyramid.

INCORPORATE ROTATIONS, MOVEMENTS, AND DIRECTION CHANGES

Rotating and traveling pyramids are guaranteed ways to score points with the judges and fans. An effective directional change that involves both rotation and movement is the "Circle to Line" formation. Stunt partners begin facing one another in a circle and flyers join arms to link the groups. One group opens up the circle by walking to the other side of the floor, bringing the groups from a circle into a line (flyers remain connected).

ADD HEIGHT VARIATIONS FOR VISUAL APPEAL

Examples of low height stunts include Thigh Stands, Shoulder Sits, and Straddle Sit at chest level or higher. Low-height stunts are classified as one-and-a-half high. Mid-height stunts hold the flyer's feet at chest level. Examples include Elevators, Hands, Shoulder Stands, and Straddle Sits. Any extended stunt like Extensions, Liberties, and Cupies are considered high-level stunts. Both mid-height and high stunts constitute two-high stunts. Two-and-a-half–high pyramids use mid-bases to support a third level of flyers. Pyramids such as Table Tops and High Liberties are examples of two-and-a-half–high pyramids. Use as many different levels as possible to give the pyramid a more visual appeal.

DISMOUNT IN STYLE

If your team has the skills to execute more difficult dismounts such as Twisting Cradles, stay away from regular Pop Downs! Creative dismounts give the crowd something to "ooh" and "ahh" over. As long as the team has enough room and the flyer can safely perform the dismount trick, any judge will tell you that clean Twisting Dismounts are better than straight ones. Don't forget though, *clean* Straight Cradles are still better than messy Twists.

STAY CLEAN

Always dismount clean and controlled. A dangerous number of teams quickly abandon their flyers at the end of the performance rather than dismounting clean. Drop this bad habit, not your flyer. Just because you're excited about hitting a perfect routine doesn't mean you can get rid of your flyer as fast as possible to hit the crowd. An unclean, unsafe dismount has the potential to bring down the overall impression of your routine. It's also unsafe, and this could result in serious injuries to flyers or even in safety infractions. Bring your flyers down safely and cleanly *before* you hit the crowd.

FEEL THE FLOW

Pyramids should be controlled and not rushed. For maximum effectiveness, you want the pyramid to load, transition, and dismount as smoothly and as cleanly as possible. Keep the stunting at a pace that's fast enough to use momentum to your advantage, but slow enough that you can use good technique and that you're not rushing. Pyramids have a tendency to topple very quickly when performed by frantic stunters.

— Building Great Pyramids —

Loading a pyramid with creativity and good technique is just as important as hitting the pyramid itself. Keep the following points in mind to ensure that you stay safe and clean when loading your pyramid.

The Set-Up

Before you begin loading a pyramid, keep in mind the same stunting precautions that apply to partner stunting. Spotters are especially important to have at the sides, front, and back of the pyramid. Because pyramids involve connecting stunt groups together, you must follow a few extra steps before putting up your pyramid. Be sure you have satisfactory answers to each of the following questions.

1. DOES EVERYONE KNOW WHAT THE FINISHED PYRAMID WILL LOOK LIKE?

If, after describing the pyramid in detail, the only response you get is a group of bewildered faces, you'll need to use visual tools to explain it again. Start by bringing the flyers forward and arranging them into their finished positions. If it is a

---

— TIP —

Most cheerleading associations require a minimum of two catchers for Cradle Dismounts over two high. Note also that flipping or twisting dismounts by the top flyer from a two-and-a-half-high pyramid cannot exceed one rotation and may require hands-on assistance.

two-and-a-half–high pyramid, use spotters for assistance. Not only does this exercise make it easier to picture how the pyramid will look in the air, but it helps the flyers become comfortable with the body positioning they are required to hit in the air. If this activity doesn't help, bring out the chalkboard.

2. CAN ALL TEAM MEMBERS HIT THEIR INDIVIDUAL STUNTS PERFECTLY?

Before attempting to link a pyramid together, individual partner stunts must be solid. (If the pyramid is two-and-a-half high, it may be impossible to have the top flyers perform this stage.) The mid-bases must be completely confident in their positions before attempting to load the top flyer. This is a vital step; don't skip it.

3. IS EVERYONE CLEAR ON HOW TO DISMOUNT?

Top flyers shouldn't be wondering how they're going to get down from a two-and-a-half–high pyramid. Each flyer should be clear on her dismount, whether it is a Double Twisting Cradle or a simple Pop Down.

Build Your Pyramid Step-by-Step

Here are ten steps to pyramid success:

1. If the pyramid has two sides, break it up into halves and build one side at a time. Be sure you have spotters in each corner. Add extra catchers when building a pyramid for the first time, especially if it is two-and-a-half high.

2. Load levels one at a time—first mid-bases and then top flyer. Don't try to load everyone all together just yet.

3. When the mid-bases are solid, load the top flyer.

4. If the flyer comes down but the mid-bases are still up, load the top flyer again. If the top flyer still hasn't hit it after trying twice, have everyone dismount and take a quick break before trying it again.

5. Once the top flyer hits the pyramid and is solid, instruct her to dismount first. Then dismount the mid-bases.

6. Repeat this procedure for the other side.

7. Once both sides have hit the pyramid perfectly a number of times, load both sides together; mid-bases first and then top flyers.

8. Dismount top flyers and then mid-bases.

9. When both groups have hit the pyramid together, break it up again into two groups and practice loading and dismounting the mid-bases and top flyer at the same time. If this isn't possible (for example, the top flyer requires both sides standing to load onto the pyramid, like in a 2-2-1), skip this step.

10. Put both sides together.

— Loading Flyers into Two-and-a-Half–High Pyramids —

Flyers can be loaded into two-and-a-half–high pyramids in a few different ways:

Elevator Toss Up

In this type of load, the flyer begins in an Elevator and is usually already connected to her mid-bases by holding onto their arms. The bases holding the Elevator sink together and toss the flyer upward onto the mid-bases. An Elevator Toss Up load would be suitable for loading pyramids such as the 4-2-1, Table Top, or Split Pyramid. This load is widely used for multiple-base pyramids.

Thigh Pop Load

This is a simple and easy way to load the top flyer onto a two-and-a-half–high pyramid. The top flyer loads into a Thigh Pop and is tossed upward onto her mid-bases. This is another commonly used load by teams that use multiple bases to stunt.

Toe Pitch/Toss Load

The Toe Pitch/Toss load is frequently used in single-base pyramids. The flyer begins with one foot in a Toe Pitch in front of her and holds onto her tosser's wrists. The flyer is then tossed up to her mid-bases.

Basket Toss Load

This is the most effective load to use when the top flyer needs lots of height to hit her position on top of the pyramid. She is loaded into a Basket Toss Load and is thrown upward and onto her mid-bases. The danger in using this load is that the bases can toss the flyer too high, causing her to jolt her mid-bases as she lands on them. If the mid-bases are jolted enough to lose their balance, there is an increased risk in the possibility of the pyramid toppling down. Additionally, a free flight up to a pyramid has less control over where the flyer lands. The Basket Toss Load is frequently used to load 2-1-1 pyramids, such as a High Liberty pyramid.

The Power Press Up/Ground Up Load

This pyramid load begins with the bases either holding the mid-bases in a low height stunt or starting from a Ground Up position (the flyer standing on her bases' feet). The mid-bases are now low enough to the ground that the top flyer(s) are able to load on without having to be tossed upward. Once the top flyers are solid on their mid-bases, the bases sink together and press the entire pyramid up to chest level. This type of load is frequently used in the Ground Up press to chest-level Wolf Wall Pyramid.

— Good Connections —

When flyers connect with one another in the air, it is imperative that they join to one another in the safest possible manner. Flyers who hold on too tightly will pull the entire pyramid down in the event that one of them falls. This is why flyers generally just touch, rather than actually hold on when connecting (there are a few exceptions). In cases where flyers join arms to link stunts together, the flyer's hands should be in Blades and just touching the other's forearm rather than grasping it.

In a two-high pyramid that doesn't require the flyer to support a top flyer's weight, flyers with extended arms or legs must hold their own limbs up. There should be minimal weight on the cheerleader who is supporting the flyer's arm or leg. This alleviates unnecessary weight on both the supporting flyer and their bases, especially in pyramids that connect together via one main flyer (such as Inside Heel Stretch Pyramids). When flyers hold their own weight, the stability of the pyramid is increased. Additionally, transitioning to another pyramid is easier when flyers aren't relying on one another for support.

In a two-and-a-half–high pyramid, additional bases are often added to the bottom of the pyramid for extra stability and support. This extra base usually assists the main base with holding the flyer or (if applicable) reaches up to support underneath the mid-bases extended leg (in a Wolf Wall pyramid, for example).

Because pyramids can become high stunts and involve multiple levels, the mid-bases must utilize good technique in order to keep the top flyer stable in the pyramid. Mid-bases should hold the top flyer in exactly the same way as if they were basing on ground level. This means keeping good posture, holding the flyer in close to the body to stabilize the stunt, and working in sync with the other mid-base(s).

For low-height stunts that connect together by holding a flyer's foot, such as a Shoulder Sit flyer holding a Hitch (which means that the flyer's leg is bent), the low-height flyer must lock her arms out above her head. This puts the weight of the flyer's foot directly over top of the low-height flyer and her base, rather than just the shoulders and arms of the flyer at the low height.

— Look Out Below! —

Yes, pyramids *can* be hazardous to your health, but *only* if you don't utilize proper safety and spotting techniques. To avoid potential injuries, follow the number one Golden Rule of pyramids (and stunting in general): *You are responsible for your own flyer.*

It's that simple. Take care of your own flyer. Don't make a crazy dive for the top flyer when your own mid-base is headed for the ground at Mach One. This is the biggest mistake made by bases and thirds when catching a falling pyramid; they reach for a flyer who isn't theirs and end up hurting themselves or leaving their own flyer unprotected. Leave the Superman rescues to the spotters; that's what they're there for.

— Pyramid Photos —

Following are some examples of the pyramids we've discussed in this chapter. Once you see them in action, you'll be more excited to learn and demonstrate them.

Two-High Pyramids

Here are examples of the Inside Hitch (figure 14.1), Outside Hitch (figure 14.2). Inside Heel Stretch (figure 14.3), Outside Heel Stretch (figure 14.4), and Outside Elevator/Liberty (figure 14.5).

Two-and-a-Half—High Pyramids

Here are examples of the 4-2-1 (figure 14.6), High Cupie (figure 14.7), Co-ed 2-2-1 (figure 14.8), High Chair (figure 14.9), Table Top (figure 14.10), Wolf Wall (figure 14.11).

— Stunt Combinations —

Here are some combinations that can be used in partner stunts or in transitions to a pyramid. Before you begin, read through the stunting guidelines on each stunt so you'll understand how to connect them with the appropriate variation. Perfect the Intermediate combinations (combinations up to one-and-a-half high) before attempting the Advanced combinations (two-high stunt combinations). Then perfect the Advanced combinations before moving onto the Elite ones (diffi-

cult two-high stunt combinations). This way, you'll have a solid foundation of technique and experience helping you to hit every stunt perfectly. Remember that while every combination may not be appropriate for your level or regulations, most combinations can easily be adjusted to meet the requirements. For example, an Extension can easily be changed into an Elevator, and a Liberty can easily be changed into a Torch.

Follow the sequence of stunts in each combination, and link them together on the timing that feels best for your group. For example, you may find that adding a double bounce gives your group more time to adjust hand positions or synchronize movements in preparation for the next stunt. Start with these combinations and test them out, then change them around and add to them. One of the greatest features of cheerleading is that you are limited only by your own creativity (and, of course, a few safety regulations).

Multiple-Base Stunt Combinations

The following lists provide examples of combinations you might choose to perform, classified according to Intermediate, Advanced, and Elite levels.

INTERMEDIATE MULTIPLE-BASE STUNT COMBINATIONS

1. Show Thigh Stand Kick + One-Foot Load + Thigh Stand Load + Straddle Sit

2. Thigh Stand Offset + Sponge to a Thigh Stand Load + Chair

3. One-Foot Load to Thigh Stand + Sponge to a Thigh Stand Load + Flatback + Leg Raise Variation

4. Ground Up Load to Flatback + Straddle Sit + Sponge + Thigh Stand Load + Shoulder Split

5. Straddle Sit + Cradle Dismount + Regrab + Thigh Stand Prep + Thigh Stand Heel Stretch

(continues on page 247)

Two-High Pyramids

Figure 14.1 *Inside Hitch.*

Figure 14.2 *Outside Hitch.*

Figure 14.3 *Inside Heel Stretch.*

Figure 14.4 *Outside Heel Stretch.*

Figure 14.5 *Outside Elevator/Liberty.*

Two-and-a-Half-High Pyramids

Figure 14.6 *4-2-1 Pyramid.*

Figure 14.7 *High Cupie.*

Figure 14.8 *Co-ed 2-2-1 Pyramid.*

Figure 14.9 *High Chair.*

Figure 14.10 *Table Top.*

Figure 14.11 *Wolf Wall.*

(continued from page 244)

6. Cradle catch + Flatback + Straddle Sit + Sponge + Thigh Stand Load + Thigh Stand

7. Walk Up Shoulder Sit on third + Sponge + Thigh Stand Load + Straddle Sit

8. One-Foot, Two-Foot Load to Thigh Stand + Sponge to One-Foot Load + Show Kick + One-Foot Load + Thigh Stand Liberty

9. One-Foot Load + Thigh Stand Offset + Pop Down + Hop 'n' Go Load + Thigh Stand Load + Thigh Stand

10. Thigh Stand Offset + Sponge into One-Foot Load + Show Kick + Liberty Thigh Stand

11. Hop 'n' Go Load + Thigh Stand Load + Chair

12. Shoulder Sit on third + Pop Off to the front + double bounce + Hop 'n' Go Load + Thigh Stand Load + Thigh Stand Offset

13. Thigh Stand Load + Shoulder Split + Sponge into a Thigh Stand Load + Show Thigh Stand + Thigh Stand Load + Chair

14. Thigh Stand Offset + Sponge into a Thigh Stand Load + Thigh Stand Offset (opposite leg than the first one) + Sponge into a Thigh Stand Load + Straddle Sit

15. Hop 'n' Go Load + Thigh Stand Load + Straddle Sit + Cradle + Flatback: Leg Raise Variation

ADVANCED MULTIPLE-BASE STUNT COMBINATIONS

1. Flyer round-offs or back handsprings into the Cradle position + Regrab + Elevator

2. Ground Up Flatback Load: Flatback Leg Raise Variation + 360-Degree Log Roll Dismount to Cradle + Regrab to Thigh Stand Load + Chair

3. Toe Touch Basket Toss or Thigh Pop + Regrab + Show Elevator or Extension + Thigh Stand Load + Chair

4. Show Kick + One-Foot, Two-Foot Load + Thigh Pop

5. Straddle Sit + Twist Dismount + Flatback + Elevator

6. Grin 'n' Bear It Shoulder Sit Load + Shoulder Sit + Elevator + Toe Touch Cradle

7. Ground Up Chair + Sponge to Standard Load + Elevator or Extension

8. Show Kick + Ground Up Torch or Liberty + Sponge to Ground Up Arabesque (90-degree turn to the side at the bottom of the Sponge. You may want to add a double bounce here.)

9. Basket Toss Toe Touch + 360-Degree Log Roll + Flatback: Leg Raise Variation

10. Elevator + Ball Out Cradle + 360-Degree Log Roll + Regrab to One-Foot Load + Torch or Liberty

11. Show Extension + Standard Load + Elevator + Flip Over into a Cradle + Regrab + Chair/Elevator/Extension

12. 180-Degree Twist Up to Elevator + Sponge to Standard Load (flyer holds front spot's hands while sponging rather than putting her hands on the base's shoulders) + Pop Over + Standard Load + Chair

13. (Base group begins facing the back) Thigh Pop 180-Degree + Standard Load + Show Extension + Flip Over (use an additional base for the post) + Regrab + Standard Load + Elevator (this is a harder variation of #11)

14. Double Back Load to Elevator + Press to Extension (continuous "and go" motion. Don't stop in the elevator but sink and press right up to an Extension) Sponge + Elevator + Assisted Front Tuck Dismount

15. One-Foot Load to Offset + Pop Down + Hop 'n' Go Load + Elevator or Heel Stretch Torch or Heel Stretch Liberty

ELITE MULTIPLE-BASE STUNT COMBINATIONS

1. Facing the side: Show Kick to Cradle + Regrab + One-Foot Load + Arabesque

2. Show Kick + Liberty + Sponge 1/4 turn to side + Scale

3. 180-Degree Thigh Pop + Standard Load + Show 360-Degree + Standard Load + One-Foot, Two-Foot Load + Elevator or Extension

4. Double Back Load to Cupie + Sponge to One-Foot Elevator Load: 1/4 turn to side + Arabesque + Twist Dismount

5. X-Out Basket Toss + Regrab + One-Foot Load + Show Kick + One-Foot Load + Heel Stretch + Twist Dismount

6. Grin 'n' Bear It + Shoulder Sit + Single-Base Hands or Extension

7. 180-Degree Thigh Pop + 180-Degree Thigh Pop; flyer lands into left splits + Elevator

8. 180-Degree Twist Up + Elevator + Sponge to Standard Load + Show 360-Degree + One-Foot Load + Liberty

9. Facing the side: Walk-In One-Foot Elevator Load + Cupie + Rotate 90 degrees to face the front + Sponge to Mid-Level: 1/4 turn to the left side on the way down + Scorpion

10. Bottle Rocket Basket Toss + 360-Degree Log Roll + Regrab to Standard Load + 180-Degree Thigh Pop + Show 360-Degree + Standard Load + 1/4 turn + Scale

11. Facing the side: Show Kick to Cradle (to your own base group) + Regrab + One-Foot Load + Heel Stretch + 3/4 turn in the Heel Stretch to face the front

12. 180-Degree Twist Up + Extension + Sponge Straddle Sit + Elevator or Extension + Toe Touch, Cradle Dismount

13. Standard Load to Single-Base Hands + Sponge to Shoulder Sit + Single-Base Liberty

14. 180-Degree Twist In + Elevator + Ball X-Out + Regrab + Flatback + Heel Stretch + Double Twist Dismount

15. Corkscrew Arabesque/Heel Stretch Liberty + Double Twist Dismount + Regrab to One-Foot Load + Elevator + Assisted Front Tuck Dismount + Hop 'n' Go + Standard Load + Extension

Single-Base Stunt Combinations

INTERMEDIATE SINGLE-BASE STUNT COMBINATIONS

1. Toss Chair + Hands + Pop Down

2. Single Back Load + Hands + Sponge + Shoulder Sit + Hands

3. Assisted 180-Degree Side Toss + Hands + Sponge to Walk Load with assisting base + Hands

4. Toss Hands + Pop Down + Double Bounce + Toss Chair

5. Single Back Load + Hands + Assisted Reverse Walk Load + Hands

6. Toss Toe Touch + Toss Chair

7. Grin 'n' Bear It + Shoulder Sit + Sponge + Hands

8. Toss Chair + Hands + Pop Down + Side Shoulder Sit

9. Toss Shoulder Sit + Forward Dismount + Double Bounce + Toss Hands

10. Walk Hands + assisted Sponge to Walk Hands Load + Hands

11. Single Back Load + Hands + Pop Down + Side Shoulder Sit

12. Toss Toe Touch + Traveling Toss Load + Toss Hands

13. Walk Reverse Hands + Sponge to Walk Load + Walk Extension (assisted)

14. Toss Toe Touch + Toss Side Shoulder Sit + Pop Down 'n' Go to Hands + Assisted Press Up + Extension

15. Walk Reverse Hands + 180-Degree Pop + Hands + Assisted Press Up + Extension

ADVANCED SINGLE-BASE STUNT COMBINATIONS

1. Toss Hands + Reverse Walk Load + Walk Liberty

2. Walk Load (Toe Pitch) Toss Up (Flyer brings her knees to her chest above the base) + Grin 'n' Bear It + Walk Load + Walk and Go Extension

3. Toss 'n' Go Liberty + Sponge to Hands + Press Up Heel Stretch + Twist Dismount

4. Toe Pitch Toss 360 Degrees + Walk Load + Walk Extension

5. Assisted 270-Degree Toe Pitch + Liberty + Toss Up 180-Degrees + Grin 'n' Bear It + Walk Arabesque

6. Back Tuck X-Out Basket Toss + Regrab Cradle to Hands + Heel Stretch + Twist Dismount + 360-Degree Prep + Toss Extension

7. Toss Hands + Sponge + Shoulder Sit + Heel Stretch + Twist Dismount

8. Back Bootie Cupie + Pop Down to the spot behind the base + Assisted Step Up Liberty

9. Assisted 270-Degree Toe Pitch + Arabesque + Cradle + Tuck In Grin 'n' Bear It + Walk Load + Extension

10. Walk Hands + Liberty to Walk Load + Walk Hands Reverse (flyer facing back) + 180-Degree Pop + Hands 'n' Go Liberty

11. Toss 'n' Go Liberty + Cradle + Regrab + Hands + Retake Walk Load + Walk 'n' Go Extension

12. Walk Load Reverse (flyer facing back) + Reverse Offset + Liberty + Cradle + Regrab to Toss Load + Toss 'n' Go Extension

13. Walk Hands + 'N Go+ Press Up Heel Stretch + Twist Cradle + Tuck In Grin 'n' Bear It + Two-Foot Load + Liberty

14. Peg Leg + Liberty + Hands + Reverse Walk Load + Walk Extension

15. Toss 'n' Go Cupie + Sponge + Hands 'n' Go X-Scale (flyer turns 1/4 to side)

ELITE SINGLE-BASE STUNT

1. Tuck Up Toss + Heel Stretch + Double Twist Cradle + 360-Degree Log Roll to Toss Load + Toss Cupie

2. Toss 360-Degree Arabesque + Double Twist Cradle + 270-Degree + Grin 'n' Bear It + Two-Foot Load + Cupie

3. One-Foot, Two-Foot Walk Load + Toss 360-Degree + Flyer lands in a Grin 'n' Bear It + Two-Foot Load + Heel Stretch

4. Toss 180-Degree Switch Split Grin 'n' Bear It + Walk Load + Show 360 Degrees + Walk Load + Heel Stretch + Double Twist Dismount

5. Walk Load Toss Up (Flyer brings her knees to her chest above the base) + Grin 'n' Bear It + Two-Foot Load + Cupie + 90-Degree Twist Cradle + 360-Degree Log Roll to Toss Load (partners are now facing the side) + Toss X-Scale (base facing forward, flyer facing forward)

6. Toss Cupie + 90-Degree Twist Cradle (base remains facing the front) + 270-Degree + Grin 'n' Bear It + Two-Foot Walk Load + Reverse Offset Load + Heel Stretch + Double Twist Dismount

7. Ball and Chain + Liberty

8. Walk Load Toss Up (Flyer brings her knees to her chest above the base) + Grin 'n' Bear It + Walk Load + Walk Arabesque + Double Twist Cradle + Regrab to Hands 'n' Go Cupie

9. J-Up + Arabesque + 90-Degree Pop inward + Grin 'n' Bear It + Walk Load + Liberty

10. Swing + 360-Degree Log Roll + Toss Load + Tuck Up Toss + Heel Stretch

11. Handstand Load + Cupie + Cradle + 270-degree turn + Grin 'n' Bear It + Two-Foot Walk Load + 270-degree turn + Scale

12. Toss Tuck Up + Heel Stretch + Double Twist Cradle + 360-Degree Log Roll to Toss Load + Toss 270-Degree Arabesque + Twist Cradle + 360-Degree Log Roll To Toss Load + Toss Star Up + Cupie + Cradle

13. Toss one-handed Liberty + Pop Down + Toss + flyer turns 180 degrees toward her

base + Grin 'n ' Bear It + Two-Foot Load + Cupie

14. Toss 180-Degree Switch Split + Grin 'n' Bear It + Walk Load + Show 360 Degrees + Walk Heel Stretch

15. Rewind + Cupie + Tick Tock + Cradle + Regrab + Scorpion

PART FOUR

Getting It Together for Competition

Choreographers' Organization and Cheerleaders' Preparation

Routine Choreography

Competition takes a lot of work—but the payoff is definitely worth it. More than ever it is important for coaches and cheerleaders to work together as a team, to the best of their abilities.

When you start choreographing a routine, first decide on the routine's major sections—which pyramids, dances, partner stunts, and cheer elements will be used, and in what order. The first part of the routine should immediately grab the crowd's attention; often a difficult partner stunt or pyramid is used for the opening. Not only is it an exciting way to begin the routine, but the athletes are fresh and have a better chance of hitting the segment with ease. The most difficult sections (tumbling, pyramids, stunts) should be performed in the first half of the routine while cheers, dances, and less difficult stunts are better suited for near the middle to the end of a routine when athletes are becoming tired. As with the opening of a routine, the ending should also be memorable to judges. Pyramids or stunt combinations are often effective endings.

— Choreography Hints —

Since choreography is the most creative aspect of cheerleading, it's more effective to provide hints than a step-by-step explanation or how to choreograph routines. Here, grouped into typical categories, are some helpful ideas:

COACHES' CORNER

BASIC STEPS OF CHOREOGRAPHY

Before choreographing a routine for a competition, review the score sheet and rules to become familiar with what the judges are looking for. Judges frequently score teams based on skill level, technique, creativity, consistency (no falls or wobbles), enthusiasm/facial expression, safety (deductions are given for poor spotting), and transitions/formation changes. After you become familiar with this, review all the competition guidelines (illegal stunts and moves, routine length, and any other stipulations), then you can begin your choreographing.

HINTS FOR CHOREOGRAPHING STUNTS

★ Choreograph the most difficult stunts near the beginning of the routine.

★ Keep the stunts at a level the team is capable of hitting. Avoid writing partner stunts into the routine that your athletes cannot consistently hit.

★ Remember that the same stunt groups should stunt together for the entire routine.

★ Transition stunts rather than just hitting one at a time. Two stunts are always better than one.

★ Be creative with loads, transitions, and dismounts.

★ Avoid having athletes hold stunts for too long. Transition or dismount stunts after they are held two to four counts.

★ Avoid using the same stunts over and over.

HINTS FOR CHOREOGRAPHING PYRAMIDS

★ Use pyramids that hit every time in practice, and avoid choreographing pyramids that are too difficult.

★ Try using a transition from pyramid 1 to pyramid 2 in the same segment. Two pyramids within one segment are visually appealing and add a level of difficulty to the routine.

★ Keep the pyramids close to the front of the performance area rather than near the back—unless tumblers or dancers are in front of the pyramid.

★ Do not repeat pyramids.

HINTS FOR CHOREOGRAPHING DANCE

★ Use "and" counts to add an element of difficulty to the routine.

★ Put the best dancers near the front.

★ Avoid dancing in one place for too long.

★ Put full team dances near the end of a routine.

★ Use dance moves that are appropriate for the age and level of the team.

HINTS FOR CHOREOGRAPHING TUMBLING

★ Choreograph the hardest tumbling lines near the beginning of a routine when athletes are fresh.

★ Avoid choreographing tumblers into the routine who do not have clean tumbling elements.

★ Put the best tumblers near the front.

HINTS FOR CHOREOGRAPHING CHEERS

★ Use signs and props.

★ Transition from motions to stunts or to pyramids and vice versa.

★ Use tumbling, jumps, and motions.

HINTS FOR CHOREOGRAPHING TRANSITIONS

★ Be discreet. The judges should never see a transition as a transition but rather as another element in the routine.

★ Transition often into different elements and formations.

★ Remember to keep the same athletes on the same side of the floor so that they don't have to run across the mat to get to their next position.

★ The floor should always look busy but not distracting. Use different timing to provide transition between elements or keep full-team transitions to an eight-count.

FINAL POINTERS

★ Add sound effects to pyramids, stunts, dances, and so on.

★ Don't try and choreograph too much into a routine. Simple and creative is often best.

★ Use a variety of (appropriate) upbeat music that changes often. Avoid using the same music for too long.

★ Encourage the team to interact with the crowd. Choreograph moves that acknowledge that the crowd is there (such as pointing).

★ Be creative, creative, and creative. Judges have seen nearly every stunt, pyramid, and dance move before. It's how you execute them that makes the difference between boring and exciting.

★ Remember to stick to the score sheet and to the rules.

— Formations and Transitions —

Great formations and effective transitions are the basis of any winning routine. Poor positioning of athletes and boring transitions will only score low points (you don't want anyone falling asleep at the judging table!). Keep the following tips in mind when writing a routine, and you will be able to create a cheerleading masterpiece in no time!

Formations

Formations are the positions in which you perform a stunt, dance, pyramid, or cheer. A routine is made up of many formations linked together by transitions. When writing a routine and creating formations, remember these points:

★ Spread your formations wide across the floor. This gives the illusion of a bigger team and is visually more appealing to the judges and crowd.

★ Be creative and unique with formations. Use each one only once in a routine.

★ Put your strongest cheerleaders at the front.

★ Don't stay in one formation too long; change it up every few eight-counts or before to keep the routine exciting.

Transitions

Because merely walking from one formation to the next lacks visual appeal, transitions are used to distract the crowd. You know you've done a great job when beginning your next formation the crowd thinks "WOW! How did they get there?" Transitions should be simple and crisp, yet effective. Remember that too much going on will take away from your next big stunt, dance, or cheer segment. Effective transitions include these:

★ Team tumbling

★ Motions while moving

★ Jumps (for example, Hurdler, Toe-Touch Back Handspring to different formation)

★ Short cheers to the beat of the music (for example: "Let's go, Bears!")

★ Clapping on the on/off beat (on the 2, 4, 6, 8 or on the 1, 3, 5, 7)

★ Spinning (such as two steps, spin in a circle, two more steps to next position)

★ Crossing or changing rows

★ Dancing to a new formation

★ Moving/spinning stunts or pyramids

Have the transition occur either during the same music as the formation before or during a voice-over or sound effect. When beginning your new segment, the music typically changes. But, there are no set rules. If you have a great music idea for a transition, go with it!

Now that you have all the formation and transition tools that you need to create a winning routine, read on for the next section on choreographing stunts and pyramids in a routine.

— Stunts and Pyramids —

When choreographing routines, stunts and pyramids must be transitioned with creativity and executed with ease. Here's an example of a pyramid transition that can be used by varsity and co-ed teams (pee-wee and junior teams can also do this pyramid by taking it down one level):

Sample Pyramid Transition

Begin with five groups connected together in an outside Hitch pyramid (for an example of this pyramid, refer to figure 14.2 on page 245). From left to right your groups are:

★ Shoulder Sit

★ Outside Liberty Hitch

★ Elevator

★ Outside Liberty Hitch

★ Shoulder Sit

Here are the steps to the pyramid transition:

1. Liberty flyers connect to the Elevator flyer with straight arms. Shoulder Sits hold the Hitch with arms extended upward.

2. Liberty Hitches sponge down 270 degrees and touch down inward (toward the Elevator). Both Liberty groups are now facing the back in a Ground Up Load. Shoulder Sits and Elevator remain in their stunts.

3. Liberty groups load back up, making a 90-degree turn as they bring the flyers into an Inside Arabesque (Arabesque flyers are facing outward). As the Arabesques are loading upward, the Elevator group sponges down and loads back up into an Elevator. The outside Shoulder Sits sink in unison with the Elevators. The Shoulder Sits come up into an Elevator facing outward (or from Shoulder Sit to Hands if this is a co-ed pyramid) at the same time the middle group sponges back up into an Elevator.

4. Arabesques hit as the other three groups hit their Elevator stunts.

5. Arabesques hold onto the shoulders of the outside Elevators for support as the middle Elevator holds the Arabesque feet above her head.

The final pyramid should look like this:

★ Elevator (or Shoulder Stand) facing outward

★ Arabesque facing outward

★ Elevator facing forward

★ Arabesque facing outward

★ Elevator (or Shoulder Stand) facing outward

Note how this pyramid utilizes different timing and direction changes to effectively move from one pyramid to the next. The same idea can be applied to stunt groups to provide transition between stunts or to transition from stunts into a pyramid or vice versa.

— Dynamic Dancing —

Crowds at games or competitions go crazy for high-energy dances and cleverly choreographed steps. Who doesn't love great music accompanied by an energetic performance?

The secret to a dynamic dance segment is pairing great moves with the use of choreographed techniques such as levels, ripples, transitions, and attitude. Remove one of these factors and you begin to negate the effectiveness of your routine.

Levels

Dancing on different levels gives the illusion that there are more dancers on the floor than there are, as well as adds visual appeal. When choreographing a dance, incorporate levels such as:

★ Kneeling (seat on the heels)

★ Kneeling upright or down on one knee

★ Bent (that is, with hands on the knees)

★ Standing upright

★ Low-level stunts (one-and-a-half high)

★ Medium-level stunts (two-high)

★ High-level stunts (two-high and two-and-a-half high)

Change levels often (at least once every one or two eight counts) to add excitement and variety to a dance segment.

— TIP —

When choreographing a routine, remember to ripple cheers/chants, tumbling, and stunting segments from left to right.

Ripples

Ripples are great for creating interesting visual effects and for keeping the pace of the dance moving quickly. When you choreograph ripples, it's important to remember not to get too carried away; simple is often best. Use big, one-count moves rather than fast "and" (double time) counts. Incorporate levels, floor work, and directional changes for maximum effectiveness.

Since people read left to right, and are used to the left to right motion, make sure that your ripples flow in that direction. Visually, it can be somewhat confusing for people to watch a ripple that goes from right to left. *Be warned:* This directional mistake can easily affect the overall appeal of your dance.

A good rule of thumb is to use a maximum of twice the number of moves as groups in your ripple. For example, if you have three groups in your ripple, six is the maximum number of moves that should be rippled. If there are too many rippled moves, the groups will start to blend together, and the movement will become a distraction rather than an effective technique.

Transitions and Formation Changes

It's a good idea to keep stationary dance at a maximum of eight counts, followed by some type of choreographed technique to keep the routine exciting. Often the easiest way to do this is to add a transition and change formations. (See the Formation section earlier in this chapter for more information on transitions.)

Dance transition ideas include:

★ Moving athletes apart into a bigger (looser) formation (lateral movements)

★ Bringing athletes closer together into a tighter formation

★ Adding a jump sequence

★ Adding a tumbling sequence (front rolls, back handsprings, back tucks, or tumbling line combinations)

> **— TIP —**
>
> Continuous movement is essential to an effective routine. Avoid staying in one formation for too long.

★ Moving forward or backward

★ Adding directional changes (spins, turns, and any movements where dancers face a direction other than front)

Dances themselves can be used to transition from one stunting, gymnastic, or cheer segment to the next.

Attitude

Let's face it. A dance without attitude is like an all-star competitive cheerleading team that doesn't perform stunts. And attitude doesn't just mean great faces and an occasional bootie shake either (more on the bootie shake is coming up). Creating a dance with attitude means choreographing a routine where the dancing style, facial expressions,

---

★ ★ ★ ★ ★ ★ ★ ★ ★ ★ ★ ★ ★ ★ ★ ★ ★ ★

Bootie Shakin'

As mentioned before, there's no doubt that attitude is an important part of any routine. However, it can be easy to get carried away. Age-appropriate choreography and music are essential for both placing well and for protecting the integrity of the sport. Be careful when adding bootie (hip) shakes, shoulder shakes, and other moves that could be classified as "controversial" or "inappropriate." When creating the routine, keep in mind the age group of your athletes and incorporate only tasteful "attitude" moves.

★ ★ ★ ★ ★ ★ ★ ★ ★ ★ ★ ★ ★ ★ ★ ★ ★ ★

and music correspond to a similar theme. Selecting music that matches the choreographed moves and adding sound effects to key points in the dance (such as kicks, jumps, or ending poses) is an easy way to boost your artistic score.

If your team is co-ed, choreograph dances that use interaction between partners. Dances that include just the "girls" or just the "guys" can also be effective as long as the rest of the team is either standing inconspicuously to the side or is performing another segment (such as a pyramid or stunt sequence).

— Teaching Dances in Ten Easy Steps —

The easiest way to teach a dance is to use two coaches or choreographers, one to "talk" the dance and one to demonstrate. The reason for this two-team teaching approach is that it's easier for both the choreographers to teach and for the athletes to learn. You don't have to turn around to talk to the team while trying to demonstrate, and the team won't get confused watching you attempt this. Follow these ten easy steps for a quick and simple way to teach a dance:

1. Show the dance first, performed full out with music.

2. Teach slowly, with one choreographer talking and the other demonstrating. Teach only one eight count at a time, or four counts if the dance involves "and" counts ("one and two").

3. Break down each count slowly, one move at a time. Walk around and make the necessary corrections before going onto the next motion.

4. Review each new eight-count a few times. After everyone is comfortable with this eight-count, review the dance from the beginning (without music).

5. Gradually speed up the counts until they're at the same tempo as the music.

Cleaning Up Dances

Often dances are mistakenly the last component to be perfected or forgotten all together, yet a clean dance is crucial to the visual impact of the routine. Good choreography is a waste if it's clouded by sloppy execution. A critical step in practicing a dance is cleaning it up—that is, breaking it down one move at a time and correcting any mistakes before moving on. Look for common errors such as these:

★ Bent, loose bodies and arms

★ Improper foot, hand, or arm positioning

★ Inconsistency in the size of movements among athletes, such as the height of kicks and the width of steps

★ Hitting moves too early or too late (that is, not on the proper count)

★ Uneven formations

Be meticulous in correcting every error, regardless of how insignificant it may seem. From tucking in thumbs right down to synchronizing the angle of head tilts, clean up every last detail until the dance is performed perfectly. The judges will reward you.

---

6. Try the dance from the beginning with music after a few eight-counts have been taught.

7. Teach the rest of the dance a few eight-counts at a time, gradually speeding it up and adding music.

8. Remove the demos.

9. Review the whole dance to counts.

10. Add music and perform the full dance.

Teaching Tips

★ Change lines often to give each athlete a chance up at the front.

★ Perform the dance in small groups while teammates watch. This is a good way to promote constructive criticism and friendly competition. Additionally, it helps athletes correct their own mistakes by learning from others.

★ To clean up the dance, go through the dance one count at a time, adjusting the moves until they're perfectly synchronized.

★ Videotape the dance and encourage feedback. Ask for suggestions to improve the performance.

Learning Dances

As an athlete, learning dances can sometimes be a frustrating experience (especially at camp when dances are taught at high speed), but there are a number of tricks you can use to make it easier:

1. *Stand near the front.*

Standing close to the instructor provides you with a better view of the moves being taught. If you stand near the back, chances are you won't be able to see how to hit the motions properly, which means you'll have to re-learn the dance later.

2. *Think about your next move before doing it.*

Concentrate on developing your "muscle memory" by consciously thinking about each move. Don't rely on following the demos. Use them only when you really get stuck.

3. *Ask questions.*

Don't be afraid to ask questions if you're not sure about a particular move. Even if you just want to go over the last eight-count one more time, speak up and let your coach know. If you're finding the teaching speed a little fast, your teammates probably are too.

5, 6, 7, 8!

Here are some last-minute pointers to dazzle the crowd and the judges with your smooth moves:

★ Keep your body tight and snap from one move to the next. Remember that each move has a corresponding count; if you're supposed to clean on "one," don't hit the motion until count "one."

★ Count in your head, but not out loud. Make sure you're not mouthing the counts or the words of the song.

★ Stay in formation. Your steps must be the same size as the steps of your neighbors or you'll be dancing out of line (literally).

★ Have fun with exaggerated facial expressions. Here's your chance to show off your attitude!

— Teaching the Routine —

Teaching the routine can be done in five easy steps.

I. WRITE OUT THE ROUTINE AND GIVE A COPY TO ALL ATHLETES

The easiest way to break down the routine is by counts.

For example:

1	2	3	4
Set for stunt	Rise on toes	Sink on 3/4	

5	6	7	8
Load in on 5/6		Pyramid loading/hitting	

1	2	3	4
Pyramid hits		All groups sink	

(continues)

5	6	7	8
Cradle down on 5/6		Catch flyers	

1	2	3	4
Flyers set down		Clap	Clean

5	6	7	8

Transition to next formation

Here's a sample sheet you can photocopy to use for writing your routines:

1	2	3	4

5	6	7	8

1	2	3	4

5	6	7	8

1	2	3	4

5	6	7	8

Transition to next formation

2. WORK ON EACH SEGMENT SEPARATELY
Add counts.

3. PUT TOGETHER SEGMENTS AND TRANSITIONS TO COUNTS
Start counting slowly, and gradually build up to the speed of the music.

4. REVIEW THE ENTIRE ROUTINE
Clean up, rewrite, and change segments that aren't working.

5. ADD MUSIC
Give a copy to each athlete to use and review at home.

Preparing for a Competition

Preparing for a competition can be stressful, and competitions test the patience of both coaches and athletes. Coaches struggle with last minute to-do lists and re-choreographing routines while athletes work hard to hit stunts consistently and stay energetic at extra practices. Rather than looking at it as a stressful event, members of the team should view it as an opportunity to show off the results of their hard work while having fun. Keeping positive attitudes, offering one another encouragement, and following the suggested preparation techniques can help channel team tension into constructive practices. Once you have accomplished this and are ready to compete, read the section Before You Take the Floor on page 264 before you leave for the event.

— Cheerleaders: Read This Before You Head to Your Competition! —

With so many things to think about before a competition, it's easy to forget something important. The following checklists contain helpful reminders for a month before, a week before, and the day of the event. Review the lists (a few times) before you leave. You can then relax, knowing you haven't left anything behind and having taken care of all the necessary tasks. It's much easier to bring home first place when you don't have to worry about last-minute details.

Cheerleader Checklist

ONE MONTH BEFORE COMPETITION

✓ Maintain healthy eating habits. (Now is *not* the time to go on a crash diet. In fact, there is *never* a time since crash diets don't work.)

✓ Modify or reduce extra weight training and conditioning workouts (especially if the coach has set additional practices) so there is less chance of physical burnout. Get your sleep, too.

✓ Get together with other teammates and review recently learned cheers and dances. This makes practices more efficient because time isn't wasted working on material you already know.

ONE WEEK BEFORE COMPETITION

✓ Go to bed early the entire week to rest up for the competition.

✓ Bring in all outstanding monies, permission forms, and releases to the coach.

✓ Give your parents a finalized copy of the schedule including important contact information. Keep a copy for yourself.

C O A C H E S '   C O R N E R

CREATING A POSITIVE AND WINNING TEAM

The best way to reduce stress before a competition is to offer encouragement. It's a good idea to encourage the athletes on your team, and to remind athletes to encourage each other. Although keeping a positive attitude can be difficult when everyone is tired and stressed, encouragement works wonders in fostering a positive environment and also helps lower tension.

Avoid swearing at or putting down your team. You must work especially hard to avoid showing any negative attitude near competition time, when emotions run high and you are tempted to let things slip.

While all participants must make an effort to encourage one another, you as a coach have additional responsibilities when competition time looms near. An extremely important responsibility is protecting athletes against both physical and mental burnout. You can do this by keeping practices near the two-hour mark (remember, not *more* practices, but more *efficient* practices) and watching for signs of exhaustion such as excessive irritability and repeated out-of-character mistakes from the athletes. Holding too many practices right before competition can overtire teams and contribute unnecessarily to anxiety they might have about the routine. Avoid holding too many extra practices or adding extra time to practices.

If stunts aren't hitting close within a week of the competition, first warn athletes that the stunts or pyramids will be removed from the routine. (If the pyramid can't hit in practice, chances are good that it won't hit in competition.) If they continue to fall, replace those techniques with easier ones that the athletes are capable of hitting 100 percent of the time. A clean routine that consists of easier skills is better than a sloppy routine with advanced skills that cannot be performed proficiently. Athletes will also feel more comfortable with the routine.

The following hints can help reduce competition nervousness and increase routine success:

★ **Clean up the routine.** Athletes will feel better about performing on the team when they are confident in their skills and movements. Take each segment and break it down one count at a time so that athletes are clear on their specific role for each count.

★ **Visualize perfection.** Have athletes envision their responsibilities in the routine by sitting down and listening to the music with their eyes closed. Every stunt should hit perfectly and every move should be sharp in their minds. This visualization exercise can make a significant difference in their stability and perfection when they actually perform the routine.

★ **Videotape the routine.** This is a great way for athletes to see what they actually look like in the routine, which gives them a chance to correct their own mistakes.

★ **Count out loud.** While this is something athletes should not do during the actual competition or performance, counting out loud during practice helps to ensure that each cheerleader is hitting the same move to the corresponding count. This drill works really well to synchronize stunts, dances, jumps, and motions.

★ **Instruct athletes to encourage one another.** Whether it's a wink, a smile, or a simple, "Let's go, Sue!" encouraging one another during the routine helps to calm one other's anxiety.

✓ Review the routine with music every night before going to bed. Know the material so well that you can do it in your sleep.

✓ Warm up and stretch well at practice. Take care of yourself so that you don't get hurt.

✓ Begin setting aside items to take on the trip. Buy small versions of your toiletries such as shampoo, conditioner, and soap so you can pack lightly!

✓ Confirm the competition dates with teachers or professors. Get assignments, homework, and lecture notes for the dates you'll be away.

✓ Do your homework *before* you go to the competition. (There won't be time to do it once you get there, and chances are it won't get done on the bus or the night you get home either.)

✓ Make Warm Fuzzies for teammates (see page 264).

WHAT TO TAKE TO COMPETITION

✓ Full uniform: shoes, bows, bloomies, shell, skirt, warm-ups, and proper socks.

✓ Make-up, curlers, and other hair accessories.

✓ Medication taken on a daily basis.

✓ Camera, film, and batteries.

✓ Walkman or Discman and the competition routine music.

✓ Pillow for the bus.

✓ Sunscreen.

✓ Alarm clock.

✓ Bathing suit.

✓ Casual clothes for the day.

✓ Dressy clothes for the "after party" or for the evening.

✓ Money, ID, passport, and important contact information and numbers (such as the coach's cell phone number).

✓ Band-Aids, tensor bandages, and pain relievers.

✓ Snacks: juice, fruit, granola bars, and bottles of water.

✓ Phone card or cell phone to call home.

✓ Insurance card.

Don't ruin your chances of having a good time by forgetting something essential!

BEFORE GETTING ON THE BUS OR PLANE

✓ Arrive on time.

✓ Be sure you have everything you need— passport/traveling documents, uniform, bags, and so on. (For a complete list, see the previous section, What to Take to Competition.)

✓ Pack healthy snacks and bottles of water. Eating at fast-food joints along the way is not only unhealthful but makes for a *very* long trip.

✓ Wear your warm-up suit or school colors to proudly represent your team.

THE DAY BEFORE COMPETITION

✓ Pack your snacks and water for the competition day.

✓ Pack anything else you'll need, such as sunscreen, change of clothes, extra socks.

✓ Lay out your uniform, shoes, and make-up so that if you get up late, you'll still be able to get ready on time.

✓ Put your hair in curlers. It's easiest to put your hair up in a ponytail first (use gel to smooth down the top) and then just curl the tail with rags or sponge rollers.

✓ Before you go to sleep, listen to your music and mentally perform your routine.

✓ Get a good night's sleep. You've put far too many hours and too much effort into your routine to perform less than your best.

BEFORE YOU TAKE THE FLOOR

✓ Take bathroom breaks and do make-up and hair touch-ups no later than a half-hour before performance time.

✓ Tie your bow and double-knot your shoelaces.

✓ Put your bag or purse in a safe spot.

✓ Put on your Walkman or sit down with the team and mentally hit your routine perfectly to music.

✓ Drink a little bit of water to wet your throat, but not enough to make you need to go to the bathroom again.

✓ Smile! It's showtime!

Boosting Team Unity with Warm Fuzzies

Warm Fuzzies are "feel-good" notes or small posters written by one teammate for another, describing what they respect, admire, or like about that person. Assign each cheerleader three or four teammates' names and have him or her make a Warm Fuzzy for each of them. Warm Fuzzies are a great way to improve team unity, especially before a competition.

COACHES' CORNER

CHECKLIST FOR COACHES

ONE MONTH BEFORE THE COMPETITION

✓ Fax or mail in all forms, confirmations, and deposits to the company or organization hosting the competition.

✓ Confirm that your school is aware of the competition and which athletes will be participating.

✓ Determine whether additional weekly practices are needed.

✓ Send Parents' Competition package home. This includes:

★ Permission forms and release forms for the competition.

★ Payment schedule, including when the last payment is due.

★ Tentative itinerary that includes contact information, the site of the competition, location and name of the hotel, and a schedule of events.

★ A schedule outlining upcoming extra practices.

★ A request for supervision helpers (depending on the age of the team).

★ Additional competition information.

✓ Hand out copies of Cheerleader Checklist to team members and instruct them to bring checklists to competition.

ONE WEEK BEFORE COMPETITION

✓ Confirm bus and hotel reservations.

✓ Confirm once more with the organization running the competition that your team is on the schedule.

✓ Request a schedule of events and performance times if you don't have one already.

COACHES' CORNER

✓ Collect outstanding monies, permission forms, and release forms. Make copies of all forms.

✓ Make any necessary amendments to the schedule and contact information (such as the hotel phone number or the coach's cell phone number) and send a copy to all parents and cheerleaders.

✓ Run the routine full out with the music (Only minor changes should be made from here on.)

✓ Encourage each team member to bring in a tape or CD and copy the routine music.

WHAT TO TAKE TO COMPETITION

✓ Boom box.

✓ Three copies of routine music; two on CD and another on Cassette Tape.

✓ First-aid kit, including tensor bandages, Band-Aids, ice packs.

✓ Cell phone for emergencies.

✓ Contact numbers, such as for the hotel and bus.

✓ Copies of all releases, competition, and insurance forms.

✓ Camera or camcorder with extra film, tapes, and batteries.

✓ Extra bows and bloomies.

✓ Itinerary and schedule.

✓ ID, passport, money.

✓ An alarm clock.

✓ The team trainer.

✓ Extra supervision (age dependent).

BEFORE GETTING ON THE BUS OR PLANE

✓ Do you have everything? Music, first-aid kit, boom box, and your own bags? (See the previous section, What to Take to Competition).

✓ Do you have everyone? Cheerleaders? Mascots? Supervisors? Bus Driver?

✓ If you're going to another country, does everyone have his or her passport and/or other required documents for traveling?

✓ If you're taking a bus, have a map ready in case the driver gets lost or takes the extra-long scenic route.

✓ Keep an eye on the weather, and plan an alternate route you can follow should bad weather render your original route unrealistic.

✓ Make sure the bus leaves on time.

✓ If you're flying, confirm your flights before heading to the airport.

THE DAY BEFORE THE COMPETITION

✓ Review the itinerary and check for schedule changes.

✓ Have team exchange Warm Fuzzies (see sidebar on page 264).

✓ Scope out the performance area. If possible, bring your team so that they can mentally prepare themselves to compete on the floor. Finding out the limits of the area could make the difference between hitting a routine with confidence and having one of your tumblers back-handspring off the stage. (Most teams are given the opportunity to map out their routine on the floor before actually competing, but you may not be able to do so.)

✓ Make breakfast plans for the next day. (Does the hotel offer a Continental breakfast? Is there a place down the street? Well-fed cheerleaders perform better than hungry ones.)

(continues)

C O A C H E S '   C O R N E R

CHECKLIST FOR COACHES, continued

✓ If you need to take a bus over to the competition area, confirm where the driver will meet you in the morning. If you're walking, make sure you know the most direct route.

✓ Schedule wake-up calls for the morning— early enough so everyone can get ready on time and eat a good breakfast.

✓ Make sure everyone is in bed early. If necessary, use the "tape trick." (Place a piece of tape across the outside of their doors. If the tape is broken or peeled off, you'll know they've been out.)

✓ Try to get a decent night's sleep.

BEFORE YOU TAKE THE FLOOR

✓ Ensure that everyone is present. It sounds obvious, but it's easy to get caught up in the excitement and lose or forget someone.

✓ Put the bags and props in a safe place, preferably with someone watching them at all times.

✓ Check with a staff member to confirm that performances are still running on schedule.

✓ Warm up the team, facing away from any other teams or distractions.

✓ Sit everyone down and mentally perform to the music.

✓ Arrive in the competition practice and competition area with a minimum of three routines to go before you're scheduled to practice or perform.

✓ Make sure the music is with the DJ and that someone familiar with your routine will be cuing the music.

Be sure you review these lists a number of times before heading out the door!

— Cheerleading Companies —

Camps, instruction, competitions.

United States

American All-Star
P.O. Box 1062
Mandeville, LA 70470
800-256-STAR
www.americanallstar.com

American Cheer Express
P.O. Box 3505
Princeton, NJ 08543
888-TEAM-XPRS
www.americancheer.com

American Cheer Power
201 Spruce
Dickinson, TX 77539
800-500-0840
www.cheerpower.com

American Cheerleaders Association
7415 Northaven
Dallas, TX 75230
800-316-8815
www.acacheerleading.com

American Cheerleading Federation
5132 69th Street
Urbandale, IA 50322
800-803-4294
www.cheeracf.com

American CheerX-treme
112 Ministry Drive
Irmo, SC 29063
877-56-CHEER

American Spirit Championships
P.O. Box 2712
Edmond, OK 73083

800-636-5272
www.ascspirit.com

America's Best Cheer & Dance
P.O. Box 25328
Dallas, TX 75225-5328
800-414-8778
www.americasbestcheer.com

AmeriCheer
20 Collegeview Road
Westerville, OH 43081
800-966-JUMP
www.americheerinc.com

Atlantic Cheer & Dance
825 Hammonds Ferry Road, Suite H-J
Linthicum, MD 21090
866-WIN-ACDC
www.atlantic-cheer-n-dance.com

Champion Cheerleading
1187 Hemphill Court
Brighton, MI 48114
810-220-1146
www.championcheerleading.com

Champion Cheerleading, Inc.
3200 Tanager Street
Raleigh, NC 27606
800-732-2309
www.championcheer.com

Cheer Ltd., Inc.
118 Ridgeway Drive, Suite 101
Fayetteville, NC 28311
800-477-8868
www.cheerltd.com

Cheer! Michigan
32802 Franklin Road
Franklin, MI 48025
800-390-0950
www.cheermichigan.com

Cheerleaders of America
3699 Paragon Drive
Columbus, OH 43228
800-252-4337
www.COAcheer.com

Cheerleading Stunt Academy
2421 Crescent Drive, Suite 4
Cedar Falls, IA 50613
888-383-5520
www.cheercsa.com

Cheerleading Technique Camps
P.O. Box 15267
Gainesville, FL 32604
800-462-8294
www.spiritteam.com

Cheersport Inc.
11011 Monroe Road, Suite C
Matthews, NC 28105
888-READY-OK
www.cheersport.net

Cheertec, Inc.
P.O. Box 5095
Carefree, AZ 85377
800-785-2433
www.cheertec.com

Christian Cheerleaders of America
P.O. Box 49
Bethania, NC 27010
877-CHEER-CCA
www.cheercca.com

Classic Cheerleading Camp
310 Elam Avenue
Ramseur, NC 27316
336-824-4222

Collegiate Cheerleading Company
1861 W. 24th St.
Erie, PA 16502
888-912-4337
www.collegiatecheerleading.com

East Coast Cheerleading Academy
20 Simpson Place
Middletown, MD 19709
410-688-2240

Eastern Cheerleaders Association
P.O. Box 475
South Hill, VA 23970
800-940-4ECA
www.ecaeda.com

Elite Cheerleading Organization
816 Grandview Avenue
Pittsburgh, PA 15211
800-456-4PEP

Excite! Cheerleading
P.O. Box 191513
Dallas, TX 75219
972-874-8500
www.excitecheer.com

Fellowship of Christian Cheerleaders
1645 Lakes Parkway, Suite H
Lawrenceville, GA 30043
800-825-6953
www.cheerfcc.org

Global Cheerleaders Association
2607 Big Woods Trail
Beavercreek, OH 45431
877-GCA-9476

JAMZ Cheerleading & Dance
P.O. Box 512
San Ramon, CA 94583
800-920-4272
www.jamzcheer.com

Mid American Pompon
24425 Indoplex Circle
Farmington Hills, MI 48335
888-477-8507
www.pompon.com

National Cheerleaders Association
P.O. Box 660359
Dallas, TX 75266
800-NCA-2-WIN
www.nationalspirit.com

New England Cheerleaders Association
P.O. Box 124
Uncasville, CT 06382
860-848-0040
www.cheerneca.com

North Coast Cheerleading
95 Karl Street
Berea, OH 44017
440-239-0696
www.northcoastallstars.com

Pine Forest Cheerleading Camp
P.O. Box 11
Olyphant, PA 18447
570-876-2664
www.cheerleadingcamps.com

Power Cheer
4200 Bangs Avenue
Modesto, CA 95356
209-545-7693
www.powercheersummercamps.com

Premier Cheerleading
742 Cambridge Crest Lane
Knoxville, TN 37919
865-692-9244
www.premiercheerleading.com

Premier Cheerleading Association, Inc.
1018 Central Avenue, Suite 300
Metairie, LA 70001
800-408-4858
www.premiercheer.com

Southern Star Resort Cheer Camps
7595 Highway 105
Beaumont, TX 77713
877-898-1496
www.southernstar.net

Southwestern Cheerleaders Association
P.O. Box 5352
Lake Charles, LA 70606
337-477-5218

Spirit 1 Elite Camps
P.O. Box 915456
Longwood, FL 32779

888-716-2287
www.spiritcheer.com

Spirit Unlimited
777 Route 3 North
Gambrills, MD 21054
888-737-2221
www.spiritunlimited.com

Spirit Xpress
4907 South Alston Avenue
Durham, NC 27713
800-286-4219
www.spiritxpress.com

U.S. Cheer, Inc.
P.O. Box 290037
Columbia, SC 29229
877-780-0800
www.gouscheer.com

United Performing Association
361 90th Avenue, NW
Minneapolis, MN 55433
800-800-6-UPA
www.unitedperformingassociation.com

United Spirit Association
11135 Knott Avenue
Cypress, CA 90630
800-886-4USA
www.usacamps.com

United States Cheer & Dance Camps
P.O. Box 1524
Washington, PA 15301
888-922-DANCE
www.cheeranddanceds.com

United States Cheerleading Association
3650 SW 10th Street, Suite 13
Deerfield Beach, FL 33442
888-414-USCA
www.uscheerleading.com

Universal Cheerleaders Association (UCA)
6745 Lenox Centre Court, Suite 300
Memphis, TN 38115
888-CHEER-UCA
www.varsity.com

US Spirit
P.O. Box 26701
Columbus, OH 43226
800-469-7878
www.us-spirit.com

US Spiritleaders
P.O. Box 32227
Long Beach, CA 90832
888-675-2999

USA Cheerleading Federation (USACF)
P.O. Box 247
Stanfield, NC 28163-0247
888-86-USACF
www.usacf.com

World Cheerleading Association
P.O. Box 220098
St. Louis, MO 63122
888-TEAM-WCA
www.cheerwca.com

Worldwide Spirit Association
P.O. Box 86430
Baton Rouge, LA 70879-6430
800-53-CHEER
www.wsacheer.com

Canada

Flygirl
#305-155 Lake Shore Drive
Toronto, Ontario
Canada M8V 2A1
416-503-8739
www.flygirl.ca

Power Cheerleading Athletics (PCA)
3 Horn Street
London, Ontario
Canada N6C 3K3
800-567-PCA1
www.powercheerleading.com

Professional Spirit Services
47 Fairwood Crescent
Toronto, Ontario
Canada M1E 3T2
416-287-6842

Stunt Factory
Ontario, Canada
866-2-1-STUNT
www.stuntfactory.com

Ultimate Leaders Corporation
10524 40th Street
Edmonton, AL
Canada T6A 1T1
877-903-2468

— Cheerleading Association/Federations —

United States

American Association of Cheerleading Coaches and Advisors (AACCA)
P.O. Box 752790
Memphis, TN 38175-2790
800-533-6583
www.aacca.org

National Federation of State High School Associations
P.O. Box 690
Indianapolis, IN 46206
317-972-6900
www.nfhs.org

National Pop Warner Headquarters
586 Middletown Boulevard, Suite C-100
Langhorne, PA 19047
215-752-2691
www.popwarner.com

Each state also has a cheerleading organization, association, federation, or governing body.

Canada

Alberta Cheerleading Association
www.albertacheerleading.ca

British Columbia Cheerleading Association
www.bccheerleading.ca

Commission Provinciale de Cheerleading (Quebec)
www3.sympatico.ca/almoncpc/indexE.html

Manitoba Association of Cheerleading
www.cheermanitoba.ca

New Brunswick Cheerleading Association
www.nbca.homestead.com

Newfoundland and Labrador Cheerleading Association
www.newfoundlandcheerleading.com

Nova Scotia Cheerleading Association
www.nscheer.com

Ontario Cheerleading Federation
www.ocf.on.ca

International

American Cheerleading & Danz Association (Chile)
www.americancheerleaders.cl

Asociacion National de Porristas de Mexico
www.anpmex.com

AusCheer (Australia)
www.auscheer.com

Australian Cheerleading Association
www.geocities.com/australian-cheer-association.org

Austria Cheerleading
Contact the International Cheerleading Federation

British Cheerleading Association
www.cheerleading.org.uk

Chinese Taipei Cheerleading Association
www.tca-cheers.org.tw

Czech Association of Cheerleading
www.cach.cz

European Federation of American Football
www.efaf.org

Finnish Cheerleading Federation
suomen-cheerleaderit.fi

German Cheerleading
Contact the International Cheerleading Federation

International Cheerleading Federation
www.icf-hdqrs.org

Japan Cheerleading Association
www.jca-hdqrs.org

Norwegian Cheerleader Committee
www.cheerleadercom.com

Russian Cheerleading (American Football in Russia)
www.kulichki.com/claf

Scotcheer (Scotland)
www.scot-cheer.org.uk

Slovenian Cheerleading & Pom Pon Association
www.zveza-znps.si

Swedish Cheerleader Federation
www.gymnastik.se/cheerleading

United Cheerleader of Switzerland
www.swisscheer.ch

United Kingdom Cheerleading Association
www.abc-ukca.co.uk

— Competition Uniform Suppliers —

United States

Cheerleader&DanzTeam (National Spirit Group)
www.nationalspirit.com

CranBarry, Inc.
130 Condor Street
East Boston, MA 02128
800-992-2021
www.cbcheer.com

Pep Threads
1141 West Katella Avenue
Orange, CA 92867
888-737-2557
www.pepthreads.com

Team Cheer
131 Main Street
Geneseo, NY 14454
800-350-1562
www.teamcheer.com

Varsity Spirit Fashions (UCA)
www.varsity.com

Many other cheerleading companies listed in the previous Cheerleading Companies section also manufacture and offer uniforms and apparel.

Canada

Active Knit Apparel, Inc.
480 Lawrence Avenue West, 4th Floor
Toronto, Ontario
Canada M5M 1C4
800-665-1102

Cheer Basics
22 Mill Street South
Waterdown, Ontario
Canada L0R 2H0
905-689-2160

Power Cheerleading Athletics
See information under Cheerleading Companies,
Canada

Europe

Cheer Store
255 Croydon Road
Wallington, Surrey
SM6 7LR, UK
www.cheer-store.com

First Cheer Uniforms & Accessories
64 Mount Pleasant
Ruislip, Middlesex
FA4 9HQ, UK

0208 426-2277
www.firstcheer.com

— Cheerleading Apparel & Accessories —

United States

CheerWarehouse.com
P.O. Box 25328
Dallas, TX 75225-5328
800-414-8778
www.cheerwarehouse.com

Cheer Zone
141 West Nepessing
Lapeer, MI 48446
800-856-8869
www.cheerzone.com

Hudson & Company (Spirit throws)
100 Irene Avenue
Roseville, CA 95678
888-429-7708
www.spiritthrows.com

Kurler-Kozy
3009 SW Captiva Court
Palm City, FL 34990
772-781-8314
www.kurler-kozy.com

Threads of Fun Spiritwear
285-A Sawdust Road
The Woodlands, TX 77380
800-496-8787
www.threads-spiritwear.com

Canada

Cheer Cutie
2059 Waterbridge Drive
Burlington, Ontario
Canada L7M 3W2
519-731-2111
www.cheercutie.com

Cheer Cutie provides cheerleaders with fun, fashionable cheerleading wear and custom practice apparel. Many of the athletes demonstrating the cheers, jumps, and stunts in this book are wearing Cheer Cutie clothing.

Power Cheerleading Athletics
See information under Cheerleading Companies, Canada

Stunt Factory
See information under Cheerleading Companies, Canada

See **www.cheerleading.net** for more uniform apparel and accessories resources

— Non-Profit Cheerleading Organizations & Companies —

USA Spirit Organization
806-798-7946
www.teamspiritusa.com

USA Spirit Organization is a company devoted to the development of young athletes involved in cheerleading and dance. The purpose of the USA Spirit Team is to provide alternatives for hard-working athletes who want to pursue careers in their favorite sports, attend unique events, and serve as role models to the worlds of cheer and dance.

— Cheerleading Events (other than competitions) —

CheerExpo
902-765-0101
www.cheerexpo.com

CheerExpo is an Expo/Trade Show event for cheerleaders, dancers, drill-teams, majorettes, baton twirlers, and all of their coaches. CheerExpo features cheerleading and dance companies from across the country and related companies including shoes, choreography, music, uniforms, props and signs, pom poms, ribbons, fundraising, trophies, and team wear. These events also include dance and cheerleading competitions, free classes for coaches and athletes, and scholarship awards. CheerExpo is held three times a year in major U.S. cities.

— Cheerleading Magazines & Books —

Magazines

American Cheerleader Magazine
www.americancheerleader.com

American Cheerleader Junior magazine
www.americancheerleaderjunior.com

Cheer Leader Magazine, British Cheerleading Association
Available online: www.cheerleading.org.uk

Books

101 Best Cheers:
How to be the Best Cheerleader Ever!
By Suzi J. Golden

Cheer Technique
By Jean Eve & Lynda Blyth-Phillips

Coaching Cheerleading Successfully
By Linda Rae Chappel and Lawrence Herkimer

Let 'Em Cheer
By Jack H. Llewellyn

The Most Excellent Book of How to Be a Cheerleader
By Bob Kiralfy, et al.

The Cheerleading Book
By Stephanie Breaux French

Ultimate Cheerleading
By Kieran Scott

— Online Cheering Resources —

www.cheerauthority.net

www.cheerleading.de

www.cheerleading.net

www.cheerleading.org

www.cheerleadingcheers.com

www.cheerplace.com

www.mspineapple.com

Index